Wilderness Wanderings

**RADICAL
TRADITIONS**

THEOLOGY IN A POSTCRITICAL KEY

*Series Editors: Stanley M. Hauerwas, Duke University,
and Peter Ochs, University of Virginia*

Radical Traditions cuts new lines of inquiry across a confused and confusing array of debates concerning the place of theology in modernity and, more generally, the status and role of scriptural faith in contemporary life. Charged with a rejuvenated confidence, spawned in part by the rediscovery of reason as inescapably tradition constituted, a new generation of theologians and religious scholars is returning to scriptural traditions with the hope of retrieving resources long ignored, depreciated, and in many cases ideologically suppressed by modern habits of thought. *Radical Traditions* assembles a promising matrix of strategies, disciplines, and lines of thought that invites Jewish, Christian, and Islamic theologians back to the word, recovering and articulating modes of scriptural reasoning as that which always underlies modernist reasoning and therefore has the capacity—and authority—to correct it.

Far from despairing over modernity's failings, postcritical theologies rediscover resources for renewal and self-correction within the disciplines of academic study themselves. Postcritical theologies open up the possibility of participating once again in the living relationship that binds together God, text, and community of interpretation. *Radical Traditions* thus advocates a "return to the text," which means a commitment to displaying the richness and wisdom of traditions that are at once text based, hermeneutical, and oriented to communal practice.

Books in this series offer the opportunity to speak openly with practitioners of other faiths or even with those who profess no (or limited) faith, both academics and nonacademics, about the ways religious traditions address pivotal issues of the day. Unfettered by foundationalist preoccupations, these books represent a call for new paradigms of reason—a thinking and rationality that is more responsive than originative. By embracing a postcritical posture, they are able to speak unapologetically out of scriptural traditions manifest in the practices of believing communities (Jewish, Christian, and others); articulate those practices through disciplines of philosophic, textual, and cultural criticism; and engage intellectual, social, and political practices that for too long have been insulated from theological evaluation. *Radical Traditions* is radical not only in its confidence in nonapologetic theological speech but also in how the practice of such speech challenges the current social and political arrangements of modernity.

Wilderness Wanderings

Probing Twentieth-Century Theology and Philosophy

Stanley M. Hauerwas

■ WestviewPress
A Division of HarperCollins*Publishers*

Radical Traditions: Theology in a Postcritical Key

Published in 1997 in the United States of America by Westview Press, 5500 Central Avenue, Boulder, Colorado 80301-2877, and in the United Kingdom by Westview Press, 12 Hid's Copse Road, Cumnor Hill, Oxford OX2 9JJ

Library of Congress Cataloging-in-Publication Data
Hauerwas, Stanley, 1940–
    Wilderness wanderings : probing 20th-century theology and philosophy / Stanley M. Hauerwas.
        p.   cm. — (Radical traditions)
    Includes bibliographical references and index.
    ISBN 0-8133-3349-0 (hardcover)
    1. Theology, Doctrinal—History—20th century.   2. Liberalism (Religion)—Protestant churches—Controversial literature.
I. Title.   II. Series.
BT28.H333   1997
230'.09'04—dc21   97-13025
                                                                          CIP

The paper used in this publication meets the requirements of the American National Standard for Permanence of Paper for Printed Library Materials Z39.48-1984.

10   9   8   7   6   5   4   3   2   1

To
Julian Hartt, Robert Calhoun, George Lindbeck,
James Gustafson, Hans Frei, Gene TeSelle,
Paul Meyer, Jaroslav Pelikan, Brevard Childs,
Rowan Greer, Liston Pope, Paul Holmer, David Little,
Robert King, Wayne Meeks, Gay Noyce

Contents

Part 3
"Journeying On": Life on the Road, or the Long Journey Homeward

Preface

I have been thinking about this book for years. Indeed, I have not just been thinking about this book for years, but for years this book has been in the process of being written. That will be obvious to the reader, as the essays in this volume span a decade. A book about time, as well as "a time," should not try to hide its own timefulness. I have never tried to write for "the ages." Those with greater intellectual power and erudition may so try to write, perhaps even successfully, but I try to remember that my talents and task are more modest. I write in the hope that a space may be provided for those still to come to do theology with a confident expansiveness that, to me and many of my generation, is largely unavailable.

One of the characters in John Updike's novel *The Couples* observed that his generation was attempting with great difficulty to "break back into paganism." That surely is the right way to put the matter. For it is no easy challenge to be a pagan in a semi-Christian world where too often Christianity has simply become another name for pagan reality. Witness, for example, the idolatry of Christian love of nation. My own work has been an attempt to imagine what it would mean to "break back into Christianity" in a world that is at best semi-Christian. Again, that is not an easy undertaking, because the very assumption that one must "break back into Christianity" means that one is robbed from the very outset of whatever confidence that "being there" might have engendered. This side of the Holocaust—a lack of confidence on the part of Christians—may, one hopes, be a sign of faith.

The series Radical Traditions, however, is designed to provide a space for those who are "back into Christianity and Judaism." That *Wilderness Wanderings* is one of the first books to appear in the series is, therefore, something of an embarrassment. I was (and am) a bit ambivalent about publishing one of my own books in a series in which I am one of the general editors. I have agreed to do so only because Peter Ochs said I should—and I do what Peter tells me. Yet I hope that this book represents what will be seen as a transitional work in a way that the other books we publish are already in many ways "beyond."

Wilderness Wanderings is transitional in several senses. The book represents my continuing battle to break free from the modes of discourse intrinsic to liberal Protestantism as well as from the modernist presumptions and practices in which that tradition remains embedded. Yet attempts to "break free" too often only reproduce that from which we flee. I do not know the exact extent to which I may remain implicated in liberal Protestantism, and in that respect this book cannot help but document transitions in my work. However, the book is also transitional inasmuch as it charts for some people how theology might be done when theologians no longer fear the prospect of living in the wilderness but embrace it instead as a challenge to "break back into Christianity."

When Peter Ochs read an earlier draft of the Introduction to this book, he observed that an "agonized I" was the author—an astute observation and challenge. If I am "thoroughly postmodern," then no such "I" should intrude itself. More important, the kind of theology this book is meant to represent, or at least move toward, requires no such "I." For such an "I" usually indicates that the author (in this case a theologian) is taking himself or herself far too seriously in presuming that the limits of his or her own subjectivity are at least as interesting, if not more so, than what the church believes. Yet it would be dishonest for me to repress or try to hide the fact that the "I" still plays a role in my work. I am, after all, by training and habit, a Protestant liberal. a la s

Habits, moreover, are hard to break. Habits of thinking are especially unyielding, since they are usually not recognized as habit. If I have discovered one thing over the years, it is that I have no ability to "will" my way free of habits of thought (or any other habits for that matter) without friends. I think it therefore important to indicate how significant it is that Peter Ochs honors me with his friendship and willingness to act as coeditor of the Radical Traditions series. That he is a Jew willing to question me on why I am not a Jew I understand to be a profound gesture of friendship. For it indicates not only that he "likes me," but more important, that he assumes that we, Jew and Christian, are bound in an inseparable embrace. I hope that Radical Traditions will allow Jews and Christians (and Islamic thinkers as well) to discover that we cannot think without one another. Without such friendship none of us will be capable of being freed from the "agonized I."

Although such an "I" is undeniably present in this book, *Wilderness Wanderings* is also about other people or, at least, conversations I am having with other people. Yet I already claimed that this is a book about time, even though the reader will find few paragraphs about time qua time. Perhaps it is in conversation with others that one best learns how to think about time, because if one tries to think about time abstractly, as if time existed apart from such conversations, one usually discovers that one has not been thinking about time. The same point holds true regarding any attempt to think or talk about God, who, as the reader will discover, is also the subject of this book. Conversations are required if we are to make the connections necessary for the display of what it means to worship a God who is as near to and as far from us as the God of Abraham, Isaac, and Jacob. Though I am often critical of those with whom I am in conversation, it should also be evident that I am so because of how deeply I respect their various attempts to understand the difference God makes for how we live, or equally, how much I admire the attempt by some to teach us how to live when there is no God.

This book is dedicated to my teachers at Yale Divinity and Graduate School. Every generation of divinity school students, I suspect, develops its own "black humor." During my time at Yale a joke circulated that, I think, was (and is) quite telling. It seems that John XXIII had an archeological team in the Holy Land. One day the head of the team called him with the news that they had discovered Jesus' tomb. There was just one problem, however; the body was still in it. After thinking and praying about the matter, John XXIII decided he would phone his old friend, Rudy Bultmann, to see if he might help him think through the implications of this monumental discovery. Even on the phone John XXIII could feel Bultmann's shocked silence on being told the news. Finally Bultmann responded, "So he really existed!" My teachers during my years at Yale taught me that if Jesus had not really existed, if the Jews were not God's promised people, then it is all smoke and mirrors. That is what this book is all about and why, I think, even at the risk of embarrassing my teachers, I dedicate it to them.

Of course, I am not suggesting that all my teachers agreed on the claim just made. The current identification as well as criticism of the so-called Yale School cannot help but strike those of us who are allegedly members of that school as funny. Those of us who studied at Yale during the time in question had no idea that our teachers had any convictions, much less represented a "school." Yet somehow we learned as their students that theology was not just about acquiring more information, but rather an activity that required practiced attention to the Christian tradition. That was a lesson for which I will always be grateful.

For some time I have known that there was a book in these essays. I could not have found it without the help of Scott Saye, Kelly Johnson, David Cloutier, and, of course, James Fodor. Scott, Kelly, and David are in the Ph.D. program in theology and ethics at Duke University. Such students make me better than I am. I am also indebted to Scott and Demry Bader-Saye for preparing the index. James Fodor originally came to Duke from Cambridge University via Canada, as a postdoctoral fellow. Canada is obviously a superior society compared to the United States, since it is willing to fund postdoctoral work in theology. I do not know if Jim has benefited from his postdoctoral work with me, but I know that I have.

Helping me to think through as well as to write this book has been, as we say in the South, a "godsend." Although I have little confidence in my ability to write theology as radical as are the hopes for Radical Traditions, I have every confidence that Scott, Kelly, David, Jim, and their colleagues and friends will be so able. Such students and friends are a source of hope and joy.

That I continue to be supported by new and old friends alike, I count as a sign of God's providence and grace. The same cast of characters—David Burrell, Reinhard Hütter, Robert Wilken, Michael Cartwright, Nancy Murphey, Jim McClendon, Greg Jones, Brett Webb-Mitchell, Charlie Pinches, Jean Elshtain, Rusty Reno, Jim Burtchaell, Alasdair MacIntyre, John Howard Yoder—and, as they say, many others—continue to make my life and work possible. Most of them are in one way or another academics. Academics are certainly important, but no less significant are friends such as Logan Jones and Kelli Walker-Jones, Julia and Larry Bowden, Kyle and Jane Childress, Adam Hauerwas and Laura Boynton-Hauerwas, Susan and Herb Allred, David Jenkins, and numerous others.

I have discovered, moreover, that I have a friend who was unexpected. She is Paula Gilbert, and she is my wife. I am not surprised that I love her. I live in wonder that she loves me. What I did not expect was that in marrying we would become such good friends. Marriage does not preclude friendship, but then neither does it require it. I am doubly blessed, therefore, that Paula is not only my wife, but my friend. I have no idea how this happened, but I thank God for having such a friend as her. She, of course, not only makes what I do possible; what is more, she makes the nonagonized "me" possible. God is great.

Stanley M. Hauerwas

Introduction: Theological
Interventions and Interrogations

Speaking Theologically

Theology is best done without apology. I therefore have no intention of apologizing for the unapologetic character of this book.[1] That I refuse to offer such an apology puts me at odds with a great deal of modern theology, which has adopted as its task to "explain"—either to our cultural despisers or to what is a growing and more characteristic population, the indifferent—what Christians believe. This explanatory enterprise is undertaken on the presumption that theologians, like Christians in general, will be more or less tolerated if they underwrite views on which general agreement prevails. The current sparsity of agreements about agreements, however, renders such a position extremely problematic. For one thing, theologians who adopt such an explanatory task often find themselves quickly out of date, having sided with agreements that often become the site of further disagreements. Accordingly, the status of theology is further undermined because of the concomitant impression that those who engage in such activities lack integrity.

The situation of the theologian mirrors the sociology of the church in social orders like that of the United States. Churches are thought to be a "good thing"—by those both within and without the church—to the extent that churches support what we care about most as a society or nation. This presumption is true for people on the political left and right. Those on the left want the churches to be "for economic justice," whereas those on the right want the churches to be good "for the family." As a result, churches find themselves in a difficult bind, particularly at the national level: They struggle to find ways to be inclusive without at the same time forgoing their distinctive "prophetic" calling to speak out or take positions on this or that issue.

That churches and theologians occupy a space that by its very nature is compromised should come as no surprise. I have no interest in blaming anyone for the harsh reality that as Christians we find ourselves in such a doubtful, ambivalent position. Rather, in this book I try only to locate a central challenge facing those of us who care about theology, namely, how theology in our time might reclaim a voice that speaks with authority, a voice whose power compels without coercion and persuades without denigration. Accomplishing such a feat requires, at the very least, a competence in writing and speaking in such a manner that our language as Christians actually does some work. By "doing work" I mean that our language is not simply a means of "saying what everyone already knows," but is deploying and engendering linguistic practices that enable Christians to discover and simultaneously to bear witness to a reality that we (and all that is) are God's good creation. In short, theological language that "does work" consists of those discourse practices that truly make a difference. (Language that "makes" a difference, of course, does so precisely because it also "reveals" important differences.)

The attempt to discover such differences has always been the animating center of my work. I have never thought, however, that the discovery of difference is an end in itself, since the discovery of difference clearly does not preclude the discovery of similarities as well. Nor have I assumed that "difference" implies that Christians are "better" than anyone else. Such moralism I find repugnant in the light of Christ's cross. Given the cosmic struggle Christians believe took place in that cross and resurrection, the idea that its significance can be reduced to who is "better" belittles both God and those of us who worship and struggle to obey God.

The project of discovering the differences has been my attempt to explore, in a modest but singularly significant fashion, how Christian claims about the world truly and faithfully display the way things are. I acknowledge that this project has put me in tension with much of contemporary theology and church practice. In an attempt to respond to the compromised position of theology, many theologians assume that their task is to show how theological speech could make sense given the epistemological presumptions of modernity—that is, they see their mandate as rendering intelligible to the world at least some of what Christians believe. A correlative politics and ethics is thus developed in the hope of putting the church on the side of what are assumed to be the most progressive aspects of our civilization. Such a politics and ethics appear quite prophetic insofar as they call, for example, for greater economic justice in the interest of egalitarian ideals. Unfortunately, the extent to which such a politics and ethics accommodate themselves to the presumptions of modernity is effectively concealed.

In contrast to this dominant outlook, I have repeatedly argued that the central theological task is to render the world intelligible to Christians. For me the question is not "How can theologians make Christianity intelligible in the modern world?" but "How can theologians make sense of the world, given the way we Christians are taught to speak in and through our worship of God?" I therefore have very little sympathy with attempts to translate Christian speech into terms that are assumed to be generally available. I resist that project not because I think there is some unchanging "core" of Christian convictions that must be protected come hell or high water,[2] but because I have a number of theological and philosophical misgivings about the very idea of translation. The notion that Christian speech can or must be translated if it is to be acceptable to modern people too often embodies simplistic views regarding the nature of language. For instance, such views of the linguistic character of the theological task fail to understand that the theologian should be trained as an adequate, skillful speaker of a language.[3] From my perspective, if Christian theological claims are no longer doing any work, they are best given up, for it is far better to abandon such futile endeavors than subject them to a resurfacing operation (a "face lift") that tries to show that they really mean something else.[4]

The theologian's task is to articulate why and in what ways certain practices are intrinsic to Christian discourse. As I suggest in Chapter 9, that was one of the reasons I became an "ethicist." I thought that ethics provided an intellectual opportunity to explore the differences Christian speech could and should make. I did not anticipate then the ways in which this project would force me to (re)discover the significance of the church as the primary set of language games not only in which Christians learn to speak, but in which our speech already is a practice with a significant difference.

Such claims about the significance of the church invite counterassertions by contemporary Christians and theologians to the effect that there have been so many different ways to be "church" or to do theology in Christian tradition. I have no reason to deny past and current differences between churches or the conflicts that theology both names and to a certain extent perpetuates. I have little use, however, for the easy affirmation of variety in the Christian tradition or for appeals to pluralism to legitimate the view that theologians get to decide what they want Christianity to be. The Christian tradition is a given, albeit a complex given, that invites and requires, rather than inhibits, argument.

That I became an ethicist first and foremost for theological reasons helps account for some of the misunderstanding, as well as the vehement criticism, generated by my work. "Ethics" was and continues to be the project of Protestant liberalism, particularly in the United States. That project, which is the Protestant project, has been to put the church at the service of making ours a society like no other. Ethics thus became the way to pursue that task to the extent that ethics purportedly named what was "really important" about Christianity in order to leave behind what was dubbed "traditional theological convictions." For me, by contrast, ethics refers to the kind of practices that shape the way Christians must live if we are to embody in our lives the confession that Jesus Christ is Lord.[5] Such language may make it difficult, perhaps even impossible, for Christians to "fit in." But I have never understood, let alone have I been persuaded by, the assumption that Christian theologians are supposed to help Christians "fit."

I hope that this book will make clear the theological agenda that has always animated my work as an ethicist. At first blush, this volume may look like just another book about other theologians and philosophers. It is at least that. Indeed, I trust that by reading the chapters on Niebuhr, Ramsey, Stout, Nussbaum, and the others treated herein, the reader will gain a greater appreciation and understanding of those thinkers. I, of course, hope the reader will also understand me better by considering my understanding of the people discussed in this book. Yet I trust it will be clear that this is not a book primarily "about other people." Rather, it is an attempt to make clear one central point, namely, that whatever my reputation may or may not be as an "ethicist," from beginning to end my concerns have always been theological. In this book not only do I try to display what I take to be the task of theology, but I actually do some theology. I have always been about the doing of theology, but here it may be present in a form more recognizable to those who are accustomed to having their theology done "straight."

For me to claim to be a theologian, of course, in no way assures greater understanding or agreement. In fact, it simply shifts the site of the controversy, since liberal theology is still theology. "Doing ethics" was one of the ways I tried to avoid the way theological questions were put in the liberal tradition—questions like "What is the experiential basis of theology?" or "What does it mean to say God acts in history?"[6] The essays in this book continue that avoidance strategy, but I hope they also help clarify why such questions are best made redundant and thus forgotten through the discovery of more interesting questions.

That I do theology in conversation with others is not accidental. It is through conversation that I discover what I think theologically. Actually the language of "conversation" is too weak to characterize the essays in this book. They are, as the title of this Introduction suggests, more like interventions and interrogations. That is to say, most of these essays are not so much "attempts at understanding" as they are interventions in another's agenda in order that I might better understand my own. But they are also interrogations, reflecting the ways in which I differ or agree or search for greater clarity. Accordingly, these essays are characterized by the kind of questioning that detectives employ when they do not know "who did it," but are equally sure that a crime has been committed.

On finishing this book the reader will not discover "who did it." For one thing, I do not know how the story will end. For another, I do not have a finished theological system nor do I believe in such a thing. I do not know what a finished theological system would look like, and even if I knew, I am pretty sure that I would not want it. My suspicion is that the desire to have such a system may indicate the theologian's lack of faith in the church. Indeed, the church across the centuries and through the communion of saints believes more than any theologian could possibly say. The theologian is therefore free to wander and wonder, knowing that the truth of what the church believes is not threatened by the theologians to "put it all together."

That the theology done in this book may seem to wander is not accidental. The essays, particularly in the first half of this book (Chapters 1–8), challenge the presumption of us Christians in America that we are finally "home"—that after two thousand years of wandering in the wilderness we have finally got to where we were meant to be. To be sure, even those of us who assume we are at home believe there are still a few kinks to work out. Christians of the left and the right have different accounts of those kinks, but it is commonly assumed that whatever the problems may be, we nonetheless have the resources to accomplish that task. In contrast, I assume that the church (and the theology that serves that church) must not be surprised or afraid to discover itself still in the wilderness. This is not a condition exclusive to the church's position in America, though America presents peculiar challenges for the church, but rather reflects the character of a church that by its very nature must always be on the way.

Wilderness theology will prove, I hope, to be a bit wild. After all, we have nothing left to lose, inasmuch as we are unsure where we are in the first place.[7] I remain convinced that nothing is quite as uncontrolled or radically unpredictable as Christian orthodoxy. To learn to see our lives (as well as the cosmos) as created; to learn that out of all the nations God chose the Jews; to learn that our destiny lies in the crucified and resurrected Jesus; all of that is to learn to see the world charged with God's grandeur. Surely a theology that has at its center a God of such wildness cannot be enclosed. I believe that these essays, even in their criticism of others, suggest the confidence that comes when Christians know that even in the wilderness we have nothing to fear except our own unfaithfulness to God.

The Plot

Theologically speaking, my primary purpose in this book is constructive. But having said that, I cannot deny that one of the reasons I have put these essays together is also to rebut the charge that I have no interest in, nor am I able to engage, those who differ from me, whether they be Christian or non-Christian. I find such criticism odd, not only because of the considerable time I spend reading and talking with those who do not share my views, but also—and just as important to me—because the way I think as a theologian is due in no small way to what I have learned from them and from those diverse engagements. It is true that I do not think there is in principle any way to ensure that the Gospel can be made intelligible to someone who is not a Christian, but that does not mean that there is nothing we have to say to each other. Oftentimes you have to wait and see (but also test and try, probe and prove) what you may have to say to each other.

For anyone interested in the question of whether those of us identified as "postliberals" can talk across traditions, the chapters in this book do not need to be read in sequence. If you want to know what I think about Iris Murdoch, for instance, you can read the chapter on her without reading any of the others. Yet the chapters are arranged with a certain plotline in mind. The first eight chapters are accounts of theological and philosophical alternatives from which I find that I must finally distance myself. Chapter 9, on Paul Holmer, marks a turning point in the book. I intended that Chapters 10–14 fill out some of the background that supports the kind of criticism I make in the first part of the book.

The book begins with "Knowing How to Go On When You Do Not Know Where You Are: A Response to John Cobb"—to his essay, "The Christian Reason for Being Progressive."[8] I know I am asking much of readers by having them begin with my reply to a piece that many of them will not have read. I think, however, that the reader can gather from my response a sufficient understanding of Cobb's position to make my criticisms intelligible. Moreover, commencing with Chapter 1 on Cobb is important because it signals the ways in which he has helped me understand how it is that Protestant liberalism bequeaths to Christians a misguided sense that they actually know where they are. Liberals are convinced that particular knowledges are certain in a manner that Christian orthodoxy cannot be. By representing the faith in a manner that will appear both intellectually respectable and politically responsible, liberal Protestants try to help the rest of us "fit in." I share Cobb's presumption that theology cannot be divorced from political and economic questions, but I obviously embrace quite a different theology and politics.

Chapters 2 and 3, on Reinhold Niebuhr ("History as Fate: How Justification by Faith Became Anthropology [and History] in America" and "The Irony of Reinhold Niebuhr: The Ideological Character of 'Christian Realism'"), exemplify the interrelation between theological and political questions discussed in the chapter on Cobb. At first glance, Niebuhr and Cobb may seem to be unlikely allies. But closer scrutiny reveals that they share a critical attitude toward the Christian tradition, all the while seeking to justify Christian support for liberal causes. Particularly important is how they both understand the relation between liberal theology and their own support of liberal political arrangements. Both authors exemplify the project of social Christianity in the United States, albeit in quite different ways.[9] I am aware that some may still find it strange to treat Niebuhr as a theological liberal, but he certainly understood himself as such and thought his liberal theological views were essential for his support of political liberalism.[10]

As I have noted above, one of the major themes running through this book is the interplay between liberal theology and liberal political theory and practice. In order for Christianity to gain intellectual and political intelligibility within the world of political liberalism, it must first be transformed into (i.e., reduced to) "beliefs." The way this transformation is accomplished is to focus on the "problem of history." History becomes the shorthand term for maintaining a causal account of human behavior to which God can only be an "externality." Such an account then produces the question "How, if at all, can God act in history?" That question presupposes that history names a world that is not God's creation.[11] It is that presumption which this book is meant to challenge.

Of course, discussions surrounding the "problem of history" were, and continue to be, more complex than the preceding paragraph suggests.[12] Yet I believe that framing the issue in these stark terms illumines the interplay between theology and politics within liberal cultures. Put quite simply, the overriding issue becomes: "How can hope be sustained in a world that is not created?" In such a world, history is but another name for resignation, the stoic acceptance of our fate. The irony, of course, is that Reinhold Niebuhr's life was one of hope that his theology belied. That such was the case is a testimony to Niebuhr's rootedness in the church. Yet for those of us not so rooted, his theology can easily become, as I think it did in the later stages of his life, a justification for the liberal presumption that "in the beginning was violence."

Chapter 4, on the work of James Gustafson ("God as Participant: Time and History in the Work of James Gustafson"), was for me an essay in discovery. Gustafson was (formerly) my teacher and is (currently) my friend. And it is precisely this friendship that impelled me to understand how it is that I find myself at such a different place than Gustafson, all the while conceding that that difference is partly due to what I have learned from him. In his spirited reply to those of us who contributed essays on his work in the *Journal of Religious Ethics*, Gustafson observes that his work, beginning with *Treasures in Earthen Vessels*, has been motivated by a desire to force Christian theologians to modify, if not correct, their exaggerated claims about the "Spirit" or the "Church," particularly when those claims are tacitly empirical ones.[13] Accordingly, he characterizes as "very naturalistic" his constructive suggestions in *Christ and the Moral Life* as well as in *Can Ethics Be Christian?*

I am extremely sympathetic with Gustafson's "empiricism," if he means by that attention to the work that theological claims in fact do. But I am not at all convinced that that requires those same claims to be construed "naturalistically." For example, Gustafson takes me to task when, in my effort to differentiate myself from him, I say, "I remain stuck with the claim that through Jesus' resurrection God decisively changed our history. Therefore I believe we must continue to begin with the 'particular,' with the historical, not because there is no other place to begin but because that is where God begins." Gustafson expresses uncertainty regarding who might be included and excluded from the pronominal "our" in that opening sentence; the second sentence he simply finds "ludicrous." He says, "I can only infer that nature is of no theological significance, and that God was absent, or something, until Jesus's resurrection. God is not sovereign over nature, I take it. Nature is also, then, of no ethical significance as a source of direction in Hauerwas's ethics. Hauerwas becomes a twentieth-century version of Marcion."[14]

Gustafson further challenges what he takes to be my "radical historicism," which I use to try to force him to choose between being a historicist or a universalist. He rightly points out that Ernst Troeltsch's and H. Richard Niebuhr's basis for being "historicist" was philosophically grounded, as they rightly saw that one cannot sustain on strictly historical grounds a claim for a radically historicist perspective. Challenging further my Christology and ecclesiology, Gustafson concludes that "Hauerwas is an intellectual and moral sectarian of the most extreme sort; thus he keeps a clear distinction between Christianity and the rest of life alive but forecloses apologetics of any kind and limits the range of the ethical. Hauerwas's God becomes the tribal God of a minority of the earth's population. I could argue cogently, I believe, that it is very unbiblical in many respects."[15]

I have recounted Gustafson's response to my article not only because I think it fair to do so, but also because I think it helps locate the argument I am trying to make. I agree that little hangs on whether one is a "historicist," given the lack of clarity surrounding that designation. Nor does much hang on the alternative between particularism or universalism. Rather, the issue is fundamentally theological, and Gustafson is right to focus on the question of creation or, more exactly, the character of our existence as determined by a God who freely creates. The claim Gustafson finds "ludicrous" concerns my remark about the God who creates as the only God worth considering, a God who is found not only in the cross and resurrection of Christ but also in the continuing working of the Spirit.[16]

The doctrine of creation only makes Christian sense as part of the doctrine of the Trinity. For Christians, the doctrine of the Trinity is necessary if we are to render the world intelligible as we find it and as we hope it will be. Such a claim is "empirical," not in the sense of being verifiable,[17] but in the sense that it requires a tradition-determined community to narrate the way the world is and, given the way the world is, how Christians must be in such a world. As I will discuss in Chapter 12, such a narrative may be "totalizing" in a manner Gustafson fears. However, Gustafson's fears are unfounded because the *content* of that narrative should, if understood rightly, prevent those who are shaped by it from forcing others into living as we do. All Christians seek to be is witnesses of that hope.[18] But it is a witness whose very possibility and efficacy resides in the certain "uncertainty" of hope. In other words, Christians are able to witness to that hope, not because they know beforehand the direction of history, but precisely because they do not.

On Gustafson's account, God gets to be a participant. Similarly, we too get to participate in the historical (and natural) processes in which we find ourselves. Unfortunately, this participation is neither a theology nor a politics that holds out any prospect of radical change. For "participation" tends to be the language of the liberal manager and bureaucrat, those who assume that the way things are is about as much as one can expect. Just as Stoicism often represented great wisdom for the Romans and for those who would rule Rome, so I think Gustafson's ethic represents great wisdom for the growing bureaucratic and managerial classes that rule liberal social orders. Were Christianity false, then clearly some form of stoicism would be the best alternative. Yet Christians cannot be stoics. For the God Christians worship creates and redeems, thereby making possible (but also making imperative) that we live in a manner fully consistent with the anticipation of God's kingdom. Somehow the language of "participation," at least as it is used in liberal social orders, represents too pale an image of the Christian God, and subsequently of the people God has called to be his own. Hence, Christians rightly believe that God requires justice and hope rather than bureaucratic "participation," which is why the poor find the proclamation of the Gospel such good news.

Chapters 5, 6, and 7 ("Can Aristotle Be a Liberal? Martha Nussbaum on Luck"; "Flight from Foundationalism, or Things Aren't As Bad As They Seem"; and "Not All Peace Is Peace: Why Christians Cannot Make Peace with Tristram Engelhardt's Peace") are about philosophers, not theologians. I have included them because not only do I admire the work of Nussbaum, Stout, and Engelhardt but also I believe each in quite different ways has helped Christians begin to imagine what our world looks like in God's eclipse. Nussbaum and Stout are serious thinkers seeking to show us how to go on in God's absence. It was soon after Nussbaum's *Fragility of Goodness* was published that I wrote the essay. I have included it, in part because in it I anticipated her increasing sympathy with Kantian modes of moral analysis and her correlative support of liberal political arrangements;[19] but more important, the essay continues to be relevant in the way it articulates perhaps the central issue in liberal moral and political theory—luck.

Liberalism is the moral passion that seeks to free our lives from the determination of bad luck, "accidents of our birth," and all other vicissitudes of history. History, from a liberal perspective, is the study of the past in order to render the past impotent for the ongoing determinations of our lives. In short, history becomes the way to put the wrongs of the past truly and irrevocably in the past through a kind of forgetfulness. The political arrangements of liberalism seek to free us from history by creating social orders in which "we can be what we want to be." Yet the means necessary to secure such "freedom" in an egalitarian manner creates societies that make our lives all the more determined by powers we do not recognize as powers.

Nussbaum, therefore, makes candid some of the ontological and political commitments that, in my essays on Niebuhr and even more on Gustafson, I began to suggest were inherent in Protestant liberalism: namely, a reconfiguration of Christianity in stoic terms. These themes are extended and deepened in Chapter 12, on Milbank, and Chapter 14, on Martin Luther King Jr. In brief, my piece on Milbank is an attempt to suggest an alternative ontology required by the Christian doctrine of the Trinity. Even more important, as I am sure Milbank would agree, is the witness of redeemed memory—as exemplified in the life and work and witness of Martin Luther King Jr., a man who refused to forget. His refusal to forget derives, of course, from the conviction that our world is constituted by a God who makes forgiveness and, thus, hope possible.[20]

Jeff Stout and Tris Engelhardt in different ways represent attempts to sustain liberal results without the epistemological conceits of liberalism. I admire Stout's attempt at *bricolage* as well as his quite sympathetic acknowledgment of those of us who persist in trying to remain Christian. However, I must confess that I am as sympathetic with his project as I am doubtful of its possibility.[21] He is right, of course, in using whatever moral resources happen to be at hand; but I remain unconvinced that such resources can be made fully intelligible, given that they remain abstracted from communities of memory necessary to form people of virtue. Stout would no doubt agree about the importance of such communities. Baseball and medicine are two important resources; but in the absence of a community (or communities) with a more determinative narrative, I do not see how they can resist distortion in the liberal market.

The chapter on Engelhardt provides an opportunity to explore the question whether the practice of medicine as the unqualified care of the sick can be sustained, given current liberal political arrangements. Engelhardt, like Stout, seeks no "foundation" that might ensure him a place to stand outside history. Rather, like his fellow Texan, Lyndon Johnson, he only asks that we "reason together," assuming that we will prefer peace to conflict. Yet I fear that the sort of peace he has in view is bought with too heavy a price; for it asks us to equate peace with the absence of violence. I doubt any society built on such an illusion can long keep more overt forms of violence at bay.

I have followed the chapter on Engelhardt with an account of Paul Ramsey, "How Christian Ethics Became Medical Ethics: The Case of Paul Ramsey" (Chapter 8). I did so not only because it continues the focus on medicine,[22] but more important because Ramsey is helpful in returning us to the presuppositions (or at least the practice) of Protestant liberal theology. Ramsey would be shocked to be counted among the Protestant liberals, since he thought of himself as more theologically and politically conservative than anyone in that tradition. But it was Ramsey who also made the mistake of assuming that Reinhold Niebuhr believed what Ramsey believed.[23] As a result, he thought he could "use" Niebuhr's realism without reproducing Niebuhr's Christology (or lack thereof). Just to the extent that Ramsey accepted the role of the "ethicist," he could not help but make his theological convictions appear as afterthoughts.

The title of Chapter 9, "How to Go On When You Know You Are Going to Be Misunderstood, or How Paul Holmer Ruined My Life, or Making Sense of Paul Holmer," is an obvious allusion to the title of this book. As I indicated above, the essay on Holmer represents something of a turn in the plot of the book. It is not so much a plot reversal as an attempt to say more explicitly and constructively what I think by directing attention to those who have taught me both what to think and how to think. The essay on Holmer in particular makes explicit the Wittgensteinian resonances that some may have already noted in this Introduction and, if they are discerning readers, in all that I have written. I do not pretend that this chapter is anything more than a gesture needing more adequate defense, but I hope the reader will nonetheless find it a helpful gesture. For if the position I have tried to argue in this book is close to being right, the only "adequate defense" is precisely the kind of display each of the chapters in this book, I hope, represents.

Chapter 10, on Iris Murdoch ("Murdochian Muddles: Can We Get Through Them If God Does Not Exist?"), may at first seem to belie my claim that the rest of the chapters in the book are about thinkers with whom I am in general agreement. Yet I hope my immense debt to Murdoch is apparent even as I disagree with her "theology." Indeed, one of the things I find most fascinating about Murdoch is her willingness to believe almost everything Protestant liberals would want her to believe, yet she does so without seeing any reason why that would entail believing in God, let alone a God who creates. At the very least, my engagement with her work has forced me to be much more candid about the metaphysical entailments required by the Christian conviction that all that is, is created.[24]

Not only will Chapter 11, on James McClendon's work ("Reading James McClendon Takes Practice: Lessons in the Craft of Theology"), give the reader a sense of what my kind of "systematic theology" might look like, but it also extends the material convictions that inform the perspective of this book. For example, McClendon's claim that war and its violence turn out to be antihistorical is exactly the kind of redescriptive work Christian speech must perform if it is to command the serious attention of Christians and non-Christians alike. Of course, such a claim invites and requires much "explanation," which turns out to be the kind of work theologians are supposed to be about. That McClendon works so patiently and well to that end is why I find his work so compelling, an important beacon in our time.

By the time readers come to Chapter 12, on John Milbank ("Creation, Contingency, and Truthful Nonviolence: A Milbankian Reflection"), they may well feel it is superfluous, since frequent reference to and use of his work appear throughout the previous chapters. In a singular way, Milbank has charted a new direction for theology for which, alas, this book is only a footnote. To be sure, Milbank's attack on the social sciences as providing theodical legitimations for the violence of liberal social orders can initially be off-putting because of its uncompromising character. Exposing the invisibility of the liberal narrative and practices (which are invisible exactly because they are now more or less identified with "the way the world is") cannot help but appear as a violent exercise. But I would contend that the violence unveiled characterizes more the subject matter than either the one doing the exposing or the methods of unconcealment. My only difficulty with Milbank is the fear that in dismantling the master's house too many of the master's tools may have been used.

Nevertheless, Milbank is surely correct in claiming that finally all one can do is provide a better narrative. I remain agnostic whether "a better narrative" requires that we "out-narrate" all comers, but there can be no question that we must learn again how to do Christian history. Indeed, Milbank's *Theology and Social Theory* may well be the closest thing we have in modern theology to Augustine's *City of God*. Such a comparison is obviously not fair to Milbank, but at least it suggests the genre within which I think his work is properly judged.

Wilderness Wanderings, the title of this book, came to me while rereading the essay describing Oliver O'Donovan's work (Chapter 13, "Remaining in Babylon: Oliver O'Donovan's Defense of Christendom"). O'Donovan has done what my criticism of Protestant liberalism suggests we must do. He has sought, not to reach an accommodation with liberal culture, but to show why liberal culture is unintelligible without the God we Christians worship. His is a Constantinian project on the grandest scale before which I can only stand in awe. Not only do I stand in awe of what he has attempted, but I also stand in much agreement. He and I concur, of course, in our assessment of liberalism and its antithetical character to Christianity.[25] But our agreements are deeper in that he too seeks no "transcendental" point that might free us from our obligation to be faithful to biblically narrated history. The crucial difficulty with O'Donovan's narrative, however, is that it attempts to help Christians recover the home we thought God had made for us in "the West." In contrast, I assume that one of the most important duties of Christians is continually to resist amnesia; that is, we must not forget the sense in which our earthly journey invariably passes through wilderness places. For a people who live between the times, it should come as no surprise that we should find ourselves, more often than not, still in the wilderness.

The book closes with Chapter 14, "Remembering Martin Luther King Jr. Remembering"—on a good Protestant liberal. At least Martin Luther King Jr. was a good Protestant liberal when he came to write his theology. King's liberalism no doubt contributed to his power, which surely is an indication that much good remains in liberal theology. Yet as I suggested above, King's life and work were shaped by a people who knew they could not forget their ancestry or their history. They could not forget those who had gone before and whose past sufferings make present memories (and identities) possible. By remembering Martin Luther King Jr., those of us who are not African-Americans are presented with a crucially important opportunity to become engrafted into a practice that makes us part of a history that, through God's grace, we might learn to acknowledge as our own. King did not and could not lead us out of the wilderness, but without him, and others like him, we would not have enough hope to sustain our wandering.

Such is this book's plot. There are subplots within the main plot that I trust some readers will find of interest. Indeed, the plot I have provided is only one way that these essays can be read and thus I am confident that some readers will find more interesting ways to plot the book. Certainly my hope is that my outline will not inhibit, obstruct, or prevent such readings—or, worst of all, discourage some readers from reading the book altogether. Perhaps one should not worry oneself overly much about things about which one has little, if any, control. Nonetheless, I would be dishonest if I did not confess that central to my aspirations for this book is that it might suggest to some readers how wonderful it is to serve a God who has more interesting things for us to do than to make our world safe.

A Few Concluding Remarks

I confess I love to write introductions like this. I keep thinking that perhaps if I persevere long enough I will be able to articulate what I have been on about, not only to myself but to others as well. Perhaps I harbor the unrealistic hope that if people just understand what I am trying to do, they will not be so critical. This book, and in particular writing this Introduction, has certainly helped me understand what I am trying to do. But the more I understand, the more I understand what yet needs doing. That seems to me a good thing, if you think, as I do, that theology, if it is to reflect truthfully on God, must remain forever unfinished.

Never being able to finish, of course, can be a frustration. Yet it can also be an invitation for others to help. I am gratified and sustained by those who are pursuing, with deeper historical knowledge and theological insight than I possess, the kind of agenda represented by this book. In particular, I am grateful to Michael Broadway, Phil Kenneson, and James Fodor for writing three of the essays (Chapters 3, 6, and 13 respectively) with me. "Writing with me" is too weak a description to do justice to their individual contributions. For each coauthored piece reflects hours of discussion before, during, and after the writing. They have taught me much.

Some may wonder why the book has no separate chapters on Alasdair MacIntyre or John Howard Yoder. One answer is that I have written so often about both of them that it would be redundant to include chapters on their respective work in this volume.[26] I think, however, the more important reason is that every chapter in this book is so dependent on what MacIntyre and Yoder have taught me that the book is, from beginning to end, about them. I say that with some hesitancy and misgiving, since I know that each of them, for quite different reasons, feels some ambiguity about their influence on my work.[27] But it would be disingenuous of me not to acknowledge their influence.

I hope that if this book does nothing else, it embodies my conviction that theology is a communal endeavor. The essays that constitute its content manifest my debt to those with whom I agree and my even greater debt to those with whom I disagree. Disagreements are precious achievements indeed, not easily had and even more rarely appreciated. Mistakes are made all the time, and we ought to be grateful to all those who are kind enough to point them out. To those people we remain indebted. But there is no greater compliment than to discover that you have made a mistake that truly matters. I hope that such mistakes as may be found in what I have done here may lead to new and greater discoveries that will help all of us know better how to think and live as Christians, as those trained to wander and wonder, with curiosity and courage, but also with faith and confidence, in the one God who has promised to guide us in places that more often look like wilderness than home.

Notes

1. William Placher has illumined these matters in *Unapologetic Theology: A Christian Voice in a Pluralistic Conversation* (Louisville: Westminster/John Knox Press, 1989). I have no reason to deny the possibility of what some, following Hans Frei, call ad hoc apologetics. I remain convinced, however, that theology is most compelling when it is done with confidence.

2. The very notion of a core of beliefs that allegedly constitutes "what Christianity is all about" is one of the most dangerous assumptions in theology. Protestant liberal theology went to ruin trying to find an "essence." This search for a core I take to be the continuing legacy of the Reformation, which gave Christians the misguided notion that they could freely range over Christian tradition deciding what we like and do not like. At the risk (albeit small) of exaggeration, the attitude that most characterizes Protestants is "How much of all the past stuff that Christians used to believe do I need to continue believing in order to still think of myself as a Christian?" In contrast, Catholics tend to think: "Goodness, look at all the great stuff we get to believe!" Catholics rightly understand that they do not have to "believe" X or Y *as an individual believer,* since that is the function of the whole church. What matters is not what the individual may believe, but what the church believes.

3. Because Christians are committed to witness, I suspect that they must by necessity learn what MacIntyre calls "second first languages." The learning of such languages always presents certain challenges, but Christians have no reason to believe that such a process will not enhance their understanding of their first first language. After all, we believe our God will be found in the stranger. See Alasdair MacIntyre, *Whose Justice? Which Rationality?* (Notre Dame: University of Notre Dame Press, 1988), pp. 364–365.

4. I certainly do not think Christian convictions are invulnerable to challenge and revision. Indeed, I think it imperative that Christian theology be responsive to the best science of the day. If you could demonstrate, for example, that physics requires matter to be metaphysically eternal, then I would be compelled to view as problematic what Christians believe about creation. Of course, what one means by 'matter' or 'eternal' is not easily determined. But in saying that I seek no easy way out; rather, I wish to get the arguments in the right context. I am extremely sympathetic with the kind of account Nancy Murphy provides of these

issues in her *Theology in the Age of Scientific Reasoning* (Ithaca: Cornell University Press, 1990).

5. Consider, for example, this quote from Max Stackhouse, who is one of the most distinguished Christian ethicists currently writing: "The ethical power of Christianity is based in the affirmation that Jesus Christ is the ontological embodiment of the loving and justifying relationship between God and humanity, the One whose life, death, and resurrection are the primary historical evidence that we are loved and justified. Thus, in Jesus Christ, we find a direct, personal relationship between the divine and the human whereby the triune reality of God reaches beyond God's internal existence and overcomes the distance between the divine and the human. Thereby, the material, psychological, social, and political realities of human existence are empowered toward the integration of ethical possibilities. This embodying event gracefully invites the fragile, easily distorted, subjective, suspicious person to believe that our existence is covenantal in character, even given the ambiguities of warranted historical evidence. This vertical intersubjective relationship thereby prompts and enables us to seek the formation of those relative covenants of justice and love possible in historical relationships that they may become channels of grace in the horizontal-intersubjective relationships of life, both in the church and in the fabric of civilization. Indeed, they are to society as the soul is to self." "The Vocation of Christian Ethics Today," *Princeton Seminary Bulletin* 16, 3 (new series, 1995): 296. Stackhouse uses "orthodox" language, but note that according to him Jesus exemplifies a "prior relationship," which makes very unclear why Jesus was put to death. Would not his birth have been sufficient? Moreover, the assumption that Trinity names God's reaching "beyond" God's internal existence can only be described as bizarre, since orthodox Christian doctrine presumes Trinity is God's internal existence. What I think the reasoning in this paragraph exhibits, and this is not peculiar to Stackhouse, is the impatience that many "ethicists" have toward theology. What these ethicists really want is to get on with working out the "relative covenants of justice and love." If that sounds a lot like Reinhold Niebuhr, it is by no means accidental.

6. Peter Hodgson, in *God in History: Shapes of Freedom* (Nashville: Abingdon Press, 1989), wishes to claim for himself a "postmodern" perspective, but as the title of his book indicates, he continues to embrace the assumption that God must somehow be fitted into "history." To be sure, he provides a quite sophisticated account of the latter, disavowing all grand theories. Yet, as he acknowledges, his position is in some ways quite similar to that of John Cobb's, as like Cobb he assumes that we need an "overview" in order to make sense of history (239). Indeed, it is not clear how Hodgson's considerable erudition does not result in underwriting a high humanism in the interest of providing a theological justification of liberal causes. For example, consider this quote: "God is present in specific shapes or patterns of praxis that have a configuring, transformative power within historical process, moving the process in determinative directions—that of the creative unification of multiplicities of elements into new wholes, into creative syntheses that build human solidarity, enhance freedom, break systematic oppression, heal the injured and broken, and care for the natural" (205).

William Thompson provides a striking contrast to Hodgson's "account" of God in his *The Struggle for Theology's Soul: Contesting Scripture in Christology* (New

York: Crossroads, 1996). Consider, for example, Thompson's meditation on the first chapter of John: "The Prologue and the entire Gospel of John are inviting us to consider that we are moving, not simply from the man Jesus to God, but from the God-become-Man Jesus to the trinitarian Word. We learn about the trinitarian Word because that trinitarian Word is as and in Jesus. The 'theologic' here is from God to humanity. That is, only God can make God known" (126). Thompson accordingly does theology with the assumption that the theologian's task is to explain our existence, not God's.

I confess I simply do not understand how theologians like Hodgson (and Cobb) became so sure that they could know where God "is present" once the language of "presence" is divorced from the people of Israel and Jesus' death and resurrection. It is as if speculative theological language has become the primary discourse of faith.

7. By "unsure" I am not calling attention to the limits of my subjectivity, though such limits are surely present. Rather, by "unsure" I mean the unceasing demand to form judgments concerning the situation, the exact specificity of which always eludes the theologian, since there is no one universal, invariant standard and since the theologian enjoys no privileged vantage point.

8. Cobb's essay, along with my response, was originally given as the Shaffer/ Mars Lecture at Northwestern University. Each essay was subsequently published in *Theology Today* 51, 8 (January 1995): 548–562 and 563–569 respectively. I also commend to the interested reader John Cobb's gracious response to my response, "Ally or Opponent? A Response to Stanley Hauerwas," in the same issue of *Theology Today*, 570–573.

9. See for example Gary Dorrien's compelling account of this tradition in *Soul in Society: The Making and Renewal of Social Christianity* (Minneapolis: Fortress Press, 1995). Dorrien rightly sees Cobb's economic views as a challenge to Niebuhr's acceptance of the capitalist market, but in many ways the kind of perspective Cobb assumes that Christians should adopt in modernity was first made possible by Reinhold Niebuhr. For an appreciative review of Dorrien's book, see my review in *Modern Theology* 13, 3 (July, 1997): 418–421.

10. In his 1914 M.A. thesis, "The Validity and Certainty of Religious Knowledge," which he wrote under the direction of D. C. MacIntosh at Yale Divinity School, Niebuhr makes the following claim: "To put it as briefly as possible we may say that the demand for religion is the demand for personality. We find ourselves in an impersonal universe. Its laws do not respect those things which are dear to us and, as we think necessary for our happiness. We cannot understand oursel[ves] except in the light of moral law. We find our life without purpose if it has not the purpose of striving for the right and the just. But the universe does not appreciate the moral order. It has no place for moral values. The laws of the external, of nature totally disregard the peculiar spiritual realities of man. It destroys them. And yet we know that there can be no morality if it be not eternal. Man could not be brought to make a single moral struggle if he were forced to believe the results he achieves to be without permanence. It does not matter now whether or not man finds permanence and eternity of the values in himself necessary or whether he can be satisfied to know that the fruits of his struggle will be conserved in the universe. But the fact does matter that man can not understand himself without the moral order nor the moral order without some warrant of permanence. This is the demand for an efficient God, for a God who insures the

moral order and the permanence of moral values and personal realities. It is the need James assumes when he calls religion a consciousness of the highest social values" (11–12). I am aware how unfair it may be to quote this early work of Niebuhr, much of which he would disavow as he grew more sophisticated. Yet I do not believe Niebuhr ever abandoned the view that "science" has rendered impossible the belief that God ever did, does, or will do things in the world. Henry Clark forthrightly acknowledges and defends Niebuhr's "insufficient Christology" on grounds that "the quest for mythopoetic profundity leads to an appreciation of the greatest insights of biblical faith and avoids the errors of fundamentalism or unyielding orthodoxy." See *Serenity, Courage, and Wisdom: The Enduring Legacy of Reinhold Niebuhr* (Cleveland: Pilgrim Press, 1994), p. 150. One wonders what could have ever led Christians to die for "mythopoetic profundity."

11. Spinoza, of course, wrote the script for this account of the world. It was not just Protestants that accepted this narrative of the world, however, but also Jews. David Novak, in *The Election of Israel: The Idea of the Chosen People* (Cambridge: Cambridge University Press, 1995), observes that even if many Jewish thinkers did not accept Spinoza's particular religio-political conclusions, they did accept his general premises—which meant they were led to alter radically "the classical Jewish doctrines of creation, election, revelation and redemption into the ideas of origin, destiny, insight and progress. Creation was changed from the founding cosmic event into the perpetual origin of cosmic process; election was changed from external choice into an intuition of one's own destiny; revelation was changed from the voice of God to man into the insight of man about God; and redemption was changed from an apocalyptic event into culmination of historical progress" (47). No better description could be given of the project of Protestant liberal theology exemplified by Niebuhr, Cobb, and Hodgson.

12. The relation between history and what historians do remains a philosophical conundrum. Though they seldom explicitly appear in my work, I have never ceased thinking about or stopped learning from the kind of issues raised by Collingwood, Dray, Gardiner, and Danto. In fact, much of what I have done in "ethics" has been an attempt to transpose what I have learned from them (and Aristotle and Aquinas) into the language of character, virtue, and narrative. Consider, for example, this wonderful passage from Danto: "The present is cleared of indeterminacy only when history has had its say; but then, as we have seen, history never completely has its say. So life is open to constant re-interpretation and assessment. It nevertheless remains the ideal of history-as-science to eradicate the discrepancies between historical reality and history-for-us. To the degree that it succeeds, we live no differently in history than we do outside history: we live in the light of historical truth. It is, of course, not altogether plain that truth is to be preferred to illusion, nor certain that it will make us free. It is only that we have no choice in the matter once we achieve historical consciousness, for we cannot will falsehood or inconsistency." See *Narration and Knowledge* (New York: Columbia University Press, 1985), p. 341. Danto suggests that we must wait for history-as-science to have its say so that we will know our past—a wan hope from my perspective. For a book that at once exhibits an honest, but unsuccessful, attempt by professional historians to wrestle with these questions, see Joyce Appleby, Lynn Hunt, and Margaret Jacob, *Telling the Truth About History* (New York: W. W. Norton, 1994).

It is to his great credit that Luke Timothy Johnson (in *The Real Jesus: The Misguided Quest for the Historical Jesus and the Truth of the Traditional Gospels* [San Francisco: HarperCollins, 1996]) exposes the philosophically questionable presumptions about history behind the so-called quest for the "historical Jesus." The resurrection constitutes history (and nature) being a "new creation," which in turn implies that historical research is not without theological significance. Indeed, it is my view that however misguided the search for the "historical Jesus" at least it served to challenge the gnosticism inherent in Protestant pietism. David Keck puts it well in *Forgetting Whose We Are: Alzheimer's Disease and the Love of God* (Nashville: Abingdon, 1996) by noting that the historical-critical method, "despite its apparent historicity, has in fact made the church less historical; over the past two or three centuries, church people have grown less and less confident about their own past" (61).

13. James M. Gustafson, "A Response to Critics," *Journal of Religious Ethics* 13, 2 (Fall 1985): 185–209 (Gustafson makes this observation about his work on p. 198). The essays on Gustafson appeared in the *Journal of Religious Ethics* 13, 1 (Spring 1985), ed. James Childress and Stanley Hauerwas. Though we meant the issue to honor Gustafson's work, he was, as we say in Texas, "none too pleased" by most of the essays.

14. Gustafson, "A Response to Critics," p. 191. I think Gustafson mistakenly assumes that a strong distinction can be made between nature and history. I assume that "nature" is not dumb but alive with God's grandeur. That it is so means no hard distinction can be drawn between nature and history because human history is nature.

15. Gustafson, "A Response to Critics," p. 196. The last sentence is subjunctive because Gustafson does not want to give the Bible such authority. For what it is worth, my own views about these matters are exactly put by David Novak in his characterization of how Jews should understand the significance of historical research. He notes that historical research cannot be rejected out of hand, any more than natural science can, without "the worldly weight of the Bible being simultaneously surrendered and the Jewish readers of the Bible being relegated to the level of obscurantists. The Bible within our tradition, where it is the primary source of truth, is also found in other contexts. This has been demonstrated convincingly by modern historical means. And the doctrine of creation surely implies that there is truth in the wider world, however subordinate it must ultimately be to the truth of revelation. Nevertheless, historical research must always be secondary precisely because the Bible is the book that Jews have never stopped reading. It is a book addressed to them in all their generations. Modern historical research on the Bible, conversely, has been conducted on the assumption that contemporary readers of the Bible are reading about someone other than themselves. Occasionally, the Rabbis too recognized the gap between the historical context of their own generations and the historical context of certain biblical texts. However, the notion that the Torah speaks just to its own time is only rarely mentioned. Much more often it is assumed that the Torah speaks far beyond the time in which it was originally uttered." David Novak, *The Election of Israel: The Idea of the Chosen People* (Cambridge: Cambridge University Press, 1995), p. 113.

16. I confess to remaining perplexed, given Gustafson's own theological constraints, about how he comes to the conclusion that God creates. Moreover, I would challenge the assumption that Christian attitudes toward "nature" are peculiar to the doctrine of creation when the latter is not displayed in relation to God's trinitarian character. I do not deny that these are complex matters, which the recent emphasis on history as *the* issue before theology has ill prepared us to face. Clearly, what must be recovered is a sense of the cosmic character of Christ's person and work. See, for example, David Yeago, "Jesus of Nazareth and Cosmic Redemption: The Relevance of St. Maximus the Confessor," *Modern Theology* 12, 2 (April 1996): 163–193. Likewise, just as I find it hard to understand why Gustafson assumes that God creates, it puzzles me that he continues to think God is one. The many powers that bear down on us are, after all, just that—many.

17. By "being verifiable" I am simply calling into question any correspondence theory of truth that presumes that an isolated proposition must fit an equally isolated fact.

18. I cannot refrain from observing how Gustafson's humility does not prevent him from providing a "naturalistic" account of Christian convictions, whether or not those holding such convictions would describe their lives as Christian.

19. Nussbaum most recently has written, "My own preferred version of the ethical stance derives from Aristotle, but everything I say here could be accommodated by a Kantianism modified so as to give the emotions a carefully demarcated cognitive role." *Poetic Justice: The Literary Imagination and Public Life* (Boston: Beacon Press, 1995), p. xvi. I have no doubt that there are readings of Aristotle and Kant that might make it possible to defend this claim, but one must wonder if a self-proclaimed Aristotelian could ever begin a sentence with the phrase, "My own preferred version of the ethical stance . . ." For her defense of political liberalism, see Nussbaum, "Aristotelian Social Democracy," in *Liberalism and the Good*, ed. R. B. Douglass, G. M. Mara, and H. S. Richardson (New York: Routledge, 1991), pp. 203–252. Nussbaum has increasingly moved to a defense of what I can only call "high humanism" and a corresponding commitment to modernist presumption about how texts should be read. In both these respects Stout represents quite a different alternative.

20. For a wonderful exposition of the Christian practice of forgiveness, see L. Gregory Jones, *Embodying Forgiveness: A Theological Analysis* (Grand Rapids: Eerdmans, 1995).

21. John Howard Yoder also has written appreciatively of Stout while questioning, as Phil Kenneson and I do, Stout's "timeless" account of slavery. Yoder points out that it is hardly news to Christians, at least Christians without Constantinian pretensions, to be told that they live "after Babel." See Yoder, "Meaning After Babble: With Jeffrey Stout Beyond Relativism," *Journal of Religious Ethics* 24, 1 (Spring 1996): 125–138. Yoder rightly sees the problem is not "Babel" but "babble"—that is, "the intentional confusing of language by human users" (127).

22. The demand that medicine do more and more to alleviate our condition is necessary if we are committed to the elimination of "bad luck" through political and economic arrangements. Sickness and death, on such a view, are so "unfair."

23. Steve Long, in *Tragedy, Tradition, Transformism: The Ethics of Paul Ramsey* (Boulder: Westview Press, 1993), provides the best account of Reinhold Niebuhr's

influence on Ramsey. In a wonderful (and appreciative) paragraph, Long suggests that "Ramsey was a casuist who worked from a particular tradition, but who did not have any institutional practices to sustain that tradition. He was a particularist forced to use the leveling, generalized putatively universal language of modernity in hopes that his particular tradition might find some room in the modern era. The end result is that his work is much too particular to Christianity to be useful as a common, universal politics of speech, and it is much too universal to be useful as a politics of speech for the creation of an alternative Christian community. Yet Ramsey's work does offer an alternative to the dominant ideology undergirding much of ethics, and his work waits for the creation of those institutional practices that will give it life" (103).

24. I continue to believe that Aquinas's account of these matters is without parallel. His refusal to separate God's essence and existence (without which any account of God's simplicity would be impossible) seems to me to remain the heart of the matter. For a powerful account of Aquinas's doctrine of God, see Eugene Rogers, Jr., *Thomas Aquinas and Karl Barth: Sacred Doctrine and the Natural Knowledge of God* (Notre Dame: University of Notre Dame Press, 1995).

25. In an odd way, O'Donovan's defense of Christendom makes him more a "sectarian" that I allegedly am. For he proposes nothing less than a restoration of Christendom in liberal cultures. Indeed, from O'Donovan's perspective my own ecclesial alternative might be far too easy for liberalism to accommodate.

26. See, for example, the chapter on MacIntyre in Charles Pinches and Hauerwas, *Christians Among the Virtues: Theological Conversations with Ancient and Modern Ethics* (Notre Dame: University of Notre Dame Press, 1997). Some years ago Paul Wadell and I wrote an extensive review of *After Virtue* in *The Thomist* 46, 2 (April 1982): 313–321. I have more recently written on Yoder in the *Christian Century* series on Christian classics. My suggested title for the article was "Why the *Politics of Jesus* Cannot Be a Classic." The article was published as "When the *Politics of Jesus* Makes a Difference," *Christian Century* 110, 28 (October 22, 1993): 982–987. I have also written on Yoder for an Australian audience in "Yoder Down Under," *Faith and Freedom* 5, 1–2 (June 1996): 44–46.

27. For example, Yoder observes (in "Meaning After Babble") that my critique of "English-Speaking Justice" as a set of "bad ideas" is too simple if pluralism as a civil arrangement is better than any of the hitherto alternatives (135). I know that many share the sentiment that I too often resort to exaggeration when I need to be more exact. Yet I do not think that Yoder is right about my critique of "English-Speaking Justice" because I am quite exact about the liberal theories of justice I am critiquing. I am not at all convinced, for instance, that Yoder is right to use "pluralism" as an accurate description of our social arrangements. I certainly cannot pretend to be as "careful" as I should be, but in spite of what some believe, I try to speak and write with care.

PART ONE

*"Taking Leave": Disclaiming
the False Security of "Home"*

1 *Knowing How to Go On When You Do Not Know Where You Are: A Response to John Cobb*

I MUST CONFESS AT THE VERY OUTSET that I just do not know as much as John Cobb. This confession does not mean that I am less knowledge-able than Cobb, though I may well be. Besides, humility has never been my long suit. Rather, what I mean is that I simply do not have the basis to know what Cobb seems to know, since I have learned to distrust the very practices that have produced the knowledge he professes.

Put differently, I think Cobb would like to be a postmodernist, but he remains caught in the discourse of modernity—discourse, for example, that would have us talk of "Christ events" in preference to talking about Jesus Christ. Of course, that is not a problem peculiar to Cobb but may well be the problem of anyone caught in a time waiting for a world to be born.

Let me try to explain these obscure remarks by calling attention to the title of Cobb's paper, "The Christian Reason for Being Progressive." One should not make too much of titles, but at the very least this title implies that Cobb has some idea of what it means to be "progressive." Moreover, the title also seems to suggest that being progressive is a good thing, something Christians should support, since anyone who is progressive appears to be squarely on the side of the "good guys." But if you already know, on grounds different from Christian practice, what the goods are, then it remains unclear why one should worry too much whether being Christian makes much difference one way or the other.

Of course, Cobb starts with the confession that he really is deeply con-servative, since he belongs to a community that faithfully shapes its life according to norms derived from ancient events. As he puts it, "To sub-mit oneself to the meanings and norms inherent in such ancient events is surely a conservative stance." I must admit I am not so sure. I am not so certain because I am unclear where exactly Cobb thinks he is standing in order to decide whether to submit. By raising this question I am not at this point questioning Cobb's account of the Christian tradition—though I will raise some questions about that later. Rather, I am wondering on what grounds he believes he can take a position for or against the tradition that will then allow him to decide whether he should submit to it. Just to the extent that he thinks this vantage is possible, he certainly knows more than I know.

Moreover, I take the knowledge that allows him to assume such a position to be characteristic of modernity and modernity's faith in progress; or, perhaps, more accurately put, the presumption of modern people that progress names a good thing. For I take it, as Christopher Lasch suggests in his *True and Only Heaven: Progress and Its Critics*, that what is so original about modernity's conception of history is "not the promise of a secular utopia that would bring history to a happy ending but the promise of steady improvement with no foreseeable ending at all."[1]

Thus Cobb celebrates the development of "modern democracy, human rights, science, technology, and historical consciousness and criticism," even while acknowledging their ambiguity. I suppose that such a litany is more or less required if you want to appear to be on the side of the good guys, to say nothing of "History." But I must confess that I am less than sure I know what such terms mean or, even more, if they are a good idea.

I need to be as candid as I can about my doubts concerning these matters, for they derive from a quite different set of theological presuppositions than those of Cobb. His is a theology shaped by the attempt to make Christian convictions amenable to the epistemological conventions underlying the modern project. The very confidence he has in knowing where he is betrays his indebtedness to modernity. By modernity, I mean the project to create social orders that would make it possible for each person living in such orders "to have no story except the story they choose when they have no story." That is to say, modernity is the attempt to so dis-embed and estrange peoples from the peculiarities, distinctiveness, and contingencies of their respective traditions as to form the illusion that the only story now worth telling is one entirely of their own devising. For on modernity's terms the past as such does not truly exist, nor can it have any bearing on our present choices. Hence, the only story countenanced by modernity is one that is predicated on the false belief that since we are unencumbered by any received story, we are truly free to fashion de novo any narrative we wish and thus make (and remake) of ourselves whatever we will.[2]

One of the main engines of the project called modernity was the division of labor that is intrinsic to those economic systems that Cobb now finds so destructive. Cobb would like to reject the economic character of modernity while preserving its cultural, theological, and political character. It is nice work if you can get it, but I think such a strategy fails to see the close relation between the political systems that Cobb seems to favor and the correlative economic systems that require constant growth. Indeed, the very presumption that we can separate economics from politics is itself a liberal invention.

The primary goal of those societies we identify as progressive is freedom. Correlatively, equality and justice are thought to be the sufficient moral norms to determine social and political arrangements.[3] Egalitarianism thus becomes the opium of the masses, insofar as it presumes, falsely, that since who we are is a matter entirely of our own choosing, we are by definition free. Of course, the irony of this project is that most modernists, like Cobb, fail to notice that they themselves did not choose their own stories—namely, they did not choose the dictum (the "story") that they should have no story except the story they chose when they had no story. Correlatively, democratic ideologies operate to hide those powers that hold us captive.

This is not to deny that Cobb is right in presuming that most Christians, whether conservative or liberal theologically, assume that they ought to be on the side of a history that favors such social systems. They do so, of course, precisely because they suppose Christianity to be a civilizational religion of which modernity is but the continuation.[4] Like their modernist counterparts, they profess to believe in freedom of religion, the importance of keeping religion out of public policy decisions, and so on. But because they are socially conscious—which is usually expressed as "the need to be responsible"—they must try to infuse the social order with the Christian spirit. Cobb thus assumes that he writes for everyone—or at least everyone who counts (which means, all good democratic liberals).

Accordingly, Christian theology is assumed to be a discourse available to anyone. That is particularly true when it comes to language about, and concomitantly knowledge of, God. In this respect, I am struck by how much Cobb knows about God. He believes, for example, "that God is working to save the creation and especially the human species," even though he does not believe "that God is Lord of History in the sense that God will unilaterally intervene to save us from the consequences of our actions." I must confess that I find such a claim baffling. I wonder how Cobb knows that. As Paul Ramsey was fond of saying, "God intends to kill us all in the end." I assume that Ramsey's assertion also included the human species. I see no reason to believe that God's salvation through Jesus' cross and resurrection was about ensuring that the human project is going to come out all right in the end.

I am aware that this appeal to cross and resurrection may suggest that I am one of those who, as Cobb puts it, clings to past embodiments of

Christ in a manner that blocks Christ's present working. I may be willing to plead guilty to that charge except I find it hard to so characterize my position, given that I am a pacifist. I believe that anyone professing to worship God revealed in Jesus' life, death, and resurrection can only do so faithfully as a nonviolent disciple. Therefore, I must say that those Christians who thought they were following the "present working of Christ" through their acceptance of violence have made a disastrous mistake. The reasons for that acceptance were various, but certainly for many it represented the attempt to be on the "progressive" side of history.

I have to confess, moreover, that I believe that Christian nonviolence is unintelligible if Jesus was but an exemplification of "creative transformation." I am always curious how those that would so construe Jesus' life account for the fact he got himself killed. If all Jesus was about was helping us see that God is that "factor in the world that introduces freedom, novelty, spontaneity, life, creativity, responsibility, and love," I cannot see why anyone would think it worth his time to kill him.

I need to be quite clear that I am not disagreeing with Cobb's suggestion that any tradition worthy of our interest is involved in constant change even when it is at its most conservative. As Stanley Fish suggests in *Doing What Comes Naturally*:

> Change is not a problem if one posits independent agents who can check their accounts and descriptions against an equally independent reality; for then change is easily explained as a function of the constraints placed by reality on our interpretations of it. But the neatness of this picture is sacrificed if one conceives of persons not as free agents, but as extensions of interpretive communities, communities whose warranting assumptions delimit what can be seen and therefore what can be described; for then the describing agent, the object of description, and the descriptive vocabulary are all transformations of one another and there would not seem to be enough room between them to make change a possibility. . . . This impasse [can be] negotiated by demonstrating that neither interpretive communities nor the mind of community members are stable and fixed, but are, rather, moving projects—engines of change—whose work is at the same time assimilative and self transforming. The conclusion, therefore, is that change is not a problem; and, indeed, to the extent that there is a problem, it would seem to be one of explaining how anything ever remains the same; or, even more precisely, how, given the vision of a system and of agents continually "on the move," can one even say that a change has occurred since the very notion of change requires, as Robert Nisbet has pointed out, "some object entity or being the identity of which persists through all the successive differences."[5]

Fish answers the problem of how we can account for continuity by observing that not everything ever changes at once. "Interpretive communities are no more than sets of institutional practices; and while those practices are continually being transformed by the very work that they do, the transformed practice identifies itself and tells its story in relation to general purposes and goals that have survived and form the basis of a continuity."[6]

I call attention to Fish's account because I think it makes clear that the question is not whether change is possible, but rather how to account sufficiently for continuity so as to enable the telling of an intelligible story. I have a problem, for example, accounting for continuity as a Christian committed to nonviolence, since it is usually claimed that most Christians throughout the history of the church have thought killing to be a permissible, if not a positive, good. Of course, as one of my feminist students pointed out, nonviolent Christians are not a minority if you recognize that most Christians, by virtue of the fact that they were women, were not allowed to fight in war. That this was perhaps nonvoluntary makes this observation no less significant.

What I find unclear in Cobb's attempt to "claim the center" in Christian theology is how "creative transformation" works to claim such a center. Indeed, once something called "creative transformation" is seen as the norm of the tradition, I see no reason why you need the Jews or Jesus for any account of that tradition. I see no reason, for example, to believe that God dwelt in Jesus in a "peculiarly intimate way." That sounds too much like making the claim that Jesus had some kind of experience— which is, to be sure, a very Methodist thing to think and thus puts Cobb in good company. But then American Methodism is surely only quite incidentally related to Christianity. (That is not to say that Methodists are without any convictions. Quite the contrary. For now that I am back among the Methodists, I have discovered that they do have a conviction: It is that God is nice. Moreover, since Methodists are a sanctificationist people, we have a correlative: We ought to be nice too. I must admit, one of the things that bothers me about Cobb's God is that she is just too damned nice!)

How one understands the significance of Jesus obviously has implications for one's understanding of God. In that respect, I cannot resist commenting on Cobb's criticism of male images for God. I wish to be clear that I have no objection to feminine imagery for God, but I do not believe that the trinitarian Father, Son, and Holy Spirit is an image. Rather Trinity is a name. Christians do not believe that we first come to know something called God and only then further learn to identify God as Trinity. Rather, the only God Christians have come to know is Trinity: Father, Son, and Holy Spirit.

I am deeply sympathetic with feminist critiques of generalized fatherhood language for God, though some feminists might object to my reasons for being sympathetic. The only possible reason I can think to call God Father is that Jesus is the Son. That means that fatherhood is not analogous to the cultural presumption that men define the nature of fatherhood. The peculiar presumption that God as father derives its intelligibility from anthropological assumptions about men as fathers was a development made possible only after Protestant liberalism gave up the conviction that Jesus is the messiah. The frequently heard claim that those who have had an abusive father have trouble calling God father may be psychologically true, but theologically uninteresting. For if you see that fatherhood is a grammar controlled by Christological convictions, then those who have a troubled relation with their biological fathers are perhaps in the best condition to worship a trinitarian God.

It is hard for us to understand this last point because of current Christian sentimentalities about the family. I confess once again that I am not nearly so confident as Cobb that Christianity has always been as patriarchal as he suggests. My doubts about that involve problems with the essentialization of gender that seem intrinsic to such claims. I do think, however, that the "familization" of Christianity since the Reformation has had disastrous results for everyone. By "familization" I mean the presumption that the first way of life among Christians is marriage and family.

Forgotten in that presumption is the Christian practice of singleness as the necessary form of the church's eschatological convictions. For the single Christian is nothing less than an indispensable reminder that the church grows, not by necessity or through biology, but by witness to the stranger. That is not because, as Cobb suggests, Christians had a negative attitude toward sex, but because by becoming God's people Christians understood that their true family was now the church. A Christian's first loyalty is always to church, not to family or nation.

In this respect, I find Cobb's praise of "covenantal relationships" as the best place for the "expression of sexuality for homosexuals and those heterosexuality inclined" to be rather charming but unconvincing. That seems to underwrite romantic conceptions of sex and marriage that I take to be creating many of our current problems. I have always assumed that one of the hardest aspects of Christianity is the admonition for Christians to love one another even if they are married. The assumption that marriage is primarily a relation between two people for their mutual fulfillment represents the depolitization of marriage in the interest of the politics of liberalism.

Again one of the disastrous aspects of this emphasis on the family as the hallmark of Christianity is what it does to our understanding of the cross. What it means for Jesus to call God father surely means that in this man's life more is at stake than spontaneity, creativity, and love. What is at stake is a battle with powers that would have us killed in the name of protecting the family.

If one believes that we are engaged in that kind of battle, then it makes sense that you need all the help you can get to survive. In particular, you will need a community of people who have the ability to transmit across generations the skills necessary for survival. That community we call church; it names a reality that is constitutive of, and not simply incidental to, being Christian. In short, that is why there is no salvation without the church.

I am aware that such claims sound imperialistic and they certainly have so sounded whenever the church has been associated with Constantinian social policy. But when you remember that I assume that the church is at most a struggling minority quite unsure where it is, then such a claim appears quite different. For example, I take it that such a church, although not opposed to dialogue with other religions, assumes that its first task is to witness to what we know rather than seek agreement about "creative transformation."

Accordingly, I do not desire nor would I know how to give Christian reasons for being "progressive." I seek, rather, to know how to go on when I do not know where I am. I assume that is not a new condition for Christians to be in, as being a member of the church becomes necessary exactly because the claims of Jesus are meant to put us out of control. However, once we Christians learn how to tame our penchant for control (or, to put it bluntly, our felt need to run the world), to pretend that we know not only where we are but also where everyone else is or should be, maybe we will be able to live such joyful lives that others may actually be attracted to the celebration we call worship.

Notes

An earlier version of this chapter appeared in *Theology Today* (January 1995). Reprinted by permission.

1. Christopher Lasch, *The True and Only Heaven: Progress and Its Critics* (New York: Norton, 1991), p. 47.

2. I am indebted to James Fodor for this way of articulating the matter.

3. For a wonderful account of how liberalism must work with a far too thin account of moral vocabularies, see Ronald Beiner, *What's the Matter with Liberalism* (Berkeley: University of California Press, 1992), pp. 39–97.

4. For my general perspective on these matters, see Stanley Hauerwas, *After Christendom?* (Nashville: Abingdon Press, 1991).

5. Stanley Fish, *Doing What Comes Naturally* (Durham: Duke University Press, 1989), pp. 152–153.

6. Ibid., p. 153.

2

History as Fate: How Justification by Faith Became Anthropology (and History) in America

Karl Löwith on Reinhold Niebuhr

"God has granted American Christianity no Reformation. He has given it strong revivalist preachers, churchmen, and theologians, but no Reformation of the church of Jesus Christ by the word of God."[1] That was Dietrich Bonhoeffer's judgment about American Protestantism—a judgment that remains one of the most insightful accounts available of Protestant Christianity in America. It is a judgment that could well have been made by Gerhard Sauter, who has patiently tried to remind his American friends that "the freedom of the church is not where it has possibilities, but only where the Gospel really and in its power makes room for itself on earth, even and precisely when such possibilities are offered to it."[2]

I think it is therefore appropriate, in an essay honoring Sauter, to call attention to Karl Löwith's critique of Reinhold Niebuhr. For Löwith, like Bonhoeffer, went to the heart of the matter by challenging Niebuhr's account of history.[3] Niebuhr has often been criticized for "anthropologizing" theology and, in particular, for justification by faith, but Löwith rightly saw that even more problematic was Niebuhr's understanding of history. For Niebuhr's account of history is devoid of an eschatology, and Sauter has rightly helped us see that such an eschatology is the necessary background for the doctrine of justification.[4]

Löwith's essay, which is only eight pages long, appears in the famous anthology on Niebuhr edited by Kegley and Bretall.[5] Most of the essays in that volume are either celebrations of Niebuhr's accomplishments or sympathetically critical of some aspect of Niebuhr's work. Löwith's piece, however, challenges not just Niebuhr's answers but the very way he poses the questions. As a result, his essay could not help but appear as the proverbial frog in the punch bowl. Polite people know that the best way to handle frogs in such circumstances is by pretending they are not there, and that, it seems, is the way Löwith's contribution was received. Yet I think the issues Löwith raised should not be ignored because they remain crucial for how we think about theological anthropology and, thus, about Reinhold Niebuhr.

Löwith begins "History and Christianity" by making some general observations about why modern man places so much significance on history as the defining mark of the human enterprise. He suggests that overestimating the importance of history is the result of our loss of any sense of human nature within nature at large. We presumptuously assume that world history is the history of the universe. But, Löwith observes:

> if history has to be defined by and delimited to man's willful enterprise, the question about its meaning is itself historically conditioned. It is a specifically Western concern which presupposes that history has a purpose as *telos* and *finis*. This belief in a final purpose has originated from the faith in the purposeful will of God with regard to his creation. With the secularization of the Christian theologies of history to the modern philosophies of history, the will of God became replaced by the will of man and divine Providence by human prevision. The possibility of a philosophy of history rests on secularized eschatology. (282)[6]

Löwith notes that classical Christian theology never assumed that history was the decisive scene for determining questions of human existence and destiny. For Christians history is not a realm of human endeavor or progress. Rather, it is a realm where sin and death reign and thus it is in need of redemption. The eschatological character of Christian conviction challenges any assumption that history can be construed as a continuous, or even progressive, process. Jesus is not a world-historical link in the chain of historical happenings, but the unique redeemer.

> What really begins with the appearance of Jesus Christ is not a new epoch in secular history, called "Christian" but the beginning of an end. The Christian times are Christian insofar as they are the last times. Because the Kingdom of God, moreover, is not to be realized in a continuous process of historical development, the eschatological history of salvation also cannot impart a new and progressive meaning to the history of the world, which is fulfilled by having reached its term. The "meaning" of the history of this world is fulfilled against itself because the story of salvation, as embodied in Jesus Christ, redeems and dismantles, as it were, the hopeless history of the world. In the perspective of the New Testament, the history of the world entered into the eschatological substance of its unworldly message only insofar as the first generations after Christ were still involved in it, but without being of it. (*HC*, 283)

Löwith does not deny that Christianity may have spanned modernity's sense of history, but that is only because the early church's eschatological outlook required a perspective toward a future fulfillment. Modern historical consciousness, in short, is the Christian sense of history's having a beginning and an end but without the belief that Jesus Christ is the beginning of the end. Thus the very idea of "Christian history" is nonsense, since Christian eschatological convictions preclude any processive account of history that can be discerned, much less an account of history as actual progress.

From Löwith's perspective, therefore, the very way that Niebuhr sets up the problem of "history" is already a mistake. Niebuhr, according to Löwith, poses the question of the relation between faith and history on the presumption that Christians have a stake in providing a general account of history as the "problem of history," thereby underwriting the assumption that something called "history" exists in ontological independence from God. That is, history is understood as the growth of man's power and freedom through which every human perplexity will be resolved; indefinite progress by itself will redeem history. Niebuhr, of course, is critical of the views of history that "absolutize the relative," yet he continues to argue that progressive views of history are closer to the Christian view of history than the ahistorical spirituality of the Greeks.

According to Löwith, for Niebuhr the

> perplexing problem of how the Christian story of salvation is embodied in the history of the world seems to be resolved in a dialectical balance between the common experience of visible history and the individual experience of faith in things unseen by the rather conventional and unexamined assertion that there are "facets of the eternal in the flux of time." Tangents of moral meaning in history are supposed to point toward a suprahistorical center. Being assured of this center of meaning and orientation by a faith which reduces the doctrines of creation, incarnation, resurrection, and consummation to mere "symbols" (which have, however, to be taken "seriously" but which would be embarrassing when taken literally), Niebuhr has little difficulty in asserting the superiority of the Christian interpretation: "It is above the alternatives of despair and complacency, evolutionary optimism and defeatism, secularism and escapism, pietistic sectarianism and Catholic institutionalism, worldliness and asceticism, and so on. The Christian interpretation of history is more adequate than alternative interpretations because it is dialectically more comprehensive." (*HC*, 285–286)[7]

Löwith observes that one cannot help but wonder if such a criterion of superiority is not more Hegelian than Christian, a manifestation of the sin of pride inasmuch as it cannot help but always be superior to the too simple alternatives.

More seriously, Löwith challenges Niebuhr's satisfaction with the "dialectical method"—that is, the assumption that the limits of virtue, wisdom, and power exist only to be answered and completed by faith. The secular thinker, after all, can respond by challenging the assumption that the contradictions and ambiguities in fact require "ultimate" resolution. On the contrary, mature stoical resignation and endurance is the appropriate attitude. If the only way to establish the truth of the Christian Gospel is "at the very limits of all systems of meaning," then theologians will have to demonstrate the validity of their apologetic on more than dialectic grounds.

Niebuhr, according to Löwith, finally tries to have it both ways; namely, he maintains that Christian love not only does not extend historical potentialities of the human project, but makes historical survival problematic. Yet he also insists that it is necessary to "incorporate" what is true in the modern discovery of history as a form of development into the truth of the Christian faith.

> Thus, the intellectual power and versatility of *Faith and History* leaves us with a profound ambiguity: The author of the book shares neither the modern, now obsolete, faith in history as such, nor the ancient faith in the Christ with whom the time was fulfilled, but makes the attempt to salvage by means of a liberal faith in symbols some fragments of the modern but shaken belief in the meaningfulness and purposefulness of the historical process. (*HC*, 287)

But the crucial difficulty with this view, according to Löwith, is that those who have faith in Christ believe neither in the ultimate nor in the provisional meaningfulness of history, but experience instead the "radical *disproportion* between the history of the world and the succession of faith as implied in the story of the great flood" (*HC*, 287).

Christians, of course, experience "history" like anyone else, but they refrain from trying to explicate the story of salvation in terms of the world's history. For they believe profane history has the character of a sign, visibly intimating that which is known only to faith. Disasters may thus be interpreted as intimations of the last judgment but the last judgment cannot be comprehended in terms of, or subsumed under, the general category "disaster." Moreover,

> since the story of salvation does not refer to historical empires, nations, and civilizations but to each human soul, one cannot dismiss the thought that Christianity, that is, faith in Christ, is essentially indifferent over against world-historical differences, even over against the differences between civilization and barbarism. Both reveal under different circumstances the same human nature, though man appears better than he really is if orderly and civilized conditions do not put him to the test. Even atomic warfare would not change what human nature essentially is. (*HC*, 289)

So runs Löwith's argument against Niebuhr. It is an argument that obviously goes to the heart of the matter, not only in terms of Niebuhr's position, but also in terms of current theological debates. For to suggest that the threat of annihilation of the human species should not change how Christians understand their faith challenges some of the most deeply held convictions by Christians. His critique is therefore not just of Niebuhr but of many who continue to share Niebuhr's sense of the Christian's stake in the survival of nations and empires. However, before addressing that set of questions, we must first ask if Löwith has been fair to Niebuhr.

Anthropology as History

It may well be objected that even if Löwith is right about Niebuhr's understanding of history, he nonetheless fails to appreciate that Niebuhr's views require a fuller account of anthropology. In other words, it is *The Nature and Destiny of Man* to which we should attend, not *Faith and History*. I think such an objection entails a far too restricted sense of anthropology and, in particular, Niebuhr's anthropology. For Niebuhr was never interested in a doctrine of man *as such* but in how anthropological reflection provided the resources for an extensive commentary on history and our contemporary situation. History, for Niebuhr, is the playground of ideas. The task of Christian theology is to understand the nature of those ideas in the hopes of sustaining the social expertise.

The Nature and Destiny of Man starts with a familiar Niebuhrian theme:

> The obvious fact is that man is a child of nature, subject to its vicissitudes, compelled by its necessities, driven by its impulses, and confined within the brevity of the years which nature permits its varied organic forms, allowing them some, but not too much latitude. The other less obvious fact is that man is a spirit who stands outside of nature, life, himself, his reason and the world.[8]

The great problem, according to Niebuhr, is how to do justice both to the uniqueness of man, usually identified with our rational capacity, and to man's affinities with the world of nature. The temptation is either to lose the individual's uniqueness by allowing it to be absorbed by universal reason or to bury it in nature or the social organism by succumbing to that romantic desire that would still the pain of self-knowledge.

This theme, which has infinite variations throughout Niebuhr's work, provides him with the perspective to get on with his primary work of cultural commentary. Therefore, the first chapter of *The Nature and Destiny of Man* is an attempt to substantiate the claim that modern culture is the battleground for the conflict between two views of man: the classical and the biblical. Modern culture, according to Niebuhr, is beset by unresolved antinomies that result from our being inheritors of these fundamental options—for example, the conflict between idealists and naturalists, the conflict between individualism and collectivism, and finally the culture's inability to deal with the problem of evil.

Though it is certainly true that Niebuhr was primarily concerned with developing an adequate anthropology, we will misunderstand him if we fail to see that his anthropological interests were subservient to this larger agenda. That agenda was nothing less than the development of a philosophy of history sufficient to sustain civilization. Niebuhr's anthropology, in fact, becomes the occasion for a romp through history in the hopes of providing a new synthesis to save "our" civilization. Thus, in the second volume of *The Nature and Destiny of Man*, Niebuhr says that "when we are confronted with the task of reorienting the culture of our day, it becomes important to discriminate carefully between what was true and false in each movement"—namely, the Renaissance and the Reformation (*ND*, 205). Niebuhr's historical judgments are often criticized, but he has little stake in whether he has rightly interpreted Augustine or Luther or whether it is even possible to make generalizations about the "classical" or "biblical" view of man. Rather, what is important for Niebuhr is whether these terms do not in fact represent eternal possibilities that we must now try to bring into a new synthesis in order to be able to save "Western civilization" as a viable enterprise.[9]

For Niebuhr history and anthropology go hand in hand. As he says in *Faith and History:*

> The whole history of man is thus comparable to his individual life. He does not have the power and the wisdom to overcome the ambiguity of his existence. He must and does increase his freedom, both as an individual and in the total human enterprise; and his creativity is enhanced by the growth of his freedom. But this freedom also tempts him to deny his mortality and the growth of freedom and power only increases the temptation. But evils in history are the consequences of this pretension. Confusion follows upon man's effort to complete his life by his own power and solve its enigma by his own wisdom. Perplexities, too simply solved, produce despair. The Christian faith is the apprehension of the divine love and power which bears the whole human pilgrimage, shines through its enigmas and antinomies and is finally and definitively revealed in a drama in which suffering love gains triumph over sin and death. This revelation does not resolve all perplexities; but it does triumph over despair, and leads to the renewal of life from self-love to love. (*FH*, 233–234)

In short, the individual is for Niebuhr but the microcosm that illumines the macrocosm of world history.

On the basis of this overview, I think that there is no question that Löwith's criticism of Niebuhr's views on history is directly relevant to questions of Niebuhr's anthropology. It is quite another matter, however, whether Löwith has in fact accurately represented Niebuhr's views. At least initially, one is inclined to doubt the fairness of Löwith's depiction of Niebuhr's views, since the very criticism he makes of Niebuhr sounds very much like Niebuhr's criticism of those who assume that some kind of fulfillment is possible in history. Löwith, in other words, has failed to appreciate the dialectical character of Niebuhr's thought and has mistakenly overemphasized Niebuhr's sense of mankind's inherent historicity. In order to see if this judgment is sound, we must look at what Niebuhr says about man's historicity.

In *Self and the Dramas of History*, Niebuhr says:

> It is obvious that the self's freedom over natural processes enables it to be a creator of historical events. Both its memory of past events and its capacity to project goals transcending the necessities of nature enable it to create the new level of reality which we know as human history. But the self is not simply a creator of this new dimension, for it is also a creature of the web of events, of which it participates. [10]

Thus history is at once the realm of freedom and fate. But the issue must be put even more paradoxically because for Niebuhr our freedom, our history, becomes our fate. Through history man is able to emancipate himself from subjection to natural necessity, but in the process he becomes subject to the means of his freedom. The assumption that we have become master of our destiny is, ironically, the source of our lack of freedom.

Löwith's contention that Niebuhr continued to presuppose a progressive view of history, therefore, seems problematic in the light of Niebuhr's constant emphasis on the theme that history cannot be its own fulfillment. As Niebuhr says:

> The problem of the meaning of history is always the problem of the meaning of life itself, since man is a historic creature involved, and yet not involved, in the flux of nature and time, but always in the position either of negating the meaning of history or of completing it falsely, if he seeks to complete it from the standpoint of his own wisdom. Yet it can be completed by a revelation, the acceptance of which is possible only through a contrite recognition of the human situation of sinfulness. Such repentance is possible, in turn, only if the judgment overhanging man is known to be prompted by love and to be crowned by forgiveness. (*FH*, 140)

Niebuhr assumes that this "problem" is precisely what justification by faith is about—namely, that judgment hangs over every human achievement.

Man thus cannot finally create a meaning that can satisfy his own ability to create meaning, that is, history. Our "historic existence can not have meaning without faith" (*FH*, 57), for the meaning of history cannot be completed with itself. Rather, the meaning of history can come only from beyond itself through a faith that apprehends the divine forgiveness, thereby overcoming our attempt to secure meaning within history. Yet we continue to resist this truth, as we do not come easily to a recognition of the contingent character of our existence.

From the perspective of Christian belief, therefore, history remains to the end morally ambiguous. That is why it is not possible to speak of a "Christian philosophy of history" or why it may not even be possible to have any adequate "philosophy of history" because such philosophies cannot help but reduce the antinomies, obscurities, and variety of forms of history to a too simple form of intelligibility (*FH*, 136). Nevertheless, there can be a Christian theology of history that "makes sense" out of life and history, but only insofar as the "final clue to the mystery of the divine power is found in the suffering love of a man on the Cross." This, of course, is "not a proposition which follows logically from the observable facts of history" (*FH*, 137), which is exactly the reason why the cross and the cross alone is able to "embody the perplexity of history into the solution" of how God has overcome human recalcitrance (*FH*, 143).

The Christian Gospel, according to Niebuhr, can finally be validated only negatively.

> The Christian philosophy of history is rational, therefore, only in the sense that it is possible to prove that alternatives to it fail to do justice to all aspects of human existence; and that the basic presuppositions of the Christian faith, though transcending reason, make it possible to give an account of life and history in which all facts and antinomies are comprehended. (*FH*, 138)

Optimists therefore rightly insist that pessimists do not appreciate the dignity of man, the integrity of human reason, the ability of man to establish provisional realms of meaning in history. The pessimists, in contrast, rightly criticize the optimists for failing to understand the misery of man in the ambiguity of his subordination to and transcendence over nature. The pessimists also criticize the optimists' false estimate of the stability of cultures, which derives from their failure to understand the destructive character of human pretensions. The wisdom of the Gospel is distinguished from both pessimism and optimism, able to comprehend both, because it is derived from a source finally not subject to the contingencies of history (*FH*, 164).[11]

Löwith's Argument Assessed

Although obviously much more can be said about Niebuhr's views on history, I think we now have sufficient basis to assess Löwith's arguments against Niebuhr. First, however, we ought to let Niebuhr speak for himself. There is precedence for this: At the end of the Kegley and Bretall volume Niebuhr responds to each of the essays in the book. Under the general heading "Friendly Critics," in distinction to "Substantive Criticisms," Niebuhr remarks that the essential difference between Löwith and himself is that the former

> finds no tangents of meaning in the historical drama which are clarified by Christian revelation. He seems to me to be saying that the drama is "full of sound and fury, signifying nothing," and that only revelation and salvation rescue life from meaninglessness. I know how easily any "Christian" interpretation of history can give it false meanings, analogous to the false meanings elaborated by Hegel or other philosophers. I know that Christ is the "light that shineth in darkness." The question between us is how absolute the darkness is. If it is as dark as he assumes, there cannot be any relevance between faith and our life as historical creatures. Professor Löwith says that responsibility is a moral and not a religious category. Is this distinction absolute? Is there not wisdom in the Christian faith which might prevent a powerful nation and a secure culture from plunging into catastrophe by its pride? Or which would prevent individual Christians from fleeing into complete irresponsibility about the fate of their civilization?[12]

Niebuhr goes on to say that it is very important to be clear on what is at stake between him and Löwith. For if "history" is declared to be totally meaningless, individuals are thereby absolved of responsibility for the culture and civilizations that make us the stuff of history. The Christian faith, as a result, offers only individual transcendence from the ambiguities of collective life. Even though "world history" is not specifically mentioned in the New Testament, Niebuhr argues that he cannot see how the meaning of the New Testament faith requires that we abandon all concern with "world history." That is particularly the case if we remember that the prophets were certainly concerned with the sovereignty of God over the history of all nations and whether such a historical drama involving nations and empires had meaning.

I cannot help but think that Niebuhr's response is a classical example of a "failure in communication." He fails to respond to the substance of Löwith's argument because he simply fails to appreciate how fundamental Löwith's criticisms are for the way he initially defined the problem of history. Löwith's challenge is not simply whether history may be read as having "tangents of moral meaning" or the question of whether Christians should assume responsibility in the cultures in which they reside, but whether the very meaning Niebuhr attributes to "history" adequately appreciates the eschatological character of the cross and resurrection of Jesus of Nazareth. If Christ is a "solution" (admittedly a "transcendent solution") to the ambiguity of history, then the cross is made to be an answer to a question the Gospel does not ask. What must be challenged, according to Löwith, is not whether the fulfillment of history comes from an immanent or a transcendent source, but whether the very notion of history as a coherent enterprise determined by human action entails a false eschatology.

It is no wonder, therefore, that Löwith and Niebuhr tend to pass each other as ships in the night. For if Niebuhr attended to Löwith's challenge, it would require a completely different understanding of what anthropology is and how it should be done in Christian theology. Rather than beginning with a general account of our being caught between nature and history, between finiteness and transcendence, Niebuhr would be forced to attend to our being caught between two times, two different histories—the one a time and history of the world, the other the time and history of God. That contrast is not, as Niebuhr would have it, between the provisional and the ultimate but between those who have and those who have not become citizens of God's kingdom initiated through Jesus of Nazareth.[13]

Löwith is therefore not impressed (and rightly so) with Niebuhr's denial that he holds a "progressive" view of history. To be sure, Niebuhr stresses the ambiguity of all historical achievements; of course, Niebuhr never tires of reminding us that the "profoundest truth may be the source or bearer of grievous error" (*FH*, 196); but such emphases continue to presuppose that we can assume a perspective on history that finally lets us read its ambiguities. It is not sufficient to appeal to the necessity of maintaining a "dialectical" perspective, as Niebuhr does, for the very ability to maintain that perspective presupposes a position that is profoundly nondialectical.

Put differently, Löwith is at once challenging Niebuhr to be less and more "historical." Niebuhr is acutely aware of the problem of historical relativism. He suggests, for instance, that historical relativism

> forces modern man, who claims to be increasingly the master of historical destiny, into periodic modes of skepticism as he analyses his dubious position as observer of history. The problem is, how a man, nation, or culture involved in the mutabilities of history can achieve a sufficiently high vantage point of wisdom and disinterestedness to chart the events of history, without using a framework of meaning which is conditioned by contingent circumstances of the class, nation, or period of the observer. (*FH*, 116)

But what Niebuhr fails to see is the very statement of the "problem" presupposes a standpoint that is radically ahistorical. In contrast, Löwith's eschatological perspective requires us to accept the contingent character of our existence in history in a more radical manner than Niebuhr is willing to do.

Such a criticism may seem extremely odd, since it is Niebuhr more than any other Christian theologian who has emphasized the centrality and unavoidability of history as a category of Christian theology. Yet ironically his very presentation of "the problem of history" results in an account of Christian convictions that renders their historicity virtually irrelevant to the meaning and/or truth of their own existence. In short, Niebuhr's account of the cross is finally but another variation of the Gnostic temptation to turn the cross into a knowledge that is meaningful separate from the actual death of a man called Jesus. It sounds like orthodoxy to claim, as Niebuhr does, that the cross is the "solution" to history, but the strength of such a claim is undercut by Niebuhr's insistence that the cross is first and last a "symbol"—namely, the name for the eternal possibility that transcends the ambiguities of history.

Niebuhr would be shocked by such criticism, as he goes to great length to disassociate himself from Bultmann, who, Niebuhr believes, mistakenly identified the *"kerygma"* (the proclamation of the Gospel) with existential philosophy. According to Niebuhr, such an identification is a mistake because all "ontological" accounts of the Christian faith undercut the temporal character of our reconciliation with God. Niebuhr therefore criticizes Bultmann for failing to distinguish between prescientific myths and permanent myths, as the latter "describe some meaning or reality, which is not subject to exact analysis but can nevertheless be verified in experience. The experience which verifies it and saves the myth from caprice is usually in the realm of history and of freedom beyond the structures and laws of existence."[14]

According to Niebuhr:

> that "God was in Christ reconciling the world unto Himself" is verifiable in the experience of everyone who experiences the mercy and new life which flows from true repentance in the encounter with God. It is also verifiable by the proof that alternative methods of explaining or dissolving the mystery and the meaning which governs and surrounds us lead to observable miscalculations in regard to the nature of man and of history.[15]

But the experience of "true repentance" is no longer the response to the cross of Jesus but rather a response to a universal human possibility that at best confirms, and at worst determines, the meaning of the cross of Jesus.

It is extremely hard to criticize Niebuhr in this manner without having a sense of being unfair. For Niebuhr so often seems to say things about the "classical" or "modern" view of history (or man) that appear similar to Löwith's criticism. Thus, for example, Niebuhr suggests that the most obvious definition of "history" is a record or memory of past events.

> More profoundly considered it is a dimension of existence in which present realities can be rightly interpreted only through the memory of past events.

Since both present and past realities did not follow necessarily from previous events, the bewildering mixture of freedom and necessity in every historical concretion is rightly understood only if the particular and unique acts which constitute the flow of events are remembered in their uniqueness. (*FH*, 18–19)

Memory is therefore the crucial power that allows us to retain unique events, whether they fit into a conceptual mold or not. If developed theologically, this sense of the significance of memory could provide Niebuhr with the resources to meet Löwith's challenge. Unfortunately, on Niebuhr's account memory is but another means we have to create freedom from nature and history.

Niebuhr suggests that

the Christian faith is not merely a faith which gives meaning to history through memory, contrasted with a philosophy which seeks abortively to give it meaning by forcing it into the mold of natural recurrence. Memory alone can not produce a universe of meaning above the level of the life of the individual or a tribe or nation. Religions of memory, whether tribal or imperial, can not rise to the level of envisaging the story of mankind in its totality. Neither can they deal with the threat to life's meaning arising from the fact that the freedom of man contains the possibility of defying and destroying the coherence of life. The significance of Christianity as a "high" religion is partly derived from the two facts, (1) that it comprehends the whole of history, and not only the story of a particular people in its universe of meaning, and (2) that it deals with the problems of evil ultimately and not merely from the standpoint of what may appear to be evil to a particular individual or collective agent in human history in the actions of competitors and foes. (*FH*, 21–22)

In the light of this quote I think that there can be little doubt that the main lines of Löwith's interpretation and critique are correct. Niebuhr cannot be satisfied with history understood as a particular community's remembered past, but history must be that which "comprehends the whole." As a result, Niebuhr is simply unable to comprehend the radical eschatological perspective found in the New Testament. His not being able to do so, I suspect, is a result of his thinking that without such a comprehensive history he will lack the means to develop a social ethic to save Western civilization, to save it from its own pride. But if Löwith is right, Niebuhr's account of history, and ironically of sin, is itself but a manifestation of that selfsame pride.

Man as Sinner

What are the implications of all this for Niebuhr's account of sin and what are the implications of our appropriation of his account to inform our work today? This is a crucial question, given the fact that most who turn to Niebuhr as a theological resource are primarily attracted to his striking analysis of sin. They assume that they rely on Niebuhr because even if the kind of criticisms developed here are correct, Niebuhr's account of sin is not fundamentally affected. Niebuhrian insights are still valid even if the theological framework in which they reside may need to be rethought. Though I think it true that many of Niebuhr's insights may be separable from his methodological assumptions—for example, his treatment of sensuality as the attempt to escape from the pain of self-knowledge—I am not convinced that his account of sin can be abstracted from this broader theological agenda.

For the irony of Niebuhr's account of sin is that almost in spite of himself he makes sin intelligible—that is, sin becomes a universal of the human condition that corresponds to and underwrites the assumption that all of history as history can be comprehended as a "problem." We sin, according to Niebuhr, because as finite creatures who can comprehend our finiteness, we are anxious. Unable to remain in a state of anxiety, we seek premature resolution by giving unconditioned loyalty to the contingent. Such an account no doubt describes for many how "sin feels," but yet I think it cannot be accepted or appropriated without qualification.

Sin is not a universal condition. Rather, it is the refusal of some to believe when confronted with the Gospel of Jesus Christ. The very assumption that we can know what sin is prior to knowledge of Christ is but a form of our sin, of our attempt to claim that we can comprehend the meaning of our existence. From this perspective, Niebuhr's account of our sinfulness is a Protestant form of natural law that attempts to make intelligible, on grounds of general human knowledge, what can only be known in the light of the kingdom established in Jesus' cross and resurrection. That is why it was possible for so many of Niebuhr's contemporaries to have been attracted to Niebuhr's account of the human condition and his corresponding political realism without sharing his theological convictions.

Anomalies internal to Niebuhr's account of sin confirm this analysis. For example, he could only assert that our finite status is not equivalent to sin; but he was never able to show why, theologically, our anxiety as creatures does not necessitate sinfulness. All he could say was that our anxiety is the "precondition" of sin, but how a precondition is different from the actuality is not easily understood (*ND*, 1, 183). Moreover, because of the necessity to treat sin as a universal condition, he had no way to mark morally different kinds of sin. As a result, he claimed that even though we are all equally sinners, we are not all equally guilty—the latter being determined primarily by the extent of bad consequences that result from our sin (*ND*, 1, 219–227). It seems rather odd, but yet nonetheless true, that Niebuhr's insightful account of sin cannot help but end underwriting a shallow utilitarian calculus.

Even more troubling is how Niebuhr's account of "our" historical condition served, and continues to serve, as an ideology for a liberal-technological social and political order. For in spite of his often telling criticism of American self-righteousness, he failed to see that liberalism is based on a philosophy of history committed to overcoming the role of chance, that is, history through technological organization.[16] The freedom Niebuhr celebrated as the equivalent to history requires an attempt to dominate all human and nonhuman relationships in order to secure the only good that liberal societies can envisage—survival. What Niebuhr failed to see, because he had accepted the liberal account of history as the imposition of human will on an accidental world, is that in such a world justice and the quest for justice become unintelligible.

On Beginning with an End

I am acutely aware that in criticizing Niebuhr I have not developed any intelligible alternative. Indeed, I am not even sure that I have succeeded in breaking the hold that Niebuhr's position has on my own imagination. For Niebuhr has been such a powerful influence because we have assumed that even if his answers were insufficient, he at least had the questions right. That assumption, of course, is what I have tried to challenge. But once you challenge the very way you have learned to put the question, it is not always clear where to go next.

My sense is that our task is not to develop an anthropology alternative to that of Niebuhr. Rather, we will only be in a position to know better what we think of the human condition when we are able, as Löwith suggests, to think from the position of the end, that is, when our sense of history reflects our eschatology rather than history becoming the form our eschatological convictions take. To do that will require not only conceptual skills, but also a different stance as Christians toward our respective social orders. Only when we learn to exist in history without the power to determine *fully* the meaning of that history will we be ready, I suspect, to know as well as articulate what it means to be human.

Notes

1. Dietrich Bonhoeffer, *No Rusty Swords*, ed. Edwin H. Robertson (New York: Harper and Row, 1965), p. 117. This is, of course, a passage from Bonhoeffer's famous essay, "Protestantism Without Reformation."

2. Bonhoeffer, *No Rusty Swords*, p. 104 (italicized in Bonhoeffer). Sauter has been unfailingly generous in his attention as well as his judgments about the church in America. Yet his unwavering Bonhoeffer-like insistence that "doctrine

matters" cannot help but be a judgment on the American churches' general disdain for doctrine.

3. Bonhoeffer was quite appreciative of Niebuhr, calling him the "sharpest critic of contemporary American Protestantism and the present social order." He notes that Niebuhr is attempting to find the "right way" between neo-orthodoxy, for which Jesus Christ becomes the ground for human despair, and a true liberalism, for which Jesus Christ is the ideal and the revelation of our essential being. Yet Bonhoeffer concludes that "a doctrine of the person and redemptive work of Jesus Christ is still missing" in Niebuhr (p. 116) He was, of course, right about Niebuhr's Christology, which, I hope to show, had a disastrous effect on Niebuhr's view of history.

4. I originally wrote this paper for a colloquy on Reinhold Niebuhr between the faculties of theology of Duke and Bonn. I was supposed to write on Niebuhr's anthropology, but I felt that the world simply did not need another paper on that all-too-commonly treated subject. I therefore used Löwith to raise questions about Niebuhr's view of history, not only because I thought the latter was more interesting, but also because I thought that many who criticized Niebuhr's anthropology continued to share the methodological presuppositions of Protestant liberal views about history. At the time, I am embarrassed to say, I did not know Sauter's work well. I now understand that I was lucky to find a way to criticize Niebuhr that was commensurate with some of Sauter's theological motifs. I am grateful to be able to publish that paper for the first time in this context, as I hope it serves to express my admiration for Sauter's work but also his character as a theologian of the church.

5. Karl Löwith, "History and Christianity," in *Reinhold Niebuhr: His Religious, Social and Political Thought*, ed. Charles Kegley and Robert Bretall (New York: Macmillan Company, 1956), pp. 281–290. All page references to Löwith's contribution therein will appear in the text preceded by *HC*.

6. Löwith's full position on the matter was worked out in his *Meaning in History* (Chicago: University of Chicago Press, 1949). There Löwith says, "The interpretation of history is, in the last analysis, an attempt to understand the meaning of history as the meaning of suffering by historical action. The Christian meaning of history, in particular, consists in the most paradoxical fact that the cross, this sign of deepest ignominy, could conquer the world of the conquerors by opposing it. In our time crosses have been borne silently by millions of people; and if anything warrants the thought that the meaning of history has to be understood in a Christian sense, it is such boundless suffering. In the Western world the problem of suffering has been faced in two different ways: by the myth of Prometheus and by the faith in Christ—the one a rebel, the other a servant. Neither antiquity nor Christianity indulged in the modern illusion that history can be conceived as a progressive evolution which solves the problem of evil by way of elimination" (3). Because Löwith assumes that all modern accounts of "history" are but forms of the Promethean myth, he later claims that "Christians are not a historical people" (195). Contrary to Löwith, Christians are a historical people, since our Christ is a Jew; but more profoundly, we are eschatological people. One of the tricks modernity has played on us Christians is that which succeeds in convincing us that history is a more basic concept than providence.

7. Niebuhr, in *Faith and History* (New York: Charles Scribner's Sons, 1951), explicitly uses the phrase "tangents of moral meaning in history" (132). As we shall see, however, more troubling to Löwith is Niebuhr's assumption that history itself is the realm of meaning created by man. Page references for *Faith and History* will appear in the text preceded by *FH*.

8. Reinhold Niebuhr, *The Nature and Destiny of Man*, vol. 1 (New York: Charles Scribner's Sons, 1949), p. 3. Page references will appear in the text preceded by *ND*. It is interesting how seldom it was noticed, at the time that *The Nature and Destiny of Man* was published, how deeply Niebuhr drew on the idealist tradition for his account of the human condition. Everyone's attention was captured by his strong stress on the inevitability and power of sin. As a result, few noticed the way in which Niebuhr assumed the broad outlines of Kant's understanding of how freedom is possible in a Newtonian world.

9. In spite of his stress on the centrality of history, there is a peculiar ahistorical character to Niebuhr's work. For what is important is how history exhibits eternal characteristics rather than how concrete historical figures or movements actually changed the world. Of course, he was not alone in this respect, as Bultmann, for example, has quite similar views.

10. Reinhold Niebuhr, *The Self and the Dramas of History* (New York: Charles Scribner's Sons, 1955), p. 41. It is hard to see how this book adds anything to the work Niebuhr had done in *Faith and History*. What is interesting about the two books, however, is how they show Niebuhr's fascination with the "problem of history."

11. As we shall see, however, if the cross is not subject to the contingencies of history, then it cannot help but be a "symbol" that lacks historical particularity. Put simply, Niebuhr's failure to appreciate the eschatological reality of the cross means that the historical character of the cross must be translated into the language of eternal possibility.

12. Reinhold Niebuhr, "Reply," in Kegley and Bretall, eds., *Reinhold Niebuhr*, pp. 439–440.

13. I suspect this is also the reason why Niebuhr never felt the necessity to develop a positive sense of the role of the church.

14. Niebuhr, *The Self and the Dramas of History*, p. 97.

15. Ibid., p. 98.

16. For a well-developed argument defending this assertion, see George Parkin Grant, *English-Speaking Justice* (Notre Dame: University of Notre Dame Press, 1985). Grant's work has revolved around the "problem of history," and he has taken quite a different tack than Niebuhr. For an excellent presentation of Grant's thought, see Joan E. O'Donovan, *George Grant and the Twilight of Justice* (Toronto: University of Toronto Press, 1984). Grant saw clearly, in a way that Niebuhr does not, that the modern sickness is marked by an insatiable but clearly contradictory hunger; namely, that most want at the same time to have the freedom offered by historicism and the consolation of a nonhistorical past.

3

The Irony of Reinhold Niebuhr: The Ideological Character of "Christian Realism"

with Michael Broadway

Revisiting Reinhold Niebuhr's Realism

Robin Lovin observes that Christian Realism names the belief that in the end truth about God must prove consistent with every other kind of truth we can know.[1] So understood, we cannot imagine a Christian who would not want to be a Christian Realist. Yet as Lovin makes admirably clear, we learn little by such a designation, since "realism" names not one but a whole family of positions. Lovin, for example, distinguishes between political, moral, and theological realism, observing that some Christian Realists have held versions of all three. Yet it is equally the case that holding one form of realism does not entail holding the others.[2]

In this essay we will explore as well as critique Niebuhr's understanding of Christian Realism as a politics. In particular, we will explore the implications of Niebuhr's realism for his understanding of the role of the church. We think this is particularly important because many wish to dissent from this or that aspect of Niebuhr's theology, all the while continuing to think his account of how the Christian should approach politics is still valid. We want to challenge that presumption by showing how Niebuhr's account of realism provides more a legitimating ideology for America's political arrangements than it does a faithful explication of a political theology rooted in Scripture. We should not be surprised that it did so, as that was exactly what Niebuhr meant it to do. That Niebuhr's "realism" proved to be such a comforting position for Christian political participation in democratic politics seems counterintuitive.[3] Niebuhr's account of realism was meant to challenge, by exposing the idealisms that hide self-interest and power, a too easy acceptance of the status quo.[4] Realism was meant to force Christians, tempted by their idealisms, to face the necessity of power and violence Niebuhr thought unavoidable in history and politics. Realism was a kind of "spirituality" intended to sustain Christian participation in politics without such participation tempting the Christian to give in to cynicism.[5] Yet we will try to show that the irony of Reinhold Niebuhr is that it is precisely his antiliberal social criticism that turns out to provide a justification of liberal politics.

To claim to be a "realist" seems such a trump against any of the alternatives. The realist seeks to see beyond appearance, is committed to unmasking illusion and, thereby, to overthrowing falsehood. Accordingly, the realist seems to assume the superior position, naming other positions as illusory, utopian, idealistic, calling them prejudice and even lies. Certainly Niebuhr's claim to be a realist functioned rhetorically to give him the high ground not only morally, but also intellectually.

Yet for us what is more troubling is the way in which Niebuhr's justification of realism reproduced the liberal presupposition that a strong distinction can be made between the spheres of religion and politics.[6] Religion became for him the realm of ideals, of personal morality, of knowledge of the creator. Politics names the realm of human nature, of human collectivities, of power and conflict. Realism assumes that any collective behavior is necessarily conflictual and thus religion cannot help but be "illusion."[7] Without the clear division between religion and politics, this ontology of conflict would quickly come into question in light of the ideals of religion. However, by separating the two, Niebuhr is able to free the political space for a discourse based on the prudential limitation of conflict.

In *The Nature and Destiny of Man*, Reinhold Niebuhr seeks to ground his political analysis further by developing a psychological account of human sinfulness as a natural foundation for his theory of social relations.[8] Finite human beings inevitably reach beyond their grasp to claim ever-expanding power and authority. This sinfulness cannot be overcome in the world; it can only be tempered and contained. Religion provides ideals for partial control of egoism, but its effectiveness is limited to individual motivations.[9] This naturalized theory of the human response to finitude merges with the politics of group conflict to flesh out Niebuhr's realism. He summarizes this argument briefly in *The Structure of Nations and Empires*:

> It is interesting that a valid psychiatry has come to the same conclusions with respect to the individual as those at which a valid political science has arrived in regard to communities. This conclusion is that it is not possible permanently to suppress, by either internal or external pressure, the concern of the self for itself. . . . A valid moral outlook for both individuals and for groups, therefore, sets no limits to the creative possibility of concern for others, and makes no claims that such creativity ever annuls the power of self-

concern or removes the peril of pretension if the force of residual egotism is not acknowledged.[10]

Claims of "realism," such as those of Niebuhr, provide the perfect setting for the development of a severe case of ideological blindness. The eventual convergence of Reinhold Niebuhr's "realism" with accepted doctrine of American foreign policy in the 1950s and 1960s[11] further confirms the suspicion that many theologians had accepted a version of reality that was easily compatible with the views of the dominant groups of the society. Noam Chomsky, certainly unsympathetic with Niebuhr, writes:

> It is easy to see why his [Niebuhr's] attitudes would generally have endeared him to postwar intellectual opinion. In his avoidance of fact and argument, and the praise that such practice elicited, Niebuhr was enjoying the luxury afforded anyone who remains firmly within conventional orthodoxies, playing the game by the rules. . . . The reverential awe his words evoked reflects, in part, the shallowness and superficiality of the reigning intellectual culture, a sign of most times and places, no doubt. But to explain his status as "official establishment theologian" we must also attend to the lessons drawn from his exhortations. [Richard] Fox comments that the Kennedy liberals "did not so much 'use' Niebuhr's name as feel indebted to his perspective. He helped them maintain faith in themselves as political actors in a troubled—what he termed a sinful—world. Stakes were high, enemies were wily, responsibility meant taking risks: Niebuhr taught that moral men had to play hardball. . . . "
>   The inescapable "taint of sin on all historical achievements," the necessity to make "conscious choices of evil for the sake of good"—these are soothing doctrines for those preparing to "face the responsibilities of power," or in plain English, to set forth on a life of crime, to "play hardball."[12]

Although Chomsky sets Niebuhr's political views in the worst possible light, he does at least point out the way that realisms can become justification for perpetuating dominant ideologies.

The rhetorical character of claims to knowledge of reality can be seen in analyzing certain uses of "real," "realistic," "really," and their cognates. Often these words make little or no difference in the content of sentences. A person might say, "The reason for X is Y," or "The real reason for X is Y." In each version of the sentence, the person claims Y as the reason for X. In the second sentence, however, "real" serves to intensify the claim, not unlike an exclamation point. It also indicates that the speaker assumes that other reasons might be given that should be disregarded. In other words, the rhetorical function of "real" in this sentence is as a claim to a privileged point of view. Certainly, that is not the only way that language of "reality" functions, but it is clearly one of its more frequent uses in everyday and in theoretical discourses, including Christian Realist discourses. In a nutshell, Niebuhr's realistic point of view expects that people are likely to do bad things to one another, and that the behavior of collectives will be even worse. Although Christians might ideally want to seek nonviolent solutions to problems, they ought really to be prepared to use the violence legitimated by the state to limit the ever-present conflict among social groups.

Though Niebuhr's realism seems to commit him to some kind of historicism, in fact his account of realism is essentially ahistorical and abstract. In all times and places the inevitable rejection of human finitude distorts social relations and leads to conflict. The proper response to this universal conflict is to balance, as best one can, one power against another. Although Niebuhr recites numerous historical cases in defense of his argument, they build anything but a historicist argument. Instead, he looks to historical study, not to reveal the superficial differences between cases and eras, but to find "some similarities under the differences."[13] From Chomsky's point of view, "He too consistently interprets history not on the basis of the factual or documentary record, but in terms of professed ideals."[14] This ahistorical reductionism characterizes his method of uncovering the perennial principles of social relations. Thus, running through Niebuhr's many examples is the same set of principles repeated over and over again: Finite human beings greedily seek to obtain more than their needs dictate, a proclivity that is made infinitely worse in collectives; therefore, the best one can hope for is to structure groups, societies, and international relations in such a way that individuals and groups can be kept under relative control; religion illuminates this condition and provides some inspiration to do better, even though the full realization of its ideals are impossible in history.

John Milbank argues that Niebuhr's account of our moral situation bears uncanny resemblance to Stoicism. Carefully exegeting Niebuhr's discussion of the early church's engagement with Stoic ethics, Milbank concludes that Niebuhr found some of its key tenets to be essential. "The basic focus of Stoic ethics is on the encounter between an absolute spiritual ideal and a 'chaotic' finite world which it does its best to regulate."[15] Like Niebuhr, the Stoics saw little chance of bringing this ideal into the external world of chaos, which is inevitably conflictual. We are sure that Milbank is right to draw a parallel between Niebuhrian realism and stoicism, but before we explore how that might affect our understanding of Niebuhr's account of Christianity, we need to suggest how completely Niebuhr stands in the American grain.

Niebuhr's Americanism

Niebuhr's realism and his correlative understanding of the place of religion in liberal societies we think can be illumined by comparing his views with those of two of the key interpreters of liberalism for the

American republic, Thomas Jefferson and James Madison. Like Jefferson, Niebuhr believed that religious beliefs are properly located in the individual conscience. Our conscience, and in particular our consciousness of sin, is a signal of transcendence. Religion accordingly is "interior" to the political, whereas politics corresponds to a dualism of interior motivation and external social behavior.[16] With Jefferson, not dissimilar views led to his argument for an absolute distinction between religion and politics:

> Believing with you that religion is a matter which lies solely between man and his God, that he owes account to none other for his faith or his worship, that the legislative powers of government reach actions only, and not opinions, I contemplate with sovereign reverence that act of the whole American people which declared that their legislature should "make no law respecting an establishment of religion, or prohibiting the free exercise thereof," thus building a wall of separation between Church and State.[17]

This famous Jeffersonian doctrine came to be a crucial, albeit controversial, canon of constitutional interpretation, especially in the twentieth century.[18]

Of course, Niebuhr's whole life was committed to convincing Christians of their social responsibility, so it may seem strange to suggest that he was an ally of Jefferson. He certainly could be critical of the kind of "optimistic liberalism" he thought Jefferson represented.[19] Yet in spite of his critique of Jefferson, his own realism could not help but underwrite the sequestering of Christian conviction from the public arena. As a result, even Niebuhr's Christian convictions became motivation for political involvement.

Because of his strong emphasis on sin, Niebuhr is usually seen as having a greater affinity to James Madison than Jefferson. Madison's argument for the necessity of balancing conflicting interest groups against one another in order to prevent majority tyranny and preserve the peace sounds like a classic Niebuhrian theme. Madison was, moreover, an unapologetic advocate of a strong central government, believing that the popular election of the government was a necessary check against the tyranny of any small group or single person who might amass power. However, a unified majority might ultimately create an even more oppressive tyranny than any monarch or group of aristocrats had ever enforced. Madison's theoretical response was to suggest that a large republic could create the conditions for multiplying factions to the point that no single faction could claim a majority of the voters. Multiple factions, combined with strong central government, could help to foster the sort of balance of power within the republic that is necessary to deal with a diversity of egoistic interests, all of which again sounds like Reinhold Niebuhr's social and political philosophy.

In "Federalist 10" and "Federalist 51," Madison argued for structuring government to promote the balancing of interested factions with reference to factions of all types, including religion. Madison may have been somewhat less optimistic than Jefferson about truth prevailing in a society where free inquiry reigns. He believed that democratic societies could rely on the existence of only the bare minimum of virtue—enough to allow self-rule through law and the vote. However, he was not confident that truth and virtue could survive factional conflict if one faction were to hold a majority.[20] Like Niebuhr, he expected interest rather than morality to be the stronger motivating force in social life.

Niebuhr may be even more pessimistic than Madison in his acceptance of the necessity of social conflict, especially between groups. He doubts that even minimal virtue can be expected of social collectives. Such virtue inevitably serves self-interest and comes into conflict.[21] Like Madison, Niebuhr believes that only a strong central government can keep the conflict under control. Niebuhr cites *The Federalist Papers* in support of this belief.[22] The kinship of his thought with Jefferson and Madison thus helps explain the appeal of Niebuhr's "realism" to an American audience well versed in the split between the realms of religion and politics, the ontology of conflict, and the control of such conflict through the balance-of-power models of liberal political arrangements.

Like Jefferson and Madison, Niebuhr more readily talks about "religion" than the church. Even when he uses the term "church," he does not always refer to the Christian church.[23] He seems to consider religion a more inclusive category than church, insofar as the former names ideals that can lead human beings to aspire to morality and justice. In contrast, church is just one more collectivity that is thoroughly self-interested. Though the church can at times exercise a prophetic role toward society, most of Niebuhr's discussions of the church returned to criticisms of its potential and actual corruption—which is to say, its tendency to serve self-interest and the interests of dominant classes.[24] (He was especially critical of Roman Catholicism, which he saw as inherently oppressive of individual freedom.[25])

Niebuhr's attitude toward the church reflects his pessimism about groups. He simply did not believe in the possibility of the exercise of authority that was not destructive of individuals. To be sure, prophetic pronouncements and actions were possible, but propheticism, for him, was the result of an individual courage that acted against rather than on behalf of communities. Propheticism, it turns out, confirms the individualistic bias of liberal politics.

Like Madison, Niebuhr assumes that people enter civil society for mutual benefit, reserving certain rights to protect their individual interests. Liberty of conscience was one such reserved right, for the consent of a majority to establish religion would run roughshod over the minority.[26] Yet the mere rational acknowledgment of the existence of the rights would not offer protection. Nor could religion itself be counted on to support the kind of virtues that would restrain the passions of a majority. In fact, religious fervor might well incite people to even greater oppression than individuals would impose.[27] Some structural means of protecting rights must therefore be enacted, and the puzzle for Madison was to identify the means to keep the state neutral in religion.

Once again, the large republic supplied the answer for Madison. An extensive enough republic would embrace a large variety of sects, none of which could either claim a majority or easily organize themselves if they were a majority. They would compete for the loyalty of the citizens and would not easily unite in any common interest with their competitors.[28] Here, Niebuhr's diminution of the church's authority and role in the lives of believers, or in society, fits neatly into his liberal notions of structures of power as the means to social justice. The church, like all other groups, must be tamed by structuring social conflict in such a way that it can inflict the least harm. The only contribution of religion is in presenting useful "illusions" of a just society that may by some slim chance guide leaders of society in the direction of more just decisions.[29]

Niebuhr's Theological Justification of the Irrelevance of Christianity

Niebuhr's realism was shaped by, but also shaped, his theology. The cross of Jesus exemplifies the impossibility of love and forgiveness being politically embodied. The "law of love stands on the edge of history, not in history, . . . it represents an ultimate and not an immediate possibility."[30]

> The religion of Jesus is prophetic religion in which the moral ideal of love and vicarious suffering, elaborated by the second Isaiah, achieves such a purity that the possibility of its realization in history becomes remote. His Kingdom of God is always a possibility in history, because its heights of pure love are organically related to the experience of love of all human life, but it is also an impossibility in history and always beyond every historical achievement.[31]

Thus, for Niebuhr, the ethic of Jesus is the norm, but also fundamentally irrelevant as a social policy. "The only adequate norm is the historic incarnation of a perfect love which actually transcends history, and can appear in it only to be crucified."[32] Love can only remain suffering love in history, even though it is the law of history, because history stands in contradiction to it.[33] The cross illuminates transcendent realities, but it cannot be effective in the struggle for justice. That is why the cross can only be a symbol of truth intrinsic to the human condition.

According to Niebuhr, the attempt to make the ethic of Jesus politically relevant drove the church to apocalypticism. As the Christians' hope for immediate establishment of the kingdom faded, they had to reconceive how to live as Christians. "They merely present Christian ethics afresh with the problem of compromise, the problem of creating and maintaining tentative harmonies of life in the world in terms of the possibilities of the human situation, while yet at the same time preserving the indictment upon all human life of the impossible possibility, the law of love."[34] Such a position Niebuhr understands to be inherently unstable, threatening to become a priestly religion that does little more than provide transcendent justification for finite social structures.

Niebuhr thinks that Apostle Paul is clearly wrong to suggest that government threatens only vice and not virtue. Although Paul may have been justified in making this argument in his own historical context where it appears that some Christians may have been flaunting the government's authority, unfortunately this teaching came to be applied indiscriminately to governments in later centuries. Niebuhr advises that "biblical observations upon life are made in a living relationship to living history." The "classical view that government was primarily the instrument of man's social nature" obscures "the fact that political life is a contest of power." Paul's "'undialectical' appreciation of government in Romans 13 has had a fateful influence in Christian thought, particularly in the Reformation."[35]

Niebuhr criticized Karl Barth as the inheritor of this Reformation tradition, suggesting that Barth's extreme doctrine of the "ultimate religious fact of the sinfulness of all men" undermined the ability to make relative moral judgments or to recognize relative moral achievements in history. This criticism sounds very much like the criticisms leveled against Niebuhr himself; namely, that he eliminates the possibility of moral judgment because of his own extreme doctrine of the ubiquity of sin in human relations. Yet Niebuhr well recognized this problem, attributing it to the "Augustinian-Lutheran theological heritage [which] has had greater difficulty in achieving a measure of political sanity and justice than the more Pelagian, more self-righteous and religiously less profound Anglo-Saxon world."[36]

Niebuhr's own solution to the problem of religious endorsement of political structures was to stress that the Bible has two paradoxical principles of politics. First, because God ordains government, its authority "reflects the Divine Majesty." Second, rulers are "particularly subject to divine judgment and wrath" because of their propensity to oppress the poor and to defy God's authority. The first principle supports order as a hedge against anarchy, and the second helps to clarify that governmental power is not equal to divine power, though it often has pretensions to absoluteness.[37] The task is at once to maintain both principles without falling into the twin temptations of conservatism or radicalism.

This attempt to hold two polar positions in tension is characteristic of Niebuhr's thought.

> It is important both to recognize the higher possibilities of justice in every historical situation, and to know that the twin perils of tyranny and anarchy can never be completely overcome in any political achievement. These perils are expressions of the sinful elements of conflict and dominion, standing in contradiction to the ideal of brotherhood on every level of communal organization.[38]

John Courtney Murray called Niebuhr's position "ambiguist," suggesting that followers of Niebuhr had a tendency to find so much ambiguity and complexity in any moral situation that constructive deliberation becomes immobilized.[39] Niebuhr was seldom immobilized, but Murray's description commends itself by Niebuhr's own admission that "modern history has given us a vivid illustration of the fact that the history of communities accentuates, rather than mitigates, the moral ambiguities of our existence, particularly the ambiguities of our common life."[40]

Indeed, earlier in the same book, Niebuhr had organized types of government according to gradations of ambiguity.[41] He did so thinking he was standing in the Reformation tradition that teaches us that it is necessary to make moral judgments between "social systems" rather than concerning specific questions of obedience to particular laws. By so doing Niebuhr provides a theological justification for why theological claims cannot and should not be made to do the work of politics. But it is not clear what Niebuhr's alternative might be. Jesus has already been rendered irrelevant and Niebuhr distrusts the casuistical use of natural law.[42] His only alternative is, in the name of balance-of-power politics, to recommend that Christians be "realistic." No doubt Niebuhr would claim that he has brought the prophetic element of religion to the forefront, but the sharp division between the realms of religion and politics intrinsic to realism served to free liberal political institutions to follow their own interests, qualified only by the hope that they will recognize the ambiguity in what they do.

The Way "Beyond" Niebuhr

A dark cloud often seems to hang over the world found in Reinhold Niebuhr's writings. In a world of nation-states, he asserts that it is nation-states that are most susceptible to the temptations of unbridled self-interest and resulting injustice.[43] However, to Niebuhr the nation-state is simply a larger, more resourceful exemplification of all human collectivities. Niebuhr's ahistorical account of politics blames the violence of modern nation-states on the timeless nature of social groups. In contrast, John Milbank argues:

> It is not enough to relate the especially dangerous selfishness of modern nation-states simply to the inherent nature of groups. It is clear that it has to do rather with the contingent, historical, growth of absolute sovereignty. Likewise the selfishness of corporations and trade unions is to be related to the market economy. In older societies where there was an organic hierarchy of interlocking groupings, "group selfishness" simply could not have made the same kind of sense.[44]

The same kind of historicism is exemplified by Anthony Giddens in his book *The Nation-State and Violence.* As part of his project to examine theories of the development of modern society, Giddens argues that what we face today is different:

> I do, however, want to claim that, originating in the West but becoming more and more global in their impact, there has occurred a series of changes extraordinary in magnitude when compared with any other phases of human history. What separates those living in the modern world from all previous types of society, and all previous epochs of history, is more profound than the continuities which connect them to the longer spans of the past. This does not mean that we cannot draw upon the study of pre-existing types of society to try better to understand the nature of the world in which we now live. But it does imply that the contrasts which can be made will often prove more illuminating than the continuities that may be discerned.[45]

Giddens states that one of the most characteristic features of the modern nation-state is its highly centralized control of society through the monopoly of violence.

Milbank's and Giddens's historicizing perspective undermines the myth of the liberal society, which Niebuhr turned into the "truth" about the human condition. Such "truths" succeed in merely naturalizing a social setting of conflict that then becomes the rationale for structures of liberal social control and those who benefit from such arrangements. Rather than regulating society into a perpetual state of equilibrium in which individuals find equality and freedom, modern nation-states have developed as ever-increasing power centers sustained by industrialized militarization. Political theories like Niebuhr's help to justify this centrifugal expansion of liberal power structures by perpetuating the ahistorical ontology of conflict assumed by liberal politics. The final irony of Niebuhr's liberalism is his claim that the ontology of groups presents an insuperable barrier to ethical perfectionism, which in turn becomes the justification for liberal optimism in the name of the free individual.[46]

Politics for liberal thought, as for Niebuhr, is expressed through the manipulation of technologies of power established in constitutional structures. By putting aside the questions of moral goodness for the sake of objective technique, liberal politics engenders an unwarranted optimism. Furthermore, if Christians are rendered politically impotent in the name of the "peace" accomplished through the mechanism of the balance of power, then Christians and non-Christians alike are robbed of a common politics.[47] Ironically, Niebuhr, the realist, who everyone agrees "took sin seriously," actually provides the bases to underwrite what is increasingly seen as an unjustified liberal optimism. Niebuhr, like many theorists of liberal politics, was not historicist. On the contrary, he proclaimed an essentialized view of the human condition and a parallel reification of the state that shut out any role in the world for the church. He, like the Stoics before him, left us without hope.

Notes

An earlier version of this chapter, entitled "The Irony of American Christianity: Reinhold Niebuhr on Church and State," written with Michael Broadway, appeared in *Insights: A Journal of the Faculty of Austin Seminary* 108 (Fall 1992): 33–46.

1. Robin Lovin, *Reinhold Niebuhr and Christian Realism* (Cambridge: Cambridge University Press, 1995), p. 240. This essay was originally written and published in 1992. As a result, we did not have the benefit of Lovin's able analysis and defense of Niebuhr's realism. We have no reason to disagree with Lovin's attempt to make Niebuhr not only a political realist but also a moral realist, that is, someone who defends the claim that "moral truth exists independent of our ideas and theories about it" (p. 68). Indeed, we are convinced that Lovin is right to position Niebuhr in the pragmaticist tradition in spite of Niebuhr's criticism of John Dewey. Of course, as Lovin well knows, it is a complex question whether the pragmaticists were "moral realists."

From our perspective it is increasingly clear that Dewey and Niebuhr held more in common than their disagreements might suggest. See, for example, Daniel Rice, *Reinhold Niebuhr and John Dewey: An American Odyssey* (Albany: State University of New York Press, 1993). Of course, that is not necessarily good news for defenders of Niebuhr, such as Lovin. For as Dewey observed in a letter quoted by Rice, "I have the impression that both he (Niebuhr) and Kierkegaard have both completely lost faith in traditional statements of Christianity, haven't got any modern substitute, and so are making up, off the bat, something which supplies to them the gist of Christianity—what they approve of in modern thought—as when two newspapers are joined, the new organ always says, 'Retaining the best features of both'" (86–87). Dewey is wrong about Kierkegaard but certainly his characterization of Niebuhr rings true in spite of Niebuhr's attempt to rescue Christianity as "true myth" about transcendence. What Niebuhr

⊘ failed to see about "transcendence" is that it is but another reductive category that makes God's choice of Israel unintelligible.

2. Lovin, *Reinhold Niebuhr and Christian Realism,* p. 241.

3. In responding to Jeff Stout's doubt that religious claims have any positive contribution to make to public discourse, Lovin says that "the point is not contribution but participation" (ibid., p. 55). In other words, the task is to get Christians to participate in "politics" on prior established grounds. From our perspective such a view sells politics short, believing as we do that the world can respond to the distinctive character of Christian witness.

4. Reinhold Niebuhr, *Christian Realism and Political Problems* (New York: Charles Scribner's Sons, 1953), pp. 198–120.

5. Dennis McCann provides the most insightful account of Niebuhr's realism as a form of spirituality. See his *Christian Realism and Liberation Theology* (Maryknoll, N.Y.: Orbis Books, 1981).

6. Reinhold Niebuhr, *Moral Man and Immoral Society* (New York: Charles Scribner's Sons, 1932), p. 263, passim.

7. Ibid., p. 81.

8. Reinhold Niebuhr, *The Nature and Destiny of Man* (New York: Charles Scribner's Sons, 1949). We realize that calling Niebuhr's account "psychological" may appear prejudicial, but it is extremely difficult to locate the kind of discourse Niebuhr employs in *The Nature and Destiny of Man.* We do not say this as a criticism, for no doubt Niebuhr's genesis and persuasive power are due to his extraordinary power of generalization.

9. John Milbank, *Nuclear Realism and Christian Reality: The Poverty of Niebuhrianism* (London: Jubilee Group Publications, 1986), p. 5. A version of Milbank's essay on Niebuhr appears in his *The Word Made Strange: Theology, Language, Culture* (Oxford: Basil Blackwell, 1997), pp. 233–254.

10. Niebuhr, *The Structure of Nations and Empires,* rpt. ed. (Fairfield, N.J.: Augustus M. Kelley, 1977), pp. 30–31.

11. Noam Chomsky, "Reinhold Niebuhr," *Grand Street* 6 (1982): 204–206.

12. Ibid., 211–212.

13. Niebuhr, *The Structure of Nations and Empires,* p. 5; for other examples of perennial truths, see pp. 215, 277.

14. Chomsky, "Reinhold Niebuhr," p. 205; however, one would not want to endorse Chomsky's implication that history can be read without preconceptions.

15. Milbank, *Nuclear Realism,* p. 6.

16. Niebuhr, *Moral Man and Immoral Society,* p. 257.

17. Thomas Jefferson, Letter to Messrs. Nehemiah Dodge, Ephraim Robbins, and Stephen S. Nelson, A Committee of the Danbury Baptist Association, in the State of Connecticut, Jan. 1, 1802, *The Writings of Thomas Jefferson,* Memorial Edition, vol. 16 (Washington, D.C.: Thomas Jefferson Memorial Association, 1904), pp. 281–282.

18. *Illinois ex rel. McCollum v. Board of Education,* 333 U.S. 203 (1948), excerpted in John F. Wilson and Donald L. Drakeman, eds., *Church and State in American History,* 2nd ed. (Boston: Beacon Press, 1987), p. 207.

19. Niebuhr, *An Interpretation of Christian Ethics,* rpt. ed. (New York: Seabury, 1960), pp. 103–104.

20. Madison, "Federalist 51," *The Papers of James Madison*, ed. William T. Hutchinson, William M.E. Rachal, et al., vol. 10 (Charlottesville: University of Virginia Press, 1977), pp. 476ff.

21. Niebuhr, *Moral Man and Immoral Society*, pp. xx, 107. It is by no means clear from whence Niebuhr thought people of virtue would come. He simply presupposes that enough widespread agreement obtains concerning what it means to be "moral" that one could continue to assume that virtue would just be "there."

22. Niebuhr, *The Structure of Nations and Empires*, p. 149.

23. Niebuhr, *Moral Man and Immoral Society*, p. 82.

24. Niebuhr, "The Christian Church in a Secular Age," in *The Essential Reinhold Niebuhr*, ed. Robert McAfee Brown (New Haven: Yale University Press, 1986), pp. 83, 87.

25. Niebuhr, *The Nature and Destiny of Man*, vol. 2, *Human Destiny* (New York: Charles Scribner's Sons, 1946), pp. 138–148; also "The Christian Church in a Secular Age," in *Essential Niebuhr*, p. 88.

26. Madison, "Memorial and Remonstrance Against Religious Assessments," *The Papers of James Madison*, vol. 8 (1973), pp. 299–300.

27. Madison, Letter to Thomas Jefferson, Oct. 24, 1787, *The Papers of James Madison*, vol. 10 (1977), p. 213.

28. Madison, "Vices of the Political System of the United States," *The Papers of James Madison*, vol. 9 (1975), p. 357.

29. Niebuhr, *Moral Man and Immoral Society*, pp. 81, 277.

30. Niebuhr, *The Nature and Destiny of Man*, vol. 1, *Human Nature*, p. 298.

31. Niebuhr, *Interpretation*, p. 19.

32. Niebuhr, *Human Nature*, p. 147.

33. Niebuhr, *Human Destiny*, p. 49.

34. Niebuhr, *Interpretation*, p. 37.

35. Niebuhr, *Human Destiny*, pp. 270–271, n. 2.

36. Ibid., p. 220.

37. Ibid., p. 269.

38. Ibid., p. 284.

39. John Courtney Murray, *We Hold These Truths: Catholic Reflections on the American Proposition* (New York: Sheed and Ward, 1960), p. 282.

40. Niebuhr, *The Structure of Nations and Empires*, p. 298.

41. Ibid., pp. 25ff.

42. Lovin rightly observes that Niebuhr failed to see how much his account of Christian realism depends on natural law and, in particular, the conviction that "right action is action that conforms to human nature" (*Reinhold Niebuhr and Christian Realism*, pp. 15–16).

43. Niebuhr, *Human Nature*, pp. 209–219.

44. Milbank, *Nuclear Realism*, p. 12.

45. Anthony Giddens, *The Nation-State and Violence*, vol. 2 of *A Contemporary Critique of Historical Materialism* (Berkeley: University of California Press, 1987), p. 33.

46. Milbank, *Nuclear Realism*, p. 12.

47. Robin Lovin, in his defense of Niebuhr's realism as "theologian in the service of ethics," puts the dilemma this way: "If one aims to speak about problems

and choices that affect everyone in society, the analysis must be made in terms that are widely accepted and understood, and it may be difficult to say anything at all about God. But if one tries to exercise the theologian's vocation to speak a distinctive word about God, those of other faiths or no faith now dismiss it as a private meditation, an esoteric religious idea that has no relevance for their lives and choices" (*Reinhold Niebuhr and Christian Realism*, p. 34). Lovin argues that "in the end" human conflict and aspirations must be understood, for Niebuhr, in relation to God who sets limits on conflict and affirms human unity. For "the idea that God is love is a symbol for an ultimate unity of lives and interests in which all proximate conflicts are resolved" (p. 36). Of course, we think everything has already gone wrong whenever it is assumed that "God is love is an idea" or, even worse, that God is a "symbol."

4 *God as Participant: Time and History in the Work of James Gustafson*

Time and History: Statement of the Problem

Many have commented that James Gustafson's *Ethics from a Theocentric Perspective* seems out of character with his past work. By that they usually mean that they are surprised that Gustafson seems so determined to place himself in a critical position vis-à-vis some of the central claims of the Christian faith. For example, it seems odd for someone who has written so sensitively about the various ways Christians have understood the relation between Christ and the moral life to write a book in which Christ plays such a subordinate role. For some, the concern to understand the relation between the "earlier" and "later" Gustafson no doubt derives from a reaction against the God that Gustafson so unrelentingly portrays in *Ethics from a Theocentric Perspective.* Such a God simply seems to lack the kind of compassion that many Christians assume is at the heart of the Christian faith. Calling attention to Gustafson's earlier work, therefore, seems to be a way of reminding Gustafson that at one time he seemed to be more "orthodox."

I am troubled by this strategy, however, as I am not convinced that there is any discontinuity between an "earlier" and "later" Gustafson—at least not in terms of his doctrine of God. Moreover, I am a bit bothered by this kind of reaction because it fails to take seriously Gustafson's theological proposal. For such a reading seems to suggest that in *Ethics from a Theocentric Perspective* Gustafson has merely laid out his personal statement of faith, which is perfectly appropriate. But it seems a bit facile to believe that the argument must end there, since when dealing with such matters you either take it or leave it. Treating Gustafson's proposal in that vein, in other words, is to fail to take seriously the strong argument that Gustafson attempts to make. For he is saying, not simply, "This is my credo," but "This is what we all ought to think about God given the available evidence."

In this essay, therefore, I want to engage Gustafson at a different level in the hope that we can better understand the methodological presuppositions that underlie *Ethics from a Theocentric Perspective*. Rather than concentrate directly on his doctrine of God, I propose to look at an issue that runs through Gustafson's work from the beginning to the present— namely, how time and history are understood to determine the methodological presuppositions by which a theologian works. It is in relation to this problem, moreover, that I think there may be some difference between the "earlier" and "later" Gustafson. Of course, even if that were the case, it by no means undermines Gustafson's later position; in fact, it may help us better understand Gustafson's current views and their implications for how all of us work as theologians.

As usual, Gustafson, the master teacher of our craft, has stated the issue more clearly than I can. In *Protestant and Roman Catholic Ethics* (1978:61) he describes the basic questions that Roman Catholic and Protestant writers share:

> What philosophical foundations are necessary and sufficient to provide conditions under which theological ethics can do justice both to the historical particularities of the Christian tradition and to the common humanity and rationality that religious persons share with all members of our species? What foundations are necessary and sufficient to provide conditions under which theological ethics can do justice both to the persistent temporal continuities of human experience (nature) and the historical changes in it (history)? What foundations are necessary and sufficient to provide conditions under which theological ethics can do justice both to the dimensions of human freedom and individual personal existence on the one hand and the limitations of freedom and co-humanity on the other?

These questions obviously do not refer to the same "problem," but they are closely interrelated. For example, those who emphasize human freedom will often downplay the significance of "nature" as a source of norms for morality. That is why Gustafson, while approving of contemporary Catholic thinkers who attempt to develop a more open moral theology, rightly reminds them that to introduce a historical dimension to human existence alters, if not discards, the traditional preoccupation with ontological accounts of human nature (1978:47). In short, Gustafson rightly reminds us that when it comes to history we cannot have our cake and eat it too. Once the temporal character of existence is accepted, there is no easy return to a universal theology or an ethic that is bared as nature.

Yet that is exactly, it seems, what Gustafson has tried to do in *Ethics from a Theocentric Perspective*. He has tried to do so not just in terms of his "ethics," but in his attempt to be a theologian who is only secondarily a Christian theologian. Of course, he is quite right that theology is the most basic activity and that "Christian" is only one possible qualifier. Plato, after all, certainly did theology. But the question that especially interests me is whether the attempt to be a theologian qua theologian is not in some tension with Gustafson's own insistence, from the beginning to the end of his work, that we are fundamentally timeful beings. That is the question I will pursue in this essay by providing a sketch of how Gustafson has developed the themes of time and history throughout his work.

The questions surrounding how time and history are understood for theological method are important not only in understanding the thought of Gustafson; they are central for all modern theology. Therefore, I assume that the approach I have taken in this essay really requires no justification. I cannot pretend, however, to have taken this tack simply because I think it can provide an interesting slant on Gustafson's work. I also have personal reasons for pursuing this subject. For by investigating this set of issues I want to try to understand how the way I work as a theologian can be so influenced by Gustafson and yet why at the same time I feel I must dissent from the position that he develops in *Ethics from a Theocentric Perspective*, not so much in terms of his doctrine of God, though certainly there are also disagreements involved there, but from the very methodological assumptions that shape his later work.

Gustafson on Time and History

In *Treasure in Earthen Vessels* (1961) Gustafson was intent, in contrast to more strictly theological treatments of the church, to emphasize that the church is a natural community. Using insights from social science, he argued that the church can fulfill its theological mission only through the same natural functions that sustain every social grouping. In short, the book was an attack on all "docetic" accounts of the church, which ignore or deny that the church survives by using the same process that all institutions use to survive. As important as this perspective was for Gustafson, that theme was, in fact, subordinate to a larger concern. For as he says in the preface, the emphasis on the "natural" character of the church is an attempt to

> show that the historical and social relativity of the Church is part of its essential character. This is so in a double sense. This relativity is of the essence of its nature as an historical community, and it is essential to the achievement of its purpose in the world. The Church is earthen—of the stuff of natural and historical life. The Church is a vessel, it is useful. The contract with man and culture is made through the social and historical media of the Church—its natural functions, political forms, etc. (1961:x)

Therefore, the emphasis on the "natural" character of the church was but an expression of Gustafson's more profound conviction of the historical character of human existence. This is clear from the appendix to the book, in which Gustafson contrasts the positions of Kant, Kierkegaard, Augustine, Bergson, Royce, Dilthey, and Mead. Gustafson's discussion clearly sides with the "Augustinian stream," because these thinkers properly emphasize "that being in time is an important aspect of being a self" (1961:26). He thus dissents from the Kantian attempt to sustain an account of man that transcends natural or rational time. There is no way to secure a sense of self or community by attempting to transcend time. Rather, we must draw on the resources of memory in order to sustain the continuity and unity of self and community.

Of course memory involves the need to reinterpret the past, which always involves a relativizing process. This is as true for the church's remembering of Jesus as it is for any other cultural symbol that provides a community with a sense of continuity with its past. Yet

> continuity in the Church as an historical community is grounded in the continuity of a center of meaning that differentiates the Church from other historical societies, e.g., the French nation, the Freemasons, or Western culture. Social continuity and identity in the Church depend upon the continued significance of this center, Jesus Christ, with his manifold meanings, for contemporary persons and churches. Continuity exists not only for the preservation of an ancient truth. The lived experience of the past that was important enough to be remembered and expressed has contemporary significance as well. The present memory of Jesus Christ is not the admiration of an antique; it is a re-living in the present of his meaningfulness. Jesus Christ continues to provide a center for personal integrity and social consensus. The Christian's "contemporaneity with Christ" occurs throughout the history of the Church. It is possible because Christ has continued to be a powerful center of integration of experience through history. The one who was the Church's center of life through centuries continues to provide the center of life in the present. (1961:81–82)

Of course, the way Jesus is remembered is affected by the personal and cultural context in which the process of understanding unfolds. That such is the case is not only unavoidable but also necessary if Jesus Christ is to be personally meaningful to a particular people. Such a process, however, does not entail a complete relativization: "There is a fairly consistent expression of the meaning of the Church's knowledge of God in the Bible, the creeds, the sacraments, and other 'objectifications.' These insure in a broad way that it is Jesus Christ who is understood and remembered" (1961:84–85).

Thus, beginning with *Treasures in Earthen Vessels*, Gustafson seems to be committed to working in a historicist perspective. *Protestant and Roman Catholic Ethics* characterizes such a perspective as the conviction that

the structure of the human mind does not correspond to the structure of reality, or more particularly to a moral order of the universe which results in
human history taking on new significance. For now all knowledge is seen to
be historically "situated" and thus relative to the history within and from
which anything is known. Therefore the enterprise of Christian ethics had to
reckon with the implications of this for any claims which writers made
about the validity of its basic standpoint, or the moral principles and values
it proclaimed. Historical accounts of past human experience disclosed alter-
ations in moral teachings, in the ordering of moral and human values, even
within the Christian tradition. This posed a problem: either change was due
to a distortion or error and history had to be overcome, or it was an unavoidable aspect of morality and had to be justified theologically and ethi-
cally. Thus under a general term, "historicism," I refer to the Protestant responses in ethics that implicitly or explicitly accept history (in contrast to
immutable nature) as the necessary starting point for ethics. (1978:65–66)[1]

Gustafson notes in *Protestant and Roman Catholic Ethics* that at least
three different kinds of Christian ethics are compatible with historicist assumptions: (1) the kind that stresses the particularity of Christian convictions to the extent that it rejects the need to show the applicability of
Christian ethics to all persons; (2) the kind that uses the phrase "God acting in history" to encourage us to try to discern God's actions; and (3) the
kind that embraces relativism and/or relationalism (1978:66–68). Although Gustafson in this book does not explicitly identify with any of
these, elsewhere he explicitly disassociates himself from (1) and (2). One
can only conclude, therefore, that his historical perspective is some version of (3).

Gustafson's stress on the importance of the church for Christian ethical
reflection is consistent with his historical commitments. Thus, the essays
in *The Church as Moral Decision-Maker* (1970) continue to be shaped by
Gustafson's conviction that ethics is not some timeless method of reflection on timeless truth or principles, but the concrete process of a particular group of people committed to testing their convictions in terms of
their current historical situation. Indeed, the importance of a historicist
perspective now involves a normative point as Gustafson develops his
account of a "Christian ethics of cultural responsibility." For the basic insight of such an ethic requires the "acceptance of the relativities of a social order and technology precisely *as relative*" (1970:31). Thus, Christians
"in the church are particularly called to interpret their existence in community as the location in time and space of their responsibility to God for
human society and for other persons. To participate in a cultural ethos, in
a moral tradition, is to have responsibility for that ethos and tradition"
(1970:71).[2] A historical perspective, therefore, seems to sustain the
"premise upon which all might agree," that the "churches by tradition

and vocation bear a responsibility for the morality of the society of which they are a part" (1970:83).

Gustafson's emphasis on the importance of the church for Christian ethics in *The Church as Moral Decision-Maker* is continued in *Christian Ethics and the Community* (1971). His emphasis on the centrality of the community for ethical reflection allows him to avoid the difficulties he believes are connected with the stress on God acting in history as the center of Christian ethics. For Gustafson, stressing God's action in history ironically tends to underwrite an ahistorical account of ethics. For on the basis of the theological claim, political judgments are made without going through concrete ethical and social analysis (1971:128). In contrast, Gustafson emphasizes the necessity of attending to a concrete community's beliefs about God, on the basis of which it may be possible to make some suggestions about how we ought to live and act.

Yet it is also with *Christian Ethics and the Community* that we begin to see Gustafson qualify, at least in terms of methodology, what appeared to be a thoroughgoing historicist perspective. I do not mean to suggest that there are no hints at such a qualification in his previous work, for even in *Treasures in Earthen Vessels* he noted that the temporal continuity of human communities raised questions about their nature (1961:4). But he did not exploit that suggestion in any sustained, systematic fashion that might qualify the stress on the importance of history. However, in his essay "The Moral Condition Necessary for Human Community," in *Christian Ethics and the Community*, we see him offering an account of the "natural virtues" of faith, hope, and love that seem to be prior to any historical construal (1971:154–163). To be sure, we may only know such "virtues" through concrete historical communities, but that does not make their existence and significance for all human communities any less invariant.

I am not sure how we should understand Gustafson's views about time and history at this point in his work. Certainly the overriding impression is that he remains committed to a historical point of view. That he does so is at least partly due to his impatience with abstract theological or philosophical claims that have no empirical grounding.[3] Thus, in *Christ and the Moral Life* (1968) he claims that

> questions of ethics, Christian or any other, can be established on the basis of both general human experience and reflection on literature in the field. It [his method] assumes that one can properly evaluate writings in theological ethics from other criteria than those established in and by revelation. When a constructive proposal is made in the last chapter, the key terms used are not drawn from revelation, or even theological literature. This is done out of the conviction that any significance of the work of Christ for the moral life takes place through such aspects of selfhood as disposition, intention, and

judgment that are common to all men. Thus some of the points used in the critical analysis in the end become normative in my attempts to make constructive Christian ethical proposals. (1968:9–10)

Moreover, Gustafson is true to his word, as we find, in the last chapter of *Christ and the Moral Life,* that basic stances (such as the conviction of the goodness of life) are "confirmed" and "symbolized" by Jesus Christ. The historic figure of Jesus and/or historic community committed to maintaining his memory no longer seems necessary to know or sustain such stances.

The essays in *Theology and Christian Ethics* (1974) continue to be marked by this ambivalence—a strong claim for the centrality of doing ethics from a historical point of view but with a hint of unease about being too thoroughgoing in accepting the implications of such a perspective. Thus, in his essay "The Relevance of Historical Understanding," he notes that the historical perspective we have inherited from Troeltsch continues to be of relevance in Christian ethics in at least three ways: "(1) the importance of knowing the historical context in which religious ethical ideas were formulated in order properly to understand them; (2) the importance of, and difficulties in, using historical analogies in formulating constructive ethical positions; and (3) the freedom to be historically situated and aware of the press of historical circumstances on one's own ethical judgments" (1974:178–179). The first way continues to be unproblematic for Gustafson, but he raises some critical questions about the others.

He is particularly critical of those who attempt to move from abstract theologies of history to politics without going through a stage of more careful ethical reflection (1974:189). While supporting the use of analogies for helping us interpret history, Gustafson is now insistent that such a procedure entails that man has a nature as well as a history; that there are "universals in human experience, which, while not denying the uniqueness and precise unrepeatability of events, nonetheless are a ground for continuities" (1974:189). Put even more directly, Gustafson asserts that the use of historical analogies "do assume continuities of experience which presuppose that man has a nature as well as a history. One cannot dispose of such continuities by appealing to the authority of scripture as the source of the proper understanding of reality. Other evidences and arguments than scriptural ones are required to settle issues as complex as this" (1974:189–190).

Gustafson makes a similar point in reference to the freedom to be historically situated. Such freedom, he notes, is the warrant for the continuing commentary on political and social events that is characteristic of Christian social journalism. The risks involved in this kind of work are ever present, however, as the very determination of a historical situation to be addressed is often shortsighted. More important, such immersion in history is extremely dangerous if there are no continuities in history, persons, and experience (1974:193). Thus, there must be serious study of ethical traditions exactly to avoid becoming lost in the variety of our histories.

We thus have the assertion that man has a nature as well as a history, but apart from hints here and there, Gustafson has not spelled out what he takes that nature to be. That brings us to *Ethics from a Theocentric Perspective* (1981 and 1984), as it is there that we can expect to discover Gustafson's mature views about time and history; or perhaps more accurately put, there we will see exhibited by the structure of his argument how he regards the significance of a historical point of view for theological and ethical reflection.

Before turning to *Ethics from a Theocentric Perspective*, however, there is one last point that can help illumine Gustafson's continuing commitment to a historicist perspective—namely, his understanding of the role of the ethicist. As so often is the case, one can almost miss the significance of a Gustafson essay because it seems so straightforward; but in fact it displays substantive presuppositions that are crucial to understanding his position. This is particularly true of his article "The Theologian as Prophet, Priest, or Participant" (1974:73–94).[4] For there Gustafson gives the most sustained account of his self-understanding as a theologian. Moreover, it is an account that draws heavily on his understanding of the necessary historical character of the theologian's work.

He notes that the attitude of the prophet is likely to be a combination of sorrow and indignation. Observing the injustices of the world, the prophet lashes out against the current state of affairs. The God appealed to is the God of wrath and judgment, a position that corresponds roughly to a "Christ against culture" paradigm. History is the story of sin and corruption in which God's Kingdom can only be a future hope. The church for the prophet can be an island in the sea of corruption or a vanguard of God's army of righteousness.

The theologian as priest may have the indignation of the prophet, but his indignation is directed against those who threaten the established order. He stands as preserver of tradition, emphasizing God as creator and ruler of an ordered life. Closer to a "Christ of culture" position, priest-preservers look on history as already bearing the fruits of the redemptive purposes of God. History is the story of God's rule and power. The Kingdom is in the historical processes, and the role of the church is to be the conserver of religious and cultural traditions.

The theologian as participant stands between the types of prophet and preserver. The participant "is wedded neither to the condemnation of the existing state of affairs, nor to the wholehearted support of them. He is however not a passive spectator of events and institutions, judging some to be worthy of endorsement and others to be worthy of reorientation and reform. Rather, he is actively involved in the shaping of events and in the development and reordering of institutions" (1974:84). Such a theologian is not simply the sage generalist with great moral sensitivity, but has specialized knowledge and discipline, developed through training, which can be passed on to future practitioners. The theologian or participant "brings to bear the insight and wisdom of the Christian community's long historical reflection about the chief ends of man" (1974:84).

Though the participant speaks from a perspective that is theologically informed, he does not announce it as truth. His attitude is a combination of dispassion and objectivity that helps him think clearly about the world in which he is active. He is hopeful but without illusions. He is more skeptical than either the prophet or the preserver regarding our ability to know God's will. Indeed, God is neither the wrathful judge nor the establisher of an immutable order; but for the participant, God can "best be spoken of as the active presence in the events to which men respond and which in turn they seek to direct." Gustafson finds such a view of God exemplified in the work of Karl Rahner and Daniel Day Williams.

For the participant, "Christ seeks neither the defense nor the abolition of the historical orders; rather, he seeks their renewal and redirection, their conversion toward their proper end and proper qualities" (1974:88). It is "Christ the transformer of culture" that guides the participant's vision. History for the participant "is not the outcome of fated, inexorably determinative processes that are impersonal and absolutely beyond the powers of men to affect. Rather, there are interstices between institutions and events, between persons, which provide the occasions for the meaningful exercises of human and other powers to give direction to the world" (1974:90). The participant denies that the Kingdom can be identified with any historical order, but that does not mean that revolution is always necessary. Rather, the "kingdom is the orientation point that gives both the disposition of hope and the vision of human fulfillment" (1974:90) by which the participant hazards opinions about the social-ethical correlates of what may be the most appropriate social order.

The participant therefore seeks to direct social change by making as clear as possible the purposes that social change can fulfill. The social and behavioral sciences are obviously of great importance for the accomplishment of that task. The role of the church is to be involved in social change, as Christians must seek to bring their spiritual resources to bear through their involvement in economic and political life. The function of the theologian in this community is to be the "leader of the moral discourse that is required if Christians are to be more effective actors" (1974:95). Gustafson candidly notes that his depiction of the participant type is not only a descriptive possibility, but also an ideal he would "wish to endorse as fitting for the theologian in our time for theological, historical, and ethical reasons" (1974:84). Moreover, it is clearly Gustafson's own understanding of his role as an ethicist and theologian. What makes this essay particularly important, then, is not what it may reveal personally about Gustafson but rather the way in which Gustafson's view of history determines how he understands his role as ethicist and theologian.

That is true because the strong claims about the historic character of all human communities and agents can now be seen to underwrite the view that there are limits to historical change. Therefore, the strong position taken in *Treasure in Earthen Vessels* concerning the historical character of all knowledge no longer determines Gustafson's basic methodology—such a strong position is the necessity of working from within a particular tradition—but rather it influences Gustafson's normative ethics in the sense that one must always accept the parameters of one's historical situation. Of course, there is no reason why one necessarily has to choose between these, and no doubt Gustafson continues to hold both, but as we shall see in *Ethics from a Theocentric Perspective*, the latter emphasis clearly becomes the more prominent.

Time and History in *Ethics from a Theocentric Perspective*

Gustafson begins *Ethics from a Theocentric Perspective* with the now familiar theme of the finiteness and limited nature of the human enterprise. "We may not be sure that there is an ultimately sovereign and purposive power governing all things, but we can be sure that we are creatures, and that we are not God" (1981:9). This general claim is expressed in several different ways throughout the two volumes of *Ethics from a Theocentric Perspective*. In relation to theological methodology it means that we must admit that truth is historically variant. But this acknowledgment of the relative nature of theological claims does not mean there are no tests of adequacy for doctrines (1981:144). Rather, it means that such tests can only be developed within the ongoing history of particularistic communities that develop canons of greater and lesser rationality.

This emphasis also has a negative side, as Gustafson is particularly critical of those philosophical positions that assume that they overcome historical particularity. From a theocentric perspective one does not presume that we are capable of

> developing an ideal moral theory, or formulating an ethical theory disregarding the implications of our embodiment as moral agents, our bearing of a particular culture, our location and involvement in society, and our interdependence in the ordering of the natural world. Such efforts to develop ideal moral theories assume a posture of spectator that I believe is not finally

possible or justifiable, though one appreciates their intellectual brilliance and learns from them. Indeed, as sociologists of knowledge and some philosophers, theologians, and intellectual historians have pointed out, such efforts are themselves part of a cultural tradition; they have their own intellectual history. (1984:146)

Gustafson is particularly critical of Kant and his followers for the ahistorical character of their work (1984:139). His constant theme is that

> visions, ways of life, and intellectual activities take place in particular historical and communal contexts. They grow out of aspects of cultural histories and societies, and can be sustained only in communities that have their distinctive symbols, languages, and rites. This is true not only of religious views and activities, but it is necessarily true of them. Communities are bound together by common interest, common loyalties, common standards, and common languages. If a community of autonomous rational moral agents, that fictive denomination into which many contemporary moral philosophers seek to convert us all, were actualized, it too would share these characteristics. (1981:317–318)

Gustafson's point, however, is not simply "methodological," because to admit the historical character of our existence means that we must also accept the fact that we are "fated." Although history, as distinguished from nature, involves those events that are the result of the choices and powers of human agents, it is nonetheless true that history "fates us." Thus,

> the range of choice of religious symbols for construing the world is limited initially by events beyond individual control. In this sense one is "fated" to be a Protestant Christian, or whatever one's religious identity early in life is. To say this, however, is not to imply that the Deity so governed all the events that led to my being what I am with a particular intention in mind for me. Nor does it mean that I must "resign" myself to this "fate." To give consent to the direction in which accidents of birth and history have turned one is to be persuaded of the adequacy of that direction, if not its eternal validity. What is true for the individual is true for the religious community as well. In some complex ways it consents to its history and its tradition. But the processes of selection from the tradition, of judging aspects of it in light of contemporary knowledge and experience, of reordering, revising, and rejecting, go on. If a community can consent to its tradition, it can dissent from it; it can select aspects to which it dissents. The test for the community or for individuals are many: lived experiences of many sorts, coherence or incoherence with other ways of construing the world, and the like. (1981:233)

We are fated and yet we are not; we do have the possibility, the grace, not to be determined by the conditions of our fatedness (1981:248). We are caught in the tension between the historical particular and its relations, and its relativities and the universal. "There is no possibility of human emancipation from the particularity of a perspective" (1981:301). Yet at times Gustafson seems to suggest, in spite of his criticism of the philosophers, that it would be good if we could be so emancipated. Thus he writes:

> To strive for the universal is not only intellectually valiant but also a necessary motivation in theological work. It is necessary for apologetic purposes; the intelligibility of the particular can be made clear and to some extent more persuasive by demonstrating that its insights and truths refer to the experiences of many if not all persons and that its justifications can be made clear in non-esoteric language. It is also necessary for purposes of internal criticism or a historical tradition. Blindness can be indicated; places where assumptions that were made in a tradition about such things as the ordering of the natural world, the motivations of human behavior, and the reliability of historical accuracy of critical texts have been made clear. The shifting within a tradition occurs in part by exposing it to lights which come from relevant knowledge, and to ideas from other movements of thought. Undue parochialism becomes clear. Where historic particularity is adduced as support for ideas which are no longer viable or are marginal to the importance of what the tradition stands for, it can be eliminated. (1981:151)

It seems, moreover, that this is exactly what Gustafson understands his task to be in *Ethics from a Theocentric Perspective*. He is striving for the universal, while acknowledging he is not free from history or the peculiarities of a particularistic tradition. Yet the crucial question is how Gustafson understands the force of that acknowledgment. For it now appears he seeks to ground theology in a manner that makes its particularistic starting point secondary. I am aware that such a claim may appear doubtful, given Gustafson's stress on the necessity of working within a tradition; but he still seems to hanker after a position that will be compelling to anyone. Thus, he says that the first task of theological ethics

> is to establish convictions about God and God's relations to the world. To make a case for how some things really and ultimately are is the first task of theological ethics. What the theologian writes about ethics must reasonably follow from these convictions. To be sure, it is impossible to have a philosophical theology, or a metaphysics, or a cosmology, based on "reason alone" from which follow ethics based on reason alone. In some respects (with qualifications made in volume 1) my work is more in accord with that intention than it is with a view that takes biblical "revelation" as the exclusive basis for theological ethics. (1984:98)

Now it may be objected that what Gustafson means by "reason alone" is certainly not what Kant meant, and that he is certainly not appealing to that "community of autonomous rational moral agents" that some philosophers mistakenly assume exists. Yet it must be asked, in what community is Gustafson standing, given his own concern to "strive for the universal"? On the surface it seems he has answered that with admirable clarity—namely, he stands within the Christian tradition and, in particular, the Reformed version of that tradition. As such it seems he is completely consistent with his insistence on a particularistic starting point. Yet his candid admission that he will develop only selected aspects of the Reformed tradition means that the question must stand: What community or tradition informs Gustafson's criteria of selection?

I am certainly not suggesting that Gustafson cannot dissent from various aspects of the Christian and/or Reformed tradition. Any substantive tradition requires arguments about what is and is not prominent for rightly understanding the tradition. So I have no disagreement with Gustafson's suggestion that a recognition of the historic character of our lives does not require consent to every aspect of the tradition in which we find ourselves. But the question remains whether the way Gustafson goes about selecting the elements of the Christian-Reformed tradition does not betray a lingering desire, if not presumption, that some ahistorical standpoint is valid or at least must be attempted.

In this respect, it is interesting to note that Gustafson sometimes speaks of "human experience" as if all people share common "senses" that are not historically determined. He thus claims that "human experience is prior to reflection" (1981:115). That seems innocent enough. But does "prior to reflection" mean prior to, or unmediated by, historical existence? If all our experience in fact is historically determined, then any clean distinction between "experience" and "reflection" seems hard to maintain. In the same way, Gustafson's insightful development of the "aspects of piety"—dependence, gratitude, obligation, remorse, purpose—in which religion is grounded seems to be an attempt to find a place "outside" history by which he can justify his selectivity vis-à-vis the Reformed tradition. Gustafson certainly has no wish to write "Religion Within the Limits of Reason Alone," but has he in fact written an account of "Religion Within the Limits of Senses of Piety" that may well have the same outcome?

I am aware that I may be trying to force an alternative that he has always tried to deny. But I think he finally cannot avoid such a choice, given the methodological presuppositions with which he works in *Ethics from a Theocentric Perspective*. Of course, he can respond that the "aspects of piety" assume a tradition and community; but if that is the case, then it is not clear whose history they represent. At least as Gustafson develops his accounts of these senses they seem to be true for anyone, not just that group of people who have been touched by or adhere to the Jewish or Christian tradition. Gustafson, of course, continues to emphasize in both volumes of *Ethics from a Theocentric Perspective* the importance of the church. Thus in volume 1 he says:

> The sustaining of a theological interpretation of man must take place in the context of a religious community, with its first-order religious language, its liturgies and symbols, and its procedures for transmitting a heritage. To be sure, the distinctive aspects of the views developed in this book are not completely at home in any particular Christian denomination, liturgy, or community. Yet they are grounded in some aspects of the rich and varied heritage of the Bible and of the Christian church and tradition. There are themes in the worship and religious life of the Christian tradition that do evoke and sustain the views I have espoused. In emphasizing some of them I am not merely attaching an idiosyncratic view onto a tradition; I am indicating various aspects of the tradition that evoke and sustain my views. (1981:318)

In like manner he maintains in volume 2 that

> the common life of the Christian community must continue to be formed in great measure by the biblical literature. The varieties of the biblical literature bear meanings of human life before God as they have come out of communities' conscientious participation in nature, history, society, and culture, felt and seen as ultimately under the governance of God. The Gospels powerfully portray Jesus as one who incarnates in his teachings, his manner, and his actions theocentric piety and fidelity. History and teachings powerfully form human life. (1984:292)

These are certainly claims that we would expect from the author of *Treasure in Earthen Vessels*, but it is by no means clear that they now have the same force. For Gustafson is not maintaining that the church or its worship is necessary in order to know what it means to live life under the governance of God; instead, the church seems merely to confirm experience that can be known in other, quite different ways. In effect, I am suggesting that Gustafson seems to presume something like what George Lindbeck has recently called the "experiential-expressive" theory of religion. Such a view "interprets doctrines as noninformative and nondiscursive symbols of inner feelings, attitudes, or existential orientations. This approach highlights the resemblances of religions to aesthetic enterprises and is particularly congenial to the liberal theologies influenced by the Continental developments that began with Schleiermacher" (1984:16). I certainly do not want to suggest that Gustafson's position is isomorphic with such a theory, but I think there are some striking structural similarities. If, moreover, I am right, then it does seem that Gustafson has decisively qualified his original emphasis on the unavoidability of a historical starting point for Christian theology.

It is to be noted, however, that in the more normative aspects of his work Gustafson continues to emphasize the unavoidability of a historical perspective.

> Man is not the proprietor of the creation, with rights of ownership that authorize us to do with all things what we choose in the light of our interests. Man is not the all-powerful emperor of the world, with the capacities to determine in detail the course of events and state of affairs. Man is part of a whole, indeed part of various "wholes" that can be designated. The past brings us to where we are in time and space, providing both limitations and opportunities for new achievements. (1984:145)

In short, we are participants, and it is the theologian-ethicist's task not to

> prescribe and proscribe the conduct of others, but to enable them to make informed choices. Agents who have responsibility for particular spheres of interdependence and action must be accountable for the choices that they make. Their roles, technical competence, experience, and character also enter into the decisions. The function of the ethician is to broaden and deepen the capacities of others to make morally responsible choices. (1984:315)

Such a perspective does not mean that all attempts to determine the "ordering of nature," as Aquinas did, are impossible. In fact, Gustafson seems to agree with Aquinas that there is a substantial "form of the human which gives us knowledge of the essence of the human" (1984:55). To be sure, that "essence" must now be put in terms of development in human evolution, but "insofar as the 'essence' indicates that there are particular potentialities and values to human life, and thus that human beings have an accountability for the ordering of life and a distinctive value within it, there is no quarrel" (1984:55).

A theocentric ethic must therefore try "to discern patterns of relationships which require compliance in order to preserve possibilities for the future developments not only of human beings but of the natural world" (1984:112). Hence, marriage and the family, for example, are grounded in biological functions, and though these are not sufficient for the development of a normative account of marriage, they must be taken into consideration for any normative theory (1984:159). Yet what such a perspective does seem to entail is the claim that no radical sense of social change—no prophetic perspective—should be the starting point of ethics.

Of course, change is not excluded. Thus, if increased respect for individuality and autonomy are to be met, then social arrangements, or conditions of the family, will also have to be changed. Yet what must be acknowledged is that

God orders the life of the world through the patterns and processes of interdependence in which human persons, institutions, communities, and the
species participate. These patterns and processes are a basis, foundation, or
ground for human ends and values and for moral principles. They are fundamentally necessary conditions which have to be met for other values and
ends to be fulfilled. They are not a sufficient basis of ethics; specific ends and
moral principles are not simply deduced from them. But they are a necessary basis for ethics; the oughtness of ends and principles is grounded in, or
based upon, their isness. (1984:298)

Thus, "the existing and developing order of life requires moral choices
that are necessarily related to particular contexts"—part of which, of
course, is the nation-state (1984:300).[5]

There can be no question that Gustafson's historic point of view remains decisive for his understanding of the role of ethics and the ethicist.
He is a wise incrementalist who knows that there is little chance to begin
history anew, but that there is great good to be done if we are willing to
work patiently within the historical contexts in which we find ourselves.
The search for ideal moral theories and correlative societies no doubt will
not abate, but finally our task is constantly to try to understand better
those "wholes" in which we have graciously been given parts to play.[6]

Final Thoughts on Time and History

I have tried to provide an internal critique of Gustafson's understanding
of time and history. I have suggested that although he has never abandoned the claims about inherent timefulness of the self begun in *Treasure
in Earthen Vessels*, he has nevertheless qualified that emphasis by attempting to ground his theology in a general account of human experience. That he has done so, however, does not in itself imply a criticism,
since one might well argue that he has rightly seen that any appropriate
account of God finally requires the qualification of a thoroughgoing historicist perspective.

In this respect, perhaps, Gustafson is only following H. Richard
Niebuhr's claim that

revelation cannot mean history, we must say to ourselves in the church, if it
also means God. What we see from the historical point of view and what we
believe in as we occupy that standpoint must be two different things. For
surely what is seen in history is not a universal, absolute, independent
source and goal of existence, not impartial justice nor infinite mercy, but particularity, finiteness, opinions that pass, caprice, arbitrariness, accident, bru-
tality, wrong on the throne and right on the scaffold. The claims of the evan-
gelists of historical revelation seem wholly inconsistent with their faith.
(1960:54)[7]

What Gustafson seems to reject, however, is H. Richard Niebuhr's consequent confessionalism that seems to bracket claims of truth. His analysis of "religious sensibilities" is his attempt to make a core for religious belief that is not confessionally specific and thus can provide critical perspective on the confessional traditions.

Put in different terms, it seems that Gustafson's convictions about the kind of God that sustains our existence forces him to work from the universal to the particular, whereas earlier he seemed, with H. Richard Niebuhr, to work in the opposite direction. One may wonder, of course, what difference it makes whether one goes the one way or the other. But Gustafson is sure it does make a difference, for as he writes:

> The central issue is that Christianity has always claimed its historical particularity—the biblical events and their record—to have universal significance and import. Certainly a substantive enterprise in theology from the biblical times forward has been to overcome and sustain that particularity at one and the same time, to stand with and for that historical particularity while insisting that its significance is universal. (1981:68)

Yet note that is not the way Gustafson works in *Ethics from a Theocentric Perspective*. He seeks instead to build a universal case for which the particular is only the illustration—the same tendency that H. Richard Niebuhr's later work often seemed to presuppose.

Gustafson does not seek to show how the particular has universal significance, as he seeks "to overcome" that particularity. That he does so is partly due to his reading of our current cultural situation as "the theological problem present in the New Testament itself, namely, how a historically particular person and set of events can have the universal meaning claimed for them, has gotten more complex through the centuries in which the provincialism of Western culture has been eroded by more and deeper knowledge of other cultures" (1981:64).[8] Yet I suspect the more basic reason he feels it necessary to "overcome" such particularity is that it fails to do justice to the kind of theocentricism he is willing to defend. Particularity underwrites an "anthropomorphic" standpoint because it cannot help but make history crucial for any account not only of our knowledge of God but also of our relation to God's presence.

But if that is the case, then it must be asked why Gustafson continues to insist so strongly on the necessity of a historical starting point. For no longer is that point a theological claim concerning the place of Israel and Jesus for our relation to God. Rather, it is now a general anthropological claim that at least in principle seems to qualify any radical account of our historicity. The very attempt to mount a philosophical case about our historical nature seems to presuppose that there is some standpoint that is not subject to history. By the very way he works in *Ethics from a Theocentric Perspective*, Gustafson seems to assume that such a standpoint exists.

There is neither space nor would it be appropriate at this point to mount any external criticism of Gustafson's understanding of time and history. However, in closing it seems clear to me that I remain stuck with the problem of history in a way different from Gustafson because I remain stuck with the claim that through Jesus' resurrection God decisively changed our history. Therefore, I believe we must continue to begin with the "particular," with the historical, not because there is no other place to begin, but because that is where God begins. So, as Gustafson argued, the question of time and history is finally a question about our understanding of God—or perhaps more accurately, it is finally a question of how we understand God's presence in our lives.

One final point: I find it is interesting that Gustafson's and my own emphasis on the significance of history tend to go in exactly the opposite directions. In terms of methodology he tries to develop a more universal standpoint, whereas I stress the necessity of beginning with the particularistic claims about Israel and Jesus of Nazareth, the Jews and the church. Normatively he develops an ethic that accepts the limitations of our cultural and social situation, whereas I try to conceive of alternatives to our situation. The church, for Gustafson, although still important, does not determine the methodological presuppositions from which he works; the church for me determines the context and the nature of ethics. I am not sure what to make of these differences, but I am at least sure that they remind us that there is more than one way to be "historical."

Notes

An earlier version of this chapter, entitled "Time and History in Theological Ethics: The Work of James Gustafson," appeared in *Journal of Religious Ethics*, 13, 1 (spring 1985): 3–21. Copyright © 1985 Journal of Religious Ethics, Inc.; all rights reserved. Reprinted by permission

I am indebted to Dr. Greg Jones and Dr. Harmon Smith for their criticism of this chapter.

1. Gustafson often tends to conflate the issues of (1) the historical particularity inherent in theological reflection and (2) the relativity and change characteristic of moral norms and judgments. The two are obviously interrelated, though it is possible to agree with (2) without necessarily accepting (1).

2. As we shall see, Gustafson's rather innocent use of "participate" as a notion governing Christian behavior in the world becomes a full-scale theory in his later work. I must confess I had not noticed before reading for this essay how significant is the notion of "participation" for understanding Gustafson's general perspective.

3. In many ways Gustafson can be understood as trying to have the results of beginning with ontological accounts of existence without doing ontology. He dislikes ontology for the same reason he dislikes Barth—it lacks empirical hold. So

he must try to find the "continuities" within history that will somehow allow him to transcend history.

4. Gustafson is so careful and so fair in his presentation of others' positions and statements of the problem that it is often hard to argue with him. In his work prior to *Ethics from a Theocentric Perspective* it was sometimes difficult to discern Gustafson's own position, as he was so intent to describe and analyze the position of others. Yet what can be overlooked is the very process of analysis Gustafson employs—such as the typological approach—may in fact reflect his constructive position. Therefore, if one wishes to join argument with him, perhaps one needs to challenge or reconceptualize the way the issues are put. For example, it may be a mistake to ask what is the relation between Christ and the moral life, as that assumes a coherent account of "the moral life" is available. Of course, that is not to question most of the analysis Gustafson provides in *Christ and the Moral Life*, but it is to note that the analysis may be better than the scheme. The same, I think, is the case in the delineation of prophet, priest, and participant for a description of the theologian's roles.

5. Given the perspective Gustafson develops in volume 2 of *Ethics from a Theocentric Perspective*, I think it would be extremely interesting for him to expose his views about war. For I do not see how he can avoid seeing war as perhaps tragic, but nonetheless one of the morally necessary institutions of our lives. I suspect, moreover, that if he turned his attention to war, we might better understand how his ethics may be in continuity and discontinuity with Niebuhrian "realism."

6. It is interesting that Gustafson assumes that a recognition of our historicity means we must work within the given possibilities of our cultural and societal contexts. Why could one not just as easily conclude that a historical perspective means we can create new possibilities by being a different kind of community and/or people?

7. How Gustafson's understanding of time and history continues and differs from that of H. Richard Niebuhr's would, I suspect, make a complex and interesting story. Certainly *Treasure in Earthen Vessels* seems to be more compatible with *The Meaning of Revelation*, whereas some of Gustafson's later views draw on *Radical Monotheism in Western Culture*.

8. This strikes me as a questionable claim, as I suspect the claim for "particularity" was even more difficult in a society where the "universal" was at the service of the state—i.e., Rome. It may be, however, that the reason we have so much difficulty articulating the universal appeal of the Gospel is due to our allowing it to be determined by the particularity of Western culture.

References

Gustafson, James M. 1961. *Treasure in Earthen Vessels: The Church as a Human Community*. New York: Harper and Brothers.

_____. 1968. *Christ and the Moral Life*. New York: Harper and Row.

_____. 1970. *The Church as Moral Decision-Maker*. Philadelphia: Pilgrim Press.

_____. 1971. *Christian Ethics and the Community*. Philadelphia: Pilgrim Press.

_____. 1974. *Theology and Christian Ethics*. Philadelphia: Pilgrim Press.

_____. 1975. *Can Ethics Be Christian?* Chicago: University of Chicago Press.

_____. 1978. *Protestant and Roman Catholic Ethics: Prospects for Rapprochement.* Chicago: University of Chicago Press.

_____. 1981. *Ethics from a Theocentric Perspective.* Vol. 1, *Theology and Ethics.* Chicago: University of Chicago Press.

_____. 1984. *Ethics from a Theocentric Perspective.* Vol. 2, *Ethics and Theology.* Chicago: University of Chicago Press.

Lindbeck, George. 1984. *The Nature of Doctrine: Religion and Theology in a Postliberal Age.* Philadelphia: Westminster Press.

Niebuhr, H. Richard. 1960. *The Meaning of Revelation.* New York: Macmillan.

5   *Can Aristotle Be a Liberal?*
Martha Nussbaum on Luck

In this essay I propose to explore the social and political implications of Nussbaum's interpretation and defense of Aristotle's ethics. In order to do that, I am going to bring her account of Aristotle's ethics into conversation with that of Alasdair MacIntyre. I think it will illumine the social and political issues to ask what standpoint Nussbaum and MacIntyre occupy that makes them think it important to reclaim Aristotle's account of the moral life.

If you are so inclined, you may describe my task as a hermeneutical exercise. However, since hermeneutics has increasingly come to encompass every intellectual activity, I am unsure how helpful that description may be. I do think, as MacIntyre and also perhaps Nussbaum think, that issues of interpretation cannot be separated from social and political questions. I am not going to attempt to assess the rightness or wrongness of Nussbaum's and MacIntyre's interpretations of Aristotle. Just as Amos denied being a prophet or a son of a prophet, I am neither a scholar nor a son of a scholar. I think I know enough not to enter the ring against two heavyweights like MacIntyre and Nussbaum on how to interpret Aristotle. I will not try to determine which of their accounts of the relation between Plato and Aristotle is most nearly correct. I am interested in knowing how one could even determine that question, as it is not clear to me that the debate can be settled on solely "scholarly" grounds—since I am unclear as to what "solely scholarly grounds" look like.[1]

My concern is rather to ask where MacIntyre and Nussbaum understand themselves to be standing to be able to rightly understand Aristotle. I recently asked a student on a doctoral examination how the recovery of Aristotle's understanding of practical reason has contributed to the "antifoundationalist" turn in recent epistemology and ethical theory.[2] I asked him to illustrate his answer by discussing the work of Lovibond, Stout, and MacIntyre. Being a very bright student, he argued that the question was wrongly put. The question should be, "What has happened in our social and political situation that makes Aristotle's account of practical reason so compelling?" That is what I am asking Nussbaum and MacIntyre, what is it about their understanding of our contemporary moral (and political) culture that makes their very different accounts of retrieving Aristotle so interesting and significant?[3]

Of course, one might say that all that has happened is that through hard scholarly work we have simply come to understand Aristotle more accurately. There is some truth to this, as anyone can testify who has read the essays in *Aristotle's Ethics*, edited by Amélie Rorty[4] or, to mention just one further work, John Cooper's *Reason and Human Good in Aristotle.*[5] Simplistic accounts and criticisms of Aristotle are no longer possible. No one is going to spend time, for example, trying to show that Aristotle's ethics present a too rationalistic account of human behavior because of his stress in Book X of the *Ethics* on contemplation as the highest form of human activity.

However, scholarship does not occur in a vacuum. Surely it is no accident that a renewed appreciation of Aristotle's willingness to begin ethical reflection with what we find, or as Nussbaum puts it, with the *phainomena,* happens after we have been schooled by Wittgenstein's work. For as James Edwards has reminded us in *Ethics Without Philosophy: Wittgenstein and the Moral Life,* Wittgenstein's thinking, "in both its periods, is [an] attempt to incarnate a vision of the healthy human life; the transmission of a moral vision—the attempt to reveal its character and to make it potent."[6] Wittgenstein's work cannot be divorced from his attempt to respond to his culture's loss of moral confidence. In a similar fashion, I suspect we are turning back to Aristotle because we are able, given our social and political context, to read him with fresh eyes.

In particular, I hope to show that Nussbaum believes that Aristotle provides an account of morality peculiarly suited for our times. It is, of course, by no means clear what is meant by "our times"—witness debates about whether we live in a modern or postmodern situation. I want as far as I can to avoid these questions, as I am unsure how to characterize the sides and even less sure what counts for evidence for either side.[7] By "our times," therefore, all I mean to do is ask whether Nussbaum believes we are able to understand and appropriate Aristotle's account of the virtuous moral life without being in profound tension with the current social and political forms of life we call liberal democracies.

I put the matter in this way, as I suspect Nussbaum's retrieval of Aristotle at least partly involves an attempt to sustain an ethos sufficient to underwrite the institution we associate with the "liberal project," that is, an allegedly limited state in service to a social economic order based on exchange relations. To use the phrase "the liberal project," of course, is to put the question in MacIntyre's terms, but that has the virtue of reminding us that the social-political question cannot be divorced from the epistemological one: Can liberalism survive the acknowledgment that it is a tradition when its epistemological commitments are based on the denial of tradition?

To put the issue in this way, at the outset, may be deeply unfair to Nussbaum, since Nussbaum should not be forced to accept MacIntyre's account of the tradition-bound character of rationality.[8] However, this way of stating the matter does provide a framework to explore the question of the social and political presuppositions that sustain Nussbaum's project. For MacIntyre makes no pretense of being able to reclaim Aristotle as part of the modern project. He points out that

> there is [for Aristotle] an important analogy between how a capacity for right judgment in respect of the good life for human beings as such is developed within the context provided by the polis and how capacities for more particular species of right judgment are developed in the context of all those more particular forms of activity within which standards of excellence are recognized. Just as an apprenticeship in sculpture or architecture is required in order to recognize what excellent performance in these arts consists in, so a capacity for identifying and ordering of all these other sets of goods requires training whose point emerges only in the course of the training. (*M*, 110)

For MacIntyre, the rational justification of the life of virtue within the community of the polis is available only to those who already participate in that life. So the *Nicomachean Ethics* is directed only at those who make up the mature citizens of the polis. If that is the case, however, then how does it stand with those of us who must read Aristotle from such a distance? MacIntyre argues:

> At the very least we are required in the first instance to identify ourselves imaginatively with the standpoint of the citizen of a well-ordered polis. A modern would-be critic of Aristotle, who necessarily has had a political and cultural education very different from that presupposed in his readers by Aristotle, will be unable to understand, let alone criticize, Aristotle's theses unless he or she discards for the moment at least the standpoint of modernity. (*M*, 111)[9]

Obviously MacIntyre, in his presentation of Aristotle's ethics, is standing, or at least thinks he is standing, outside modernity. It is by no means clear that Nussbaum thinks such a standpoint necessary or desirable for rightly reading Aristotle. She notes that the tragic poem is

> available equally to all readers as they consult about the good life. It is furthermore a carefully crafted working-through of a human story, designed to bring certain themes and questions to each reader's attention. It can therefore advance the conversation among readers that is necessary to the com-

pletion of the Aristotelian project, whose aims are ultimately defined in terms of a "we," of people who wish to live together and share a conception of value. A tragic poem will be sufficiently distant from each reader's experience not to bring to the fore bias and divisive self-interest; and yet (if we do the hard historical work required to bring out the extent to which we do and do not share the perplexities of the Greeks) it can count as a shared extension of all readers' experience. (*N*, 14–15)[10]

Nussbaum seems to suggest that our moral existence is inextricably timeful and, thus, fragile, although she maintains that we can have such knowledge in a timeless manner. Of course, such insight into our condition is won only through "hard historical work," but such work is not an end in itself. Nussbaum is clear: Her interrogations of Aristotle's texts are done against the background of a particular understanding of our cultural situation. She confesses:

I shall simply assert here my belief that Nietzsche was correct in thinking that a culture grappling with the widespread loss of Judaeo-Christian religious faith could gain insight into its own persisting intuition about value by turning to the Greeks. When we do not try to see them through the lens of Christian beliefs we can not only see them more truly; we can also see how true they are to us—that is, to a continuous historical tradition of human ethical experience that has not been either displaced or irreversibly altered by the supremacy of Christian (and Kantian) teaching. The problems of human life with which this book deals have not altered very much over the centuries; and if we do not feel required to depict the Greek responses to them as primitive by contrast to something else, we can see how well the Greeks articulate intuitions and responses that human beings have always had to these problems. We will see the element of continuity best, however, if we are careful to point out the respects in which history has altered the face of the problem. (*N*, 15)

I am sure Nussbaum is right that Christians, in order to make use of Aristotle, are required to reconfigure his work in ways he would find extraordinary, if not offensive. Yet I am equally sure that the way Christian theology "distorts" Aristotle is quite different from the way those influenced by Kant do so—though there have been Christian Kantians who read, or largely failed to read, Aristotle through Kantian eyes. However, just to the extent that Nussbaum assumes that Christianity and Kantianism share a common misreading of Aristotle, she betrays continuing philosophical and cultural presuppositions that have more in common with Kant, or at least with the Enlightenment, than her overall project would suggest.

These are complex matters, and I do not want to deny that Kant provides philosophical expressions for some tendencies in Christian theology, particularly Protestant theology, that have a common distorting effect for reading Aristotle. For example, Nussbaum suggests that Kantians believe that "there is one domain of value, the domain of moral value, that is altogether immune to the assaults of luck" (*N*, 4). Some Christian theologians in their concern to protect the universality and unavoidability of God's grace have seen Kant's account of morality as a resource exactly in the manner Nussbaum suggests. Grace simply becomes a word denoting the unavoidability of our relation to God that remains sure, irrespective of the quality of our lives. Of course, this is an issue any Christian theology must confront. Christians at once affirm God as the source and sustainer of all life and maintain the necessity of the transformation of our lives if we are rightly to worship God. Christians can therefore never lose hold of the affirmation that God will choose those whom God will choose in a manner that cannot help but be offensive to people with Kantian sensibilities, for whom the necessity of a people, Israel, or a person, Jesus, for salvation can only appear absurd.

Nussbaum is wrong to identify Christianity and Kant in this way, and her own interpretation of Aristotle still betrays Kantian influences. The ghost of Kant is hard to shake for any of us—even Nussbaum. Our anti-Kantianism often continues to presuppose the structure of Kant's position. I suspect this is due to the commitment to underwrite the project of political liberalism based on the Kantian presumption that we share, or we at least have the potential to share, a common humanity. Without such presumptions we fear we cannot sustain the institutional arrangements necessary to secure reasonable stability among people who do not believe they have a common destiny or who believe they have no destiny.

Nussbaum rejects the Kantian presumption that our common humanity can be grounded in rationality qua rationality. Such a project is far too grand or presumptuous for the more modest project of Aristotle, who Nussbaum rightly thinks never wanted us to be more than or less than human. Yet in *The Fragility of Goodness*, Nussbaum confesses that she is attempting to deal with problems that have not altered very much over the centuries (*N*, 15). We turn to the Greeks because of their intuition and articulation of these very problems, which human beings have always had. Thus she writes:

> I begin this book from a position that I believe to be common: the position of one who finds the problems of Pindar's ode anything but peculiar and who has the greatest difficulty understanding how they might ever cease to be problems. That I am an agent, but also a plant; that much that I did not make goes toward making me whatever I shall be praised or blamed for being; that I must constantly choose among competing and apparently incommensurable goods and that circumstances may force me to a position in which I cannot help being false to something or doing some wrong; that an event that simply happens to me may, without my consent, alter my life; that it is

equally problematic to entrust one's good to friends, lovers, or country and to try to have a good life without them—all these I take to be not just the material of tragedy, but everyday facts of lived practical reason. (5)

But it surely seems odd to call such matters "facts." That such facts are said to exist at all only seems intelligible this side of Kant—in short, it seems intelligible only if one still has a commitment to something like what MacIntyre calls the "liberal tradition" and its corresponding epistemological alternatives.

I hope it is clear that the question I am trying to pose concerning Nussbaum's methodological presuppositions betrays a profound admiration for her work. The suggestion that she is a "liberal" is not an attempt to put a label on her. Liberalism is, of course, a far too protean phenomenon to allow for such labeling. Certainly it is not sufficient to indicate her disagreement with MacIntyre to make her part of the "Enlightenment project." She may have no greater stake in the liberal project than MacIntyre, but she certainly seems to have a more hopeful view of our social alternatives.

My suspicion is that Nussbaum is trying to help us discover a chastened and more profoundly complex account of the moral life necessary to sustain those institutions that have been created by our liberal ancestors but that can no longer be sustained by our ancestors' philosophical presumptions. She is trying to "save our appearances" through a recapturing of the fragility of our existence so that we will be rescued from the excesses of cynicism and utopianism—the great project of the Stoics. Yet this surely seems an odd interpretation for anyone defending Aristotle against Kant, particularly if that defense is about the recovery of the significance of the passions. However, by contrasting the broad outlines of Nussbaum's and MacIntyre's interpretation of Aristotle, I hope to show that I have some grounds for the suspicion that Nussbaum has made Aristotle a liberal.

In drawing a contrast between MacIntyre and Nussbaum it is important that we not overlook their considerable agreements. Indeed, it is critical to the case I want to make that they agree in broad outline about Aristotle's ethics. Each wants to rescue Aristotle from Kantian interpretation. In particular, their common interest in recovering Aristotle's richer account of our existence challenges those who try to enforce the Kantian distinction between moral and nonmoral issues. Only then can we appreciate the tragic character intrinsic to the life of excellence. As Nussbaum observes, the Kantian, like Creon, tries to make "a deliberative world into which tragedy cannot enter. Insoluble conflicts cannot arise, because there is only a single supreme good and all other values are functions of that good" (*N*, 58). In their effort to make the world safe for morality, both the Creons and the Kants impoverish our existence.

According to MacIntyre and Nussbaum, Aristotle rightly saw the necessary interdependence of happiness, virtue, and friendship and the correlative complexity of our moral existence. We cannot know what should make us happy until we have been formed by the virtues that make it possible for us to be people capable of friendship. Friendship is intrinsic to the moral life, for without it we cannot have the self-knowledge necessary to make our habits our own. Such a life is, of course, the life of passion, for contrary to modern accounts of morality, we must not only do the good, we must feel the right passion and pleasure in doing so.

So MacIntyre and Nussbaum have an equal stake in defending Aristotle's account of practical wisdom. Practical wisdom is not a faculty that can be divorced from our desires or from our formation by the virtues. That is why it is a mistake to reduce Aristotle's account of practical reason to the practical syllogism. Although practical reason embodies "some syllogistic reasoning, it is not and could not be exclusively syllogist" (*M*, 135). *Proairesis* unites the agent's desire for the object and his or her true good in such a manner that reasoning cannot be abstracted from the one doing the reasoning. Practical wisdom is a matter of perception that comes from being well trained, in a society that can sustain such training.

MacIntyre captures the complexity of this account of practical wisdom in his arresting image of the hockey player who "in the closing seconds of a crucial game has an opportunity to pass to another member of his or her team better placed to score a needed goal":

> Necessarily, we may say, if he or she has perceived and judged the situation accurately, he or she must immediately pass. What is the force of this "necessarily" and this "must"? It exhibits the connection between the good of that person and hockey player and member of that particular team and the action of passing, a connection such that were such a player not to pass, he or she must either have falsely denied that passing was for their good qua hockey player or have been guilty of inconsistency or have acted as one not caring for his or her good qua hockey player and member of that particular team. That is to say, we recognize the necessity and the immediacy of rational action by someone inhabiting a structured role in a context in which the goods of some systematic form of practice are unambiguously ordered. And in so doing we apply to one part of our social life a conception which Aristotle applies to rational social life as such. It is thus only within those systematic forms of activity within which goods are unambiguously ordered and within which individuals occupy and move between well-defined roles that the standards of rational action directed toward the good and the best can be embodied. To be a rational individual is to participate in such a form of social life and to conform, so far as is possible, to those standards. It is because and insofar as the *polis* is an arena of systematic activity of just this kind that the *polis* is the locus of rationality. And it was because Aristotle judged that no form of state but the *polis* could integrate the different systematic activities of human beings into an overall form of activity in which

the achievement of each kind of good was given its due that he also judged that only a *polis* could provide that locus. (*M*, 140–141)

Nussbaum, I think, is on the whole in agreement with MacIntyre's image of how practical reason works in Aristotle. There is no point outside human experience that we can begin our moral reflection—we must begin in the *phainomena* if we are to begin at all. There is no refutation of the skeptic if we accept the skeptic's grounds. We can only begin with our experience even if our practical wisdom leads us to see our convictions in a new light or transform them. But as Nussbaum insists, that does not mean Aristotelian practical wisdom is a type "of rootless situational perception that rejects all guidance from ongoing commitments and values. The person of practical wisdom is a person of good character, that is to say, a person who has internalized through early training certain ethical values and a certain conception of the good human life as the more or less harmonious pursuit of these" (*N*, 306).

According to Nussbaum, for Aristotle, to have "*nous*, or insight, concerning first principles is to come to see the fundamental role that the principles we have been using all along play in the structure of a science":

> What is needed is not to grasp the first principles—we grasp them and use them already inside our experience. We move from the confused man of the appearances to a perspicuous ordering, from the grasp that goes with use to the ability to give accounts. There is no reason to posit two philosophical methods here, one dealing with appearances, one resting on the a-priori; dialectic and first philosophy have as Aristotle insists in Metaphysics IV, 2 exactly the same subject matter. The appearances, then, can go all the way down. (*N*, 251)

Nussbaum explicitly rejects the need for an Archimedian point where we might begin ethical reflection. "If objectivity is to be attained it must be by patient explicitness about the possible sources of bias in the inquiry" (*N*, 17). In this respect, it is important we understand that Nussbaum wants the very reading of her book to be a moral exercise. She is engaged in a profoundly moral project to assemble reminders capable of directing our attention to poetry that can enrich our lives. Like Aristotle, she hopes thus to initiate a dialogue through which we can come to agreement, which will be as close as we can get as humans to the truth—a truth, as she puts it, that is anthropocentric but not relativistic (*N*, 11). She notes:

> Aristotle and Socrates believe that the best articulation of each individual's internal system of belief will also be an account shared by all individuals who are capable of seriously pursuing the search for truth. This is so because they believe that the outstanding obstacles to communal agreement

are deficiencies in judgment and reflection; if we are each led singly through the best procedures of practical choice, we will turn out to agree on the most important matters, in ethics as in science. I believe that this position is substantially correct. (*N*, 11)

Here I think we come to the nub of the matter between Nussbaum and MacIntyre. The problem is not the circularity that seems inherent to moral developments. Nussbaum very helpfully says:

An element of circularity is probably bound to be present in any complex moral theory. But in the end our feeling about the circle, as to whether it is small and pernicious, or large and interesting, will depend upon our sense of whether Aristotle has indeed done well what his method dictates: to work through the complexities of our beliefs concerning choice, correctly describing the conflicts and contradictions they present, and to produce the ordering that will save what we most deeply consider worth saving. (*N*, 312)

The problem is, "Who is the 'we' who turns out to agree on the most important matters?" To be sure, it is not the abstract "we" or "I" of Kant, but it is still hard to know what social place this "we" occupies and what, if any, difference that social place makes for whether Pindar (or Aristotle) ought to be read in the first place and if so, how they are to be read.[11] I think it would be unfair to suggest that this "we" is the readership of the *New York Times*, which MacIntyre wickedly described as the "parish magazine of affluent and self-congratulatory liberal enlightenment" (*M*, 5), but it still seems to be a fairly small group who live lives untouched by the economic deprivation of advanced capitalist societies. There is too much wisdom in Nussbaum's book to justify such a characterization, but we must remind ourselves that we (that is, people capable of reading, or who want to read, *The Fragility of Goodness*) are members of an intellectual elite, who justify our elite position by our ability to appreciate such wisdom.

Nussbaum is aware that Aristotle's account of the moral life is in deep tension with the presumption of democratic society. She notes that Aristotle's distinction between the citizen and the free alien only makes moral sense when we see it against the well-functioning *polis* in which each citizen had a real share in shaping a public conception of the goods, where no one was alienated except by choice and where civic friendship was not attenuated by numbers or distance. Against such a background, modern democracies cannot help but appear as societies of free aliens in which the successful distributing of the social condition of self-respect is missing. Nussbaum suggests that our alienation from active governing makes us more like Aristotle, who was not a citizen of Athens, than like those whose situation he praises.[12]

Nussbaum rightly suggests that given the lack of training for most in our society, we cannot rely on the majority to give us moral (or political) guidance. Rather, we must "rely on the intuition of people who have somehow earned the right to be regarded as competent practical judges—who have displayed the requisite strength of character, intellect, and imagination and have done enough of the practical work of considering and working through alternative moral conceptions to find themselves in a good position to make sound judgments."[13] But it must be asked, "How are we to locate these people?" Is it not the case that "we" assume "we"—that is, people capable of reading *The Fragility of Goodness*—are such people? Moreover, if we are the "we," is not our ability to understand why the life of virtue must create its own vulnerability due to our presumption that we have the economic security to protect us from outrageous luck?

Nussbaum is well aware that there is a kind of self-fulfilling prophecy to her (and Aristotle's) account of the moral life. She notes that Aquinas, sensing Aristotle's appeal to the *phronimos* was circular, tried to solve the problem by appeal to Divine Law. We have denied ourselves this solution, according to Nussbaum, but that does not mean we are without resources: "If we really make ourselves think through and feel in some detail what the alternatives are like and what a life based on them can be for us, we can hope to emerge with at least a better understanding of why autonomy is important to us and just how important it is. It is not clear that moral argument can accomplish more than this."[14]

But what saves Nussbaum from believing, as Nietzsche believed, that such autonomy must result in a knowledge of its own arbitrariness? MacIntyre notes that "the Enlightenment believed and believes that we have to overcome partiality and one-sidedness from the beginning, even if beginning is something that we have to do over and over again, while the pre-Enlightenment traditions believe that it is only at the end that they will be overcome." note ?

But ever since Nietzsche, both these types of view have been confronted by the claim that partiality and one-sidedness can never be overcome: "As though there would be a world left over once we subtracted the perspectival," there are no facts as such, but only interpretations, and all interpretation is from a point of view. Thus, apparently rival interpretations are not in fact in conflict, for neither is able to vindicate a claim that this-is-how-it-is, but only that this-is-how-it-appears-from-this-point-of-view, and this latter is not at all inconsistent with matters appearing very differently from some other point of view. What has disappeared from view is any conception of truth which would be capable of generating this kind of inconsistency. And Nietzsche well understood this: "Truths are illusions which we have forgotten are illusions, worn-out metaphors now impotent to stir the sense, coins which have lost their faces and are considered now as metal rather than currency." But Nietzsche's Anglo-Saxon heirs have from a variety of motives wanted to retain the idiom of truth while still rejecting what Nietzsche had rejected of its substance. So they have attempted to revise the notion of truth by making it equivalent—more or less, that is—to warranted assertibility. The true is no more or less than what we are prepared to commit ourselves to at the present juncture; the contrast between timeless truth and what merely we take to be here and now rationally justified has been obliterated. But both more and less radical post-Nietzscheans—or some of them at least—have taken one further step to separate themselves from both the Enlightenment and the pre-Enlightenment traditions. For they have contended that we ought to regard different bodies of theory much as we regard works of art and that we ought to understand historical movements from the acceptance of one particular type of philosophical, and perhaps also even some scientific theory to its replacement by another much in the same way as we understand changes from, say, the baroque to the classical.[15]

What is not clear to me is where Nussbaum is situated in this respect. She is clearly not a pre-Enlightenment thinker; nor does she want to identify with those forms of post-Enlightenment thought that make everything a matter of interpretation (interpretation is but another form of free construction through which I create myself). Nor does it seem she wants to identify with MacIntyre's tradition-formed account of rationality. Instead, what we seem to get is the claim that by reading Aristotle we can recapture the essential human insights about the finiteness and fragility of our lives that are simply there. If I am right about this, then it seems that Nussbaum is not far from the view that she is giving us the Aristotle of "objective scholarship" whose objectivity is ensured because all with appropriate sensitivities must have the same insight if they rightly read Pindar, Aeschylus, Sophocles as now seen through Aristotle.

In this respect, I think it is interesting to see how Nussbaum and MacIntyre situate Aristotle in relation to the Greek dramatists. On the surface their accounts appear very similar, stressing how the Greek plays explored the necessary conflicts of social obligation and the virtues. Yet MacIntyre's account, particularly in *Whose Justice? Which Rationality?* locates the dramatists as but part of the political struggle of Athens to resolve the question of who should rule (*M*, 38). The tension between excellence and effectiveness, the question of whether justice is only that which is in the interest of the strong, these are fundamentally political questions. The "sense of tragedy" we find in the Greek dramatists and Aristotle cannot be separated from the moral tensions inherent in Greek social and political life.

I am well aware that this tells Nussbaum nothing she does not already know, knows far better than I do, and, perhaps, even MacIntyre knows.

But the issue is not what she knows, but how she knows it and to what purpose. To recover a sense of the fragility of our excellence, of how luck determines our moral possibilities abstracted from the social and political context that makes that knowledge make sense, means that a sense of our "fragility" becomes but another "insight" for a cultural elite.

Nussbaum is not Richard Rorty recommending that we enjoy the fact we live in a society where we can be light-minded aesthetes.[16] She is far too serious-minded for that. Yet her attempt to recover a sense of the unavoidability of the contingent for a life of excellence as a free-standing truth can be seen as very profound advice for tired liberals who no longer believe in the Enlightenment project but who know that they are condemned to live it out. That is, they are devoid of any profound convictions other than that all convictions are finally arbitrary. Is luck, in such a context, another name for discovering that we can accept the fact that we are among the powerful and that is all right as long as we work to make the same opportunity available to others?

MacIntyre returns to Aristotle because as a Christian he cannot read Aquinas without him. MacIntyre owes us an account as to why he stands in Augustinian Christian tradition, and he must spell out the social and political factors that make such a stance possible. At least MacIntyre gives us the basis for challenging him to provide such accounts. Nussbaum's account seems to prevent such questions from being raised.

I simply do not want to be capable of acknowledging luck. I am not even sure I think it a good idea to talk about the fragility of our lives as if it were a general condition. The cross of Jesus is not a symbol of the fragility of a virtuous life, but the result of the expected conflict of God's messiah with the powers. Because of that cross Christians are taught that they are not subject to fortune in a manner that makes them impotent. Rather, through the resurrection of Jesus of Nazareth they have been given the charge to rage against fortune—particularly when it takes the form of injustice that we are constantly tempted to call "fate." I am aware such claims are stark, but I need to make them in order to make clear that my deepest worry about Nussbaum's account is whether there is any basis for such rage.[17]

Notes

An earlier version of this chapter appeared in *Soundings: An Interdisciplinary Journal* 71, 4 (winter 1988): 683–699. Reprinted by permission.

I am indebted to Professor Ken Surin, Dr. Steve Long, Dr. Phil Kenneson, and Dr. Kathy Rudy for their critical response to this chapter. Dr. Rudy, in particular, pressed me on issues that forced me to read Aristotle with a more critical eye.

1. MacIntyre, I think, rightly sees Aristotle in more continuity with Plato than Nussbaum does. But he does so because he interprets the dramatist, Plato, and Aristotle as struggling with moral-political tensions of Greek society. Nussbaum sees more discontinuity because her account is concerned with how the dramatist, Plato, and Aristotle deal with universal human problems that just happen to be articulated by the Greeks. Therefore, attempts to settle the question of the relation between Plato and Aristotle depend on the framework in which the interpretation of their work is situated. That is why criticisms of Nussbaum, like that of T. H. Irwin (*Journal of Philosophy* 85 [July 1988]: 376–383), are so unsatisfactory, as he assumes such matters can be settled simply because he thinks he knows Plato's text better than Nussbaum.

2. I have put quotes around "antifoundational" to indicate my unease with the widespread assumption that epistemologically our only two options are foundationalism or antifoundationalism. Though my sympathies lie with the antifoundationalist, if I have to choose, I am bothered by the assumption that the foundationalist—that is, those people vaguely associated with the Cartesian project—have the right to set the terms of the debate. Thus I have tried to argue for a kind of realism that assumes that that which is known requires a corresponding transformation by an ongoing community of people. See, for example, my *Christian Existence Today: Essays on Church, World and Living In-Between* (Durham: Labyrinth Press, 1988).

3. For a substantial and important treatment of the recovery of practical reason in modern philosophy, see Joseph Dunne's book: *Back to the Rough Ground: "Phronesis" and "Techne" in Modern Philosophy and Aristotle* (Notre Dame: University of Notre Dame Press, 1993).

4. Amélie Rorty, ed., *Essays on Aristotle's Ethics* (Berkeley: University of California Press, 1980).

5. John Cooper, *Reason and Human Good in Aristotle* (Cambridge: Harvard University Press, 1975).

6. James Edwards, *Ethics Without Philosophy: Wittgenstein and the Moral Life* (Tampa: University of South Florida, 1985), p. 4.

7. I am impressed, however, by Anthony Giddens's account of the discontinuity in the change from the absolutist to the modern nation-state in his *The Nation-State and Violence* (Berkeley: University of California Press, 1987).

8. Alasdair MacIntyre, *Whose Justice? Which Rationality?* (Notre Dame: University of Notre Dame Press, 1988). MacIntyre's agreement concerning rationality and tradition cannot be abstracted from the execution of the display of tradition in his book—i.e., you cannot appreciate his account of or significance of an "epistemological crisis" separate from his analysis of Aquinas's attempt to understand Aristotle through Augustine. Henceforth references to MacIntyre will appear in parentheses in the text preceded by *M*.

9. "Discards the standpoint of modernity" does not mean, however, that the interpreter can occupy a perspective of "anyone." Rather, it means that interpreters must acknowledge that their interpretations work within an ongoing tradition of interpretation. I must admit I am unclear exactly what MacIntyre's position is on the place, significance, and interpretation of the "classic." Elsewhere he notes that

the presentation of "Virgil-as-he-and-his-poems were" was assumed central to the humanistic task. It is thus assumed within the humanistic tradition that in moments of crisis the tradition can be renewed by returning to these texts. Yet MacIntyre then notes that it is no longer possible to decide which texts should be considered as classics or the relation we should expect students to make between such texts and the rest of their own lives. "The Humanities and the Conflicts of and with Tradition" (Unpublished Paper, 1986), pp. 17–18. I think what MacIntyre is suggesting here is that those in the humanistic tradition who believe Virgil can speak for himself must themselves be part of the argument, even though they do not recognize "speak for himself" is a tradition. I do not think, however, that he believes that there is, thereby, a better reading we can give of Virgil than Dante's.

10. Martha Nussbaum, *The Fragility of Goodness* (Cambridge: Cambridge University Press, 1986), p. 15. All further references will be in parentheses in the text preceded by *N*.

11. MacIntyre, *Whose Justice? Which Rationality?* (p. 169), raises the question of how such a "we" works in reference to those who defend truth primarily in terms of "warranted assertibility." That is to say, the view that any understanding of any reality in relation to which truth or falsity is to be understood must be integral to our web of concepts and beliefs. Such a view assumes skepticism is unintelligible, since it presupposes that our scheme of concepts can be known to be false. The problem with such a view of truth, and the corresponding defeat of skepticism, is the assumption that there is only one overall unanimity of inquiry. What happens, MacIntyre asks, "if there appears a second community whose tradition and procedure of enquiry are structured in terms different, largely incompatible and largely incommensurable concepts and beliefs, defining warranted assertibility and truth in terms internal to its scheme of concepts and beliefs"?

Though I find MacIntyre's account persuasive, I did not learn to ask the question concerning the identity of the "we" from him but from John Howard Yoder. If one is convinced that one can never use violence, the counter usually is to ask, "But what are we to do if . . . ?" One soon learns that the moral shame and presumptions behind that "we" become the crucial issue.

12. Martha Nussbaum, "Shame, Separateness, and Political Unity: Aristotle's Criticism of Plato," in Rorty, *Essays on Aristotle's Ethics*, p. 420.

13. Ibid., pp. 423–424.

14. Ibid., p. 424.

15. MacIntyre, "The Humanities," pp. 22–23.

16. I am thinking in particular of Rorty's "The Priority of Democracy to Philosophy" in *Philosophical Papers*, Volume 1: *Objectivity, Relativism, and Truth* (Cambridge: Cambridge University Press, 1991), pp. 175–196.

17. Nussbaum's paper, "Non-Relative Virtues: An Aristotelian Approach," in *Midwest Studies in Philosophy*, p. 13; *Ethical Theory: Character and Virtue* (Notre Dame: University of Notre Dame Press, 1988), pp. 32–53, had not been published when I originally wrote this essay. I refer the reader to it because it makes explicit Nussbaum's view that there are in fact "grounding experiences" that provide a sufficient basis for assuming that there are family relatedness and overlap between societies and moral traditions. Without denying that, we are speaking of

matters that are experienced differently in different contexts. Nussbaum identifies features that she believes constitute our common humanity—morality, the body, pleasure and pain, cognitive capability, practical reason, early infant development, affiliation, and humor. The question, however, is not whether we in fact have these "grounding experiences" in common, but who it is and in what tradition they are standing that makes it important for them to so name such experience and to what end they do so. Nussbaum, although denying that she is attempting to ground moral reflection on any Archimedian point, nonetheless thinks that such "grounding experiences" are sufficient to provide a starting point for cross-cultural reflection. My only response is, "What else would you expect a representative of the liberal tradition to say?"

6 Flight from Foundationalism, or Things Aren't As Bad As They Seem

with Phil Kenneson

In his book *Flight from Authority* Jeffrey Stout established himself as a philosophically sophisticated interpreter of contemporary moral and theological discourse.[1] Later, in *Ethics After Babel,* he builds on that reputation by deftly combining social, ethical, and epistemological concerns to develop an important and provocative alternative to both standard Kantian accounts of moral discourse and more contemporary accounts such as that of Alasdair MacIntyre. As its title suggests, Stout's project is set up by the dilemmas (or perceived dilemmas) created by moral diversity. He describes his proposed solution as one of self-conscious moral *bricolage*—a term he borrows from Claude Levi-Strauss without accepting the latter's distinction between the savage mind and the rest of us. *Bricolage* names the necessity of making do with whatever is at hand. Of course, what is at hand bears no necessary relation to the current project or any particular project, "but is the contingent result of all the occasions there have been to renew or enrich the stock to maintain it with the remains of previous constructions or destructions" (74, quoting Levi-Strauss). Though such *bricolage* could be about farming, cooking, or most anything, Stout thinks it peculiarly relevant to the work of ethics. All great creative ethical thinkers (e.g., Aquinas) begin by taking stock of problems and using all available resources to solve them. Their works become "systems" only retrospectively.

Stout's definition of *bricolage* seems modest enough, but in fact his book aims at nothing less than overcoming one of the major impasses within contemporary moral and social theory. Stout uses his considerable analytical skills to show how a proper understanding of moral rationality can avoid being impaled on the horns of either foundationalism or relativism, while likewise escaping the social alternatives of nihilism or communitarianism.

In defending what he calls a "modest pragmatism" (265), Stout sets out to demonstrate that once one sees the philosophical issues clearly, the all-out war against relativism and nihilism turns out to be little more than tilting at windmills. Relativism, for example, can be made less terrifying by being divided into several distinguishable senses. The first step in unmasking "vulgar relativism" is to distinguish it from philosophically defensible and nonthreatening forms of relativism such as "environmental relativity," "relativity of expressibility," and "relativity of distance." Such distinctions provide a welcome degree of precision that has too long been absent from many discussions of relativism; those who desire to join the contemporary retreat from foundationalism would be wise to employ and further refine them in their own attacks against their foundationalist detractors.

Stout also mounts a similar, though more extended, argument against nihilism. He begins by assuming that "the facts of moral diversity are at least a leading cause, if not the leading cause, of nihilistic or skeptical compulsions in ethics" (15). Given this assumption, the rest of the book serves a rather modest purpose: to demonstrate that neither nihilism nor skepticism need necessarily follow from the facts of moral diversity, a recognition that in turn suggests that persons need not abandon the notions of moral truth and justified moral belief (14). He later returns to the notion of truth, arguing for a constructive realism informed by a sophisticated understanding of the nature of moral language. On the one hand, such an understanding recognizes that persons are "given" a moral language in which they express true moral propositions, and hence in some sense they "discover" moral truth; on the other hand, such a position recognizes, following Richard Rorty, that where there are no sentences, there are no truths, and hence because languages are a human creation, humans can be said in some sense to create truth (77).

Stout also helpfully discusses the issue of epistemic justification, rightly noting that foundationalism fails to recognize Wittgenstein's observation that persons do not have to be able to justify a proposition to be justified in believing it. Whatever they might say in support of such a proposition would be less certain than the proposition itself (35). Furthermore, Stout takes pains to show that moral diversity and moral disagreement are sometimes a function of epistemic context, not the relativity of moral truth in a strong sense. This is seen most clearly in Stout's continual reference to the proposition "slavery is evil" as the paradigmatic instance of a moral truth.

Since Stout admits that a good deal of ambiguity surrounds the notion of slavery and since he desires to limit his use of the term "proposition" to interpreted sentences, he offers a definition of slavery: "the coercive practice of buying, selling, and exercising complete power over other hu-

man beings against their will" (21). Given such a definition, Stout believes it becomes intelligible to assert that the proposition "slavery is
evil" is true and has always been true, regardless of what people in the
past have believed, regardless of whether they were justified in such beliefs, and regardless of whether they were worthy of blame for such beliefs.

Such a move is critical, for by distinguishing questions of truth from
those of justification, Stout believes that he can explain away many of the
disagreements that shake modern confidence in speaking of moral truth.
Thus, when Stout takes up the apparent conflict between the contemporary views of U.S. citizens and those of third-century Athenians on the issue of slavery, he shows that it becomes possible to affirm that the proposition "slavery is evil" has always been true even when the third-century
Athenians didn't believe it was true. So what looked like a case of moral
disagreement that called into question the very notion of moral truth
turns out, according to Stout, to be primarily about epistemic and moral
justification, with the concept of moral truth left untouched.

We can now begin to appreciate the sophistication of Stout's position:
Here is a moral philosopher who rightly eschews both radical relativism
and foundationalism without abandoning talk about truth. But Stout's
position is even more complex, for he goes to great lengths to define it in
relation to that of MacIntyre as developed in *After Virtue*.[2] Like MacIntyre, Stout insists that no simple opposition exists between tradition and
critical reason, that the complexities and contingencies of traditions are
essential to ethical thought (73). Furthermore, Stout seems to agree with
MacIntyre concerning the tradition-dependent nature of rationality. Stout
goes as far as to assert that "rationality of any kind involves the acquisi-
tion of particular skills and virtues" (53). Unfortunately, Stout does not
develop this point in any detail, but it has strong surface affinities with
the thesis of MacIntyre's later work.[3] In fact, much of the later part of
Ethics After Babel is an attempt to salvage what Stout thinks is best from
MacIntyre's earlier project—specifically the account of moral practices.

But what Stout has no desire to salvage, and where he explicitly parts
company with MacIntyre, is the latter's insistence that the present moral
climate is at best hideous and at worst hopeless. Although Stout agrees
that "complete absence of agreement on the good would render rational
moral discourse impossible" (211), he denies that society has reached this
point. He insists that purveyors of such doom and gloom simply fail to
appreciate the widespread moral agreements that societies as a whole do
share and, even more important, that they must share, if they are to have
meaningful moral disagreements. This Davidsonian argument functions
as the linchpin of Stout's refutation of MacIntyre, for it aims to demonstrate the degree to which MacIntyre has exaggerated our moral predica-

ment by focusing on our disagreements and suppressing the significance of our agreements, particularly as they are embodied in moral platitudes (210–219).[4] Although Stout agrees that society lacks any overriding conception of the good, he insists that its "relatively limited" agreement on the good is "nonetheless real and significant" (212).

The presence of such limited agreement, according to Stout, should not be viewed as the nadir of a predictable downward spiral touched off by the policies of liberalism; rather, such agreement is the necessary condition for the possibility of peaceful coexistence in pluralistic societies. Stout not only refuses to apologize for this limited agreement, he actually insists that it is part of the genius of liberal institutions that they embody such a provisional "self-limiting consensus" on the good:

> Certain features of our society can be seen as justified by a self-limiting consensus on the good—an agreement consisting partly in the realization that it would be a bad thing, that it would make life worse for us all, to press too hard or too far for agreement on all details in a given vision of the good. We can define our shared conception of the good as the set of all platitudinous judgments employing such terms as good, better than, and the like. We can define a platitude, echoing David Lewis, as a judgment that only the philosophers (and the morally incompetent or utterly vicious) among us would think of denying. The set of all such platitudes would include far too many to mention. (212–213)

Stout insists repeatedly on the centrality of such a self-limiting conception of the good. For him, one of the great strengths of pluralism is that it does not force agreement "too far down," since such a policy inevitably leads either to vacuous "verbal" agreement or to violence. This refrain about forcing agreement echoes throughout Stout's book in his assertion that any account of the role played by liberal institutions in Western ethical thought cannot be divorced from the history of theological ideas and religious conflicts that have often made the institutions necessary to sustain pluralism not only possible, but also desirable. Hence, the disillusionment evoked by the failure of religious people to resolve their conflicts without resorting to violence was largely responsible for the emergence of a secularized form of moral discourse, a fact that Stout rightly notes MacIntyre fails to develop in *After Virtue*.[5]

But the inadequacy of the communitarian account is not limited to its failure to recognize the part it played in its own demise; in addition, it suffers from what Stout refers to as "terminal wistfulness," what he regards as its inherently utopian character. Thus, although Stout acknowledges that communitarian critics rightly point to many of the shortcomings of liberal society, "they very rarely give us any clear sense of what to do about our misgivings aside from yearning pensively for conditions we are either unwilling or unable to bring about" (229). But Stout is likewise unhappy both with standard defenses of liberal society that fall prey to the problems of all foundational accounts, and with the more sophisticated nonstandard (nonfoundational) defenses of liberalism, such as those by Rorty or Meilaender. The problem with Rorty is that although he rightly points to liberal arrangements as the best currently available, he too often responds to the communitarians' legitimate criticisms of such arrangements with an air of smugness. The problem with Meilaender is his too pessimistic view of the potential of the political, a view that fails to see that a public life in which citizens find some part of their identity directed to the common good is possible. What Stout seeks is a path between what he sees as liberalism's privatization of life and communitarianism's tendency toward totalitarianism, a path that would provide a way to "describe our situation in such a way that 'liberal' and 'communitarian' no longer seem like meaningful options" (236).

Stout bases his own constructive proposal on a dialectical movement between retrieval and critique that not only acknowledges the importance of platitudes and other moral agreements as a basis of society's provisional and self-limiting consensus about the good, but also recognizes the need to reincorporate certain aspects of particular moral traditions as a critique of contemporary moral discourse. Stout's most provocative example of moral *bricolage* is his attempt to reclaim the language of virtue while holding on to traditional liberal concepts (such as rights language). Specifically, Stout attempts to salvage MacIntyre's account of practices, focusing on the latter's distinction between internal and external goods, in order to develop a "stereoscopic social criticism" that "brings social practices and institutions, internal and external goods, into focus at the same time" (279). The impetus behind such a move is plain: Stout rightly recognizes the need both to acknowledge the necessary role of institutions in embodying and sustaining particular practices, and to concede that such institutions, because they traffic so heavily in external goods, paradoxically jeopardize the integrity of those very practices. Thus, for example, society needs a way of seeing that the institutions in this country that sustain the practice of medical care (such as medical associations, commercial hospital chains, the capitalist market, and government agencies) also trade heavily in goods external to those practices (such as wealth, power, and status), a situation that too easily lends itself to the supplanting of goods internal to such practices (274).

The outcome of Stout's experiment in moral *bricolage* is that he secures a powerfully descriptive set of concepts and vocabulary in which to inscribe the moral tensions and conflicts that afflict contemporary moral discourse and practice. By so doing, Stout helpfully provides pluralist society with some of the resources necessary to criticize and transform itself from within (288). But in the end, some readers may find themselves wondering if moral *bricolage* is anything more than a fancy name for being able to have your cake and eat it too (and a lot of cake at that).

The suspicion that Stout wants more cake than he is entitled to stems more from what Stout fails to discuss than from what he explicitly states. For example, whereas many will rightly applaud Stout's desire to reclaim the language of virtue, one may legitimately question whether he has offered an account rich enough to make such language intelligible. Following MacIntyre, Stout's discussion of the virtues moves through three stages: first, a stage focusing on the concept of goods internal to a practice; second, a stage that concerns the "good of a whole human life"; and third, a stage that takes up the question of "an ongoing tradition" (266). MacIntyre does not understand these three stages in simple linear fashion, as if stages two and three merely enrich and supplement a self-standing notion of virtue made possible by the investigation of social practices. Rather, as MacIntyre went to great lengths to explain in the postscript to the second edition of *After Virtue*, "no human quality is to be accounted a virtue unless it satisfies the conditions specified at each of the three stages."[6] Stout appreciates the importance of this point, but because agreement is unlikely to be secured at the latter two stages, he argues that the notion of practice is enough to generate the moral *bricolage* necessary to sustain life in a pluralistic society. Thus, he spends no less than twenty pages discussing social practices (267–286), but commits only three paragraphs to the second aspect, and a single paragraph to the third (287–288).

Such imbalance could be excused if Stout either had clearly demonstrated why he is justified in separating what MacIntyre insists cannot be divided or had shown why a discussion of the final two aspects is unnecessary. As it stands, Stout does neither, although the rhetoric of the pertinent passages suggests that he believes he has done the latter. Thus, with respect to the importance of an ongoing tradition, Stout merely acknowledges that he thinks "pluralistic society" has already achieved sufficient continuity over time to be regarded as a tradition (288). It remains unclear by what means or with respect to what Stout is measuring such continuity. But more important, Stout skillfully dodges the question of the content of this pluralistic tradition; he does not even offer a satisfying account of the notion of pluralism. One might understand what it would mean to say that Judaism is a pluralist tradition, but one has little, if any, idea what it means to say "America" is such a tradition. Stout overlooks what a more careful analysis might divulge: What he refers to as the pluralistic tradition functions, or aspires to function, as a metatradition that tends to level the distinctions among other identifiable traditions and make their coexistence a good in itself.

By functioning at the level of a metatradition, the pluralistic tradition inevitably loses its historical character, a loss that in turn insulates it from criticism. Stout might have constructed a history of pluralistic tradition, a task that MacIntyre, interestingly enough, has begun in *Whose Justice? Which Rationality?*[7] Such a project would have made it possible to inquire what ends the liberal, or pluralistic, tradition was intended to serve, and whether it continues to serve the same or different ends. MacIntyre, for example, insists that through the course of history, "liberalism, which began as an appeal to alleged principles of shared rationality against what was felt to be the tyranny of tradition, has itself been transformed into a tradition whose continuities are partly defined by the interminability of the debate over such principles," an interminability that has itself become for many a kind of virtue.[8] If Stout believes such an historical reconstruction is skewed, then he is obliged to offer a more convincing one.

But Stout is unlikely to take up such a project, for it would entail tracing the roots of liberal "virtues" to historical accounts of "the good," accounts that remain unintelligible apart from their embodiment in the practices of concrete traditions. Curiously, in this book Stout shuns the detailed work of historical reconstruction, a task he did so well in *Flight from Authority*, choosing instead to drive most of his argument with hypothetical examples about such things as "Stout worship" (50f.) or about imaginary disagreements between peoples such as the Old World Corleones and the Modernists (62). This may seem to be a small point, but it quickly cuts to the core of the debate between Stout and MacIntyre. In *Whose Justice? Which Rationality?* MacIntyre engages in the painstakingly slow process of historical reconstruction in order to demonstrate his claim that no such thing as rationality-as-such or justice-as-such exists, but that all such notions are dependent on a narrative tradition for their content and intelligibility. From MacIntyre's point of view, Stout's moral *bricolage* remains completely unintelligible as long as the latter refuses to attend to those narrative traditions, background beliefs, and views of the good that give the moral positions within such a *bricolage* their standing. Thus whereas Stout accuses MacIntyre of proceeding much too fast in assuming that society's situation is hopeless, a strong case can be made that it is Stout who has moved too hastily, since he has not taken the time to display the history that gives these fragments within the *bricolage* their intelligibility.

If Stout were to take up such a historical investigation of liberalism and pluralism, it would likely reveal that the liberal, or pluralistic, tradition in this country is highly parasitic on other historical traditions and narratives for its justifications. It purportedly functions as a metatradition, but it cannot give a satisfactory account of why certain elements of those other narrative traditions are to be revered and others to be discarded.

This is one reason why Stout distinguishes between truth and justification; he wants to be able to separate liberal society's moral truths from their justifications, justifications that are bound up with much that Stout wants to leave behind. A prime example of such unacknowledged plundering of moral truth is found in Stout's discussion of MacIntyre's second aspect, the good of a whole human life:

> Take, first of all, the good of a whole human life. We are unlikely to secure perfect agreement on this topic in our lifetimes. Still, as I argued earlier, we needn't profess belief in the God of Moses and Calvin to be persuaded that our loves ought to be ordered toward genuine goods, each in proper proportion. From our various points of view, we can in fact recognize many genuine goods as such, including goods internal to such social practices as medical care and democratic self-government. We can also see that a life dedicated entirely to the pursuit of external goods degenerates into narcissism and idolatry, often ending in meaninglessness and despair. Finally, we can grasp that certain internal goods and the practices in which they are pursued deserve protection from the tyranny of external goods.
>
> So we have reason to suppose that a good human life is not likely to flourish under conditions where the tyranny of external goods goes unchecked— reason, in other words, to protect such social practices as medical care, baseball, family life, and democratic government from being overwhelmed and corrupted. (287)

Despite Stout's continual use of "we" and "our" (a practice that he follows throughout the book), it is more than a little difficult to discern whom he envisions as his audience. Who is this "we" that can so clearly see that a life dedicated to the pursuit of external goods "degenerates into narcissism and idolatry, often ending in meaninglessness and despair"? And what unacknowledged resources enable these unnamed persons to make such a recognition? And finally, is Stout justified in employing such language as "narcissism," "idolatry," "meaninglessness," and "despair" without offering a tradition-based account of how such tradition-rich language is to be understood, or without owning up to the theological/anthropological implications of such usage? In fairness to Stout, he does provide an extended discussion of abominations—for example, cannibalism, bestiality—which he characterizes as behavior that threatens to disrupt the natural-social order (150). Therefore, sexual intercourse with beasts threatens our "social identity" (152) in the same way that cannibalism makes problematic our status as "human beings." But given Stout's own epistemological commitments, how could one ever know what it means to be a human being as such, and even more, what one's "social identity" might or should be? In this regard we find particularly puzzling Stout's account of sodomy as relative to masculine and feminine roles (which certainly may be relevant) rather than to a community's understanding of the appropriate context for sexual activity. Curiously, Stout even makes appeals to "morality as such" (44, 192), though he never reveals what practices could ever justify such language. At times Stout seems to want to be more than pluralism's master *bricoleur*.

Closely related to Stout's unwillingness to acknowledge that moral discourse risks unintelligibility as long as it remains separated from a tradition-based narrative context is his failure to appreciate fully how moral descriptions are similarly generated. For example, when Stout uses the language of "cannibalism" (87f.), "pointless cruelty" (42), and "torturing of innocents" (245), he seems to imply that such usage is transparent. Thus he can make the seemingly innocent remark that "new types of pointless cruelty would, of course, be greeted with abhorrence by everybody who (a) qualifies as a competent moral judge and (b) does not suffer from false empirical and metaphysical assumptions" (42). Such an observation, Stout believes, supports his case against those who exaggerate the degree of moral diversity and disagreement within society.

On the contrary, such an observation actually goes a long way toward illustrating the very problem to which MacIntyre and others have pointed. For although it is true that in the United States a broad agreement might be reached on the proposition "all morally competent judges abhor pointless cruelty," such apparent agreement hides disagreement about the proper application of the description "pointless cruelty." But even this is not quite right, for limiting the level of disagreement to one of application, as this last statement seems to imply and as Stout seems to suggest with his example of "torturing innocents" (326, fn. 3), again tends to exaggerate the level of agreement. As Stout acknowledges in his better Wittgensteinian moments, there is no such thing as "meaning" or "understanding" apart from one's grasping how certain words function in a language and learning to use them oneself. If this is the case, then it is odd that he ignores such a picture of understanding when he considers the meaning of phrases like "pointless cruelty." Thus, the significance of "our" supposed agreement over pointless cruelty itself begins to evaporate when one takes account of the fact that people whom Stout would consider reasonable disagree over what kinds of things should count as instances of such cruelty. Some people believe that abortion counts as pointless cruelty, others believe the same about capital punishment, others about the killing of animals for food, as well as experimentation on animals, and still others about bullfighting and boxing.

Stout would undoubtedly minimize such disagreement by saying that these are just the hard cases, that society lacks the conceptual tools or the epistemic context that would make the elimination of such disagreements possible. In other words, Stout insists that society does enjoy significant agreement about important moral matters (such as the truth of abhorring pointless cruelty) even if it disagrees on the minor details of particular applications and interpretations. Perhaps he is right. Perhaps some readers will be convinced that this picture is an accurate portrayal of society's predicament. But it might be more honest to admit that these disagreements are real and that they can be traced to disagreements about what our lives are to be about and how the goods that characterize such lives are to be ordered. Such a recognition would in turn likely force persons to acknowledge that such disagreements about the good cannot be separated either from one's view of the good of a whole human life or from an ongoing narrative that gives such a view intelligibility. As for Stout's treasured moral truth, "slavery is evil," were it historically possible, Stout could probably have acquired agreement on this proposition (given his definition) from nineteenth-century southern plantation owners as well as third-century Athenians. Yet the first group would not consider their practice to be slavery, since their workers were not human beings but possessions, and the second group would likely not view their practice as coercive and reprehensible, but generous and beneficent. It seems that we are left with a rather empty notion of agreement.

In the end, then, Stout papers over what in Wittgensteinian perspective should be considered different understandings of phrases such as "pointless cruelty," thereby reducing many supposedly substantive agreements to merely verbal ones. So although Stout rightly praises pluralism for not pushing agreement too far down, since doing so often leads to violence or to merely verbal agreement, he remains blind to the flip side: By not pushing agreement far enough down into practices, views of the good, and ongoing narratives, pluralistic societies themselves rest on uneasy and shallow verbal agreements.

Stout's purpose in refocusing the debate on our limited but significant agreements is that it allows him the opportunity to offer an apology for pluralism. In the end, Stout's apology raises more questions than it satisfactorily answers. For example, he never clearly articulates who is responsible for doing the work of moral *bricolage* and what resources they rely on to do this task. That this work is parceled out in some way is suggested by Stout's reliance throughout on the metaphors of "spheres" and "division of labor." But such metaphors hide the fact that few people view themselves as participating on such a moral assembly line, doing only part of the moral task that needs to be done and dependent on someone else (the moral philosophers undoubtedly) to put it all together; rather, most see themselves as struggling with the whole moral project at once, cognizant of the fact that compartmentalization or specialization merely increases rather than decreases the tensions within the *bricolage*.

Similarly, Stout has given us little reason to hope that pluralism has the resources to stop or even slow the corruption of practices that he readily acknowledges is occurring. Given a pluralistic system whose purpose has been transformed from one of extending debates and protecting minority debaters to one of glorifying the debate itself, even suggesting at times that debate is by nature interminable, Stout has not convincingly demonstrated why we should expect people to see the corruption of practices as being simply that—corruption.

Furthermore, Stout has not clearly articulated why anyone should be so impressed with agreement on certain platitudes, since he has not shown how or even if such platitudes figure into our disagreements over more-intractable matters. At times one senses that Stout's advice on these matters is simply to wait, to wait for the conceptual or epistemic tools to find one's way out of such impasses, while resting comfortably on the assurance provided by moral platitudes. But surely such advice will ring hollow to those who find themselves in the midst of agonizing moral situations. One of the roots of Stout's problem is his heavy reliance on Davidson, and although a full explication of that would require an entire article, one point may be noted. Stout's reliance on Davidsonian arguments does little more than push the question one step further back—to the question of what counts as meaningful agreement and disagreement. Although Davidson may be helpful in showing that there can be no meaningful disagreement that is at the same time complete disagreement, it remains unclear why such a recognition should stand as a vindication of Stout's entire project.[9] After all, MacIntyre would probably admit that on some matters—such as the nature of justice—he might not be able to have a meaningful disagreement with Stout, a possibility that Stout seems to exclude a priori.

Then there is the question of how one might have a meaningful theological disagreement with Stout. Those familiar with *Flight from Authority* know that Stout is one of the most sympathetic and musical interpreters of theology, even though he does not claim a "theocentric vision." His work has been particularly helpful in freeing religious ethicists from reductionism in their accounts of convictions. In *Ethics After Babel*, Stout's fairness to and sensitivity for the work of theology is further evidenced by his sympathetic analysis of the thought of James Gustafson. Indeed, Stout seems to be the kind of philosopher of religion who makes it possible for theologians to enjoy being theologians. Stout denies that there are knockdown arguments that should compel theologians to stop doing theology—a denial that accounts for his withering attack on Kai Nielsen. If every person functions from within a tradition or an intersection of traditions, then it seems implausible that those traditions that include belief in God could be shown to be unintelligible *tout court*.

Stout affirms that belief in God may be morally significant in some traditions; indeed, he suggests that we might understand the logical relationships between religion and morality only after we study specific traditions of religious ethical discourse (121). But then he goes on to make two curious remarks: first, that "the best account of ethical wrongness cannot be determined in isolation from other matters—including what independent grounds we may have for believing or disbelieving in a loving God"; and second, that "the best account of ethical wrongness will be part of the best account of everything, on the whole" (122). It seems that Stout's language, which normally displays considerable philosophical precision and sophistication, has here gone on holiday. He divulges neither what resources one relies upon when juggling weighty matters to arrive at "the best account of everything," nor what such "independent grounds" look like (or what exactly they are "independent" of). Stout does note that none of the "aspects of piety" Gustafson thinks so important for sustaining the theocentric vision—wonder, awe, gratitude, a sense of the power that bears down upon us—give him any reason to associate such piety with belief in God. That does not mean there are no grounds for militant atheism, but rather that atheism, like theism, has simply lost its point.

Stout's account of the modern religious situation is descriptively powerful—see in particular his map of contemporary theological options (185). Moreover, there is even reason to take Stout's word that though his secular piety is analogous to Gustafson's, Stout has no reason to construe such piety theocentrically and, given Gustafson's own account, monotheistically. Rather, Stout would have his readers simply accept that they are finite, historically situated beings (142), soberly accepting their place in the vast and unknown universe.

Stout is not trying to exclude or deny the importance for some people of religious beliefs. He simply thinks no good reason can be given in "our" kind of world for holding such beliefs. That seems fair enough. Yet to leave the matter there is too easy both for us and for Stout. In this respect, it is no accident that Stout makes Gustafson his main theological conversation partner, for the latter has already pared down Christian convictions to the essentials he thinks consistent with the world as he knows it. More interesting would be a full-scale engagement between Stout and positions that are less apologetic. Surely John Howard Yoder's more Christologically determined ethic is not to be excluded from discussion simply because he provides no "independent" ground for believing in God. Equally challenging, we believe, would be the work of Nicholas Lash, work that argues that a trinitarian account is unavoidable if persons are rightly to worship God as Christians. We are not suggesting that Stout would be at a disadvantage in encounters with these theologians; rather, such encounters might help us better understand what it is about the current situation that makes Stout think Christian convictions about God are irrelevant and maybe even unintelligible.

Finally, social and economic issues are far more central to the contemporary moral predicament than Stout's analysis suggests. It may be no accident that Stout makes MacIntyre a primary conversation partner, for both tend to focus on the history of ideas and thinkers in isolation from socioeconomic considerations. Whereas MacIntyre's more historical and sociological approach (every ethic presupposes a sociology) has some resources with which to engage people like Bryan S. Turner, Anthony Giddens, and Michel Foucault, we are unsure how Stout would do so. Yet to bring Stout fully into conversation with these critics would require that we take up a position outside of that space jointly inhabited by Stout and MacIntyre. The resulting external critique would, of course, look very different from the more internal critique we have offered. Yet such an external critique may be the more promising avenue, since it is in encounters with such social critics that we suspect lie our most decisive theological challenges.

Notes

An earlier version of this chapter appeared in *Soundings: An Interdisciplinary Journal* 72, 4 (winter 1989): 675–691. Reprinted by permission.

We are indebted to Mr. Paul Lewis and Professors L. Gregory Jones, Thomas Langford, and Kenneth Surin for commenting on an earlier draft of this chapter.

1. Jeffrey Stout, *The Flight from Authority: Religion, Morality, and the Quest for Autonomy* (Notre Dame: University of Notre Dame Press, 1981).

2. Alasdair C. MacIntyre, *After Virtue* (Notre Dame: University of Notre Dame Press, 1981; 2nd ed., 1984).

3. See, for example, Alasdair C. MacIntyre, *Whose Justice? Which Rationality?* (Notre Dame: University of Notre Dame Press, 1988). This book, of course, did not appear in time for Stout to engage it directly in *Ethics After Babel*.

4. Stout, of course, is depending on Donald Davidson's classic article, "On the Very Idea of a Conceptual Scheme," in *Proceedings and Addresses of the American Philosophical Association* 47 (November 1974): 5–20.

5. The oft-made claim that the Enlightenment was a response to the religious wars is challenged by Bill Cavanaugh in "A Fire Strong Enough to Consume the House: The Wars of Religion and the Rise of the State," *Modern Theology* 11, 4 (October 1995): 397–420. Cavanaugh argues that the wars of religion did not necessitate the birth of the modern state; rather they were the birth pangs of that state.

6. MacIntyre, *After Virtue*, p. 275; original emphasis. Thus, it seems more than a little misleading for Stout to refer to MacIntyre's final two stages as merely "qualifications" of his initial definition of virtue, which focuses on the notion of goods internal to practices (see Stout, *Flight from Authority*, pp. 268–269).

7. See particularly the chapter entitled "Liberalism Transformed into a Tradition," *Whose Justice? Which Rationality?* pp. 326–348.

8. MacIntyre, *Whose Justice? Which Rationality?* p. 335. Stout wants to abstain from describing society as liberal and he may be right that American society does not entail the psychology of the atomistic self or the necessity of all human relations being manipulative à la MacIntyre, but he must show this to be the case, not merely allege that it can be the case.

9. See, for example, MacIntyre's remarks on Davidson in *Whose Justice? Which Rationality?* pp. 370–371.

7 Not All Peace Is Peace: Why Christians Cannot Make Peace with Tristram Engelhardt's Peace

Who Wrote the Second Edition of *The Foundations of Bioethics?*

I begin with a confession. Like most confessions it is difficult to make. Moreover, it involves others, and in particular Tris Engelhardt, whom I am honored to call a friend. I am hesitant to cause him embarrassment, but I simply can no longer live with the deception. Tris Engelhardt is not the author of the second edition of *The Foundations of Bioethics*. I am the second edition's author. I admit, it was a clever idea for me to write the second edition, and on the whole, I am pleased with the execution. But I now see that the truth should prevail. I am, of course, indebted to Tris for his cooperation, and I hope I have not damaged his well-deserved reputation.

You may well ask, "How did you ever come up with such an outrageous idea?" Actually it is all Robert Paul Wolff's fault. It was he, you will recall, who wrote a devastating review of Allan Bloom's *The Closing of the American Mind* in which he suggested that Bloom's book was actually written by Saul Bellow.[1] According to Wolff, Bellow wrote

> an entire coruscatingly funny novel in the form of a pettish, bookish, grumpy, reactionary complaint against the last two decades. The "author" of this tirade, one of Bellow's most fully realized literary creations, is a mid-fiftyish professor at the University of Chicago, to whom Bellow gives the evocative name, "Bloom." Bellow appears in the book only as the author of an eight-page "Foreword," in which he introduces us to his principal and only character. *The Closing of the American Mind* is published under the name "Allan Bloom," and, as part of the fun, is even copyrighted in "Bloom's" name.

Wolff proceeds to show that Bellow has written this novel to make fun of the Straussians and, in particular, Strauss's strange theory of concealment.

When I read the first edition of Engelhardt's *Foundations*, not only did I think his account of what a secular bioethics entails was right but I also was impressed that others found his position persuasive. Yet the real irony is that whenever I say what Engelhardt says, I am dismissed as an unreflective Christian theologian. For example, when I say that there is no reason on secular grounds to prohibit suicide or even to call it suicide, I am accused of being "against the world." When I have suggested that attempts to ground secular ethics in "reason" have not been successful, I am accused of fideism. When I argue that liberal political arrangements cannot provide an account of legitimacy, I am described as a "sectarian." In short, whenever I say what Engelhardt says, I am classified as an indiscriminate basher of liberalism and the Enlightenment.

So I got this great idea. Why should I not write a new edition of the *Foundations*, confessing my Christian faith, but trying to show constructively what a secular world can or ought to say about ethics, in particular, bioethics? I would not have to create a fictional character, as Wolff alleges Bellow had to, because we all know that Engelhardt is all too real. I only hope that I did not misuse Engelhardt's charitable spirit by assuming he would approve of my use of his name, but I saw no other way I could ever expect to get a hearing. Without such a strategy I fear I would always be accused of wanting to make matters worse than they are in order to make Christians and the church look better than they are. So, assuming Engelhardt's persona, I rewrote the *Foundations*.

Accordingly, I argued that all attempts to justify a content-full secular ethic could not help but fail because any such content unavoidably begs the question of the standard by which the content is selected (41).[2] I confess I took particular pleasure in showing how Kant smuggled moral content into his attempt to ground ethics in reason alone, but it was even more fun exposing Kant's absurd views about masturbation (105–108). I could even claim, with some hope of being heard, that "we live in a century in which more people have been slaughtered in the cause of secular visions of justice, human dignity, ideological rectitude, historical progress, and purity than have ever been killed in religious wars" (15).

It was an absolute joy to write the chapters dealing with issues like abortion, death, informed consent, refusal of treatment, and the distribution of health care, all the while assuming the permissive character of secular bioethics. Moreover, I was able to show on purely secular grounds that there was little reason to prohibit what many continue to assume are reprehensible actions and results. That meant that I could end each chapter with a paragraph like this:

> The difficulty is that in the ruins of a collapsing Judeo-Christian moral vision it is difficult for individuals to assemble coherent moral intuitions regarding how one should approach life and death decisions. Once moral sen-

timents are disarticulated from the content-full moral and metaphysical framework in which they had once been embedded, they no longer can provide reliable guidance. On the one hand, in general secular terms it will appear as if there is nothing morally improper in assisting suicide or supporting voluntary euthanasia. On the other hand, since this life will appear to be all there is, it can take on an absolute significance. Previous moral concerns regarding murder and in favor of the respect of human life may be transferred to a particular content-full moral assertion regarding the importance of saving lives at all costs. However, even in secular terms, individuals may have values that outweigh their concerns to preserve their own lives. In the absence of a coherent, content-moral vision, there will be at best confusion within which the only general secular guidance will be that derivable from the consent of those involved. (344)

By indicating some of the anomalies produced by the consistent working out of a secular ethic, I was not trying to make people "Christian" or even to make them appreciate Christian practices. Rather, all I wanted to do was remind those Christians who continue to be so enthusiastic about secular arrangements that we may be losing our soul. To suggest that a secular ethic offers no coherent reason for having children, for instance, is not to judge those who represent such an ethic. On the contrary, it is to remind Christians why it is so important for us to maintain the church's distinctiveness and integrity, that is to say, communities in which such practices are not lost (277). Indeed, "Engelhardt's" second edition gave me no small hope that my oft-made suggestion would not be so easily ignored; namely, that Christians must begin to think again about what a Christian practice of medicine might look like.[3] I could say more about the various strategies I employed in writing the second edition, but I am sure enough has been said to convince you that in fact I am the author.

Why You Cannot "Choose" to Be a Christian

Now that I have completely convinced you that I am the author of the second edition of the *Foundations,* I must own up; I have been putting you on. I did not write the second edition. Engelhardt must be given credit for that feat and accept the praise, but also the criticism, that he so richly deserves. I realize that you may be a bit put out at me for so skillfully convincing you that I wrote the second edition, but I did so only because serious philosophical and theological issues were and are at stake. By suggesting to you that I could have written the second edition, I was hoping to show why some people (and perhaps most of all, Engelhardt!) may think that Engelhardt's and my views are similar. Nothing could be further from the truth, but why that is so difficult to make clear is a primary motive behind this dissimulation. Therefore, having convinced you that I could have written the second edition, I must now indicate to you why I could not have done so.

I begin with what I take to be the deepest difference between us—namely our understanding of Christianity. Our difference is not simply that Engelhardt is Orthodox, whereas I represent the more ancient tradition of Methodism. Rather, our difference is quite simply this: I think that being Christian is more like being Texan than Engelhardt does. Let me explain by quoting a paragraph from the preface to the second edition, which I think is destined to become one of the most famous in contemporary philosophical literature.

> If one wants more than secular reason can disclose—and one should want more—then one should join a religion and be careful to choose the right one. Canonical moral content will not be found outside of a particular moral narrative, a view from somewhere. Here the reader deserves to know that I indeed experience and acknowledge the immense cleft between what secular philosophical reasoning can provide and what I know in the fullness of my own narrative to be true. I indeed affirm the canonical, concrete moral narrative, but really it cannot be given by reason, only by grace. I am, after all, a born-again Texan Orthodox Catholic, a convert by choice and conviction, through grace and repentance for sins innumerable (including a first edition upon which much improvement was needed). My moral perspective does not lack content. I am of the firm conviction that, save for God's mercy, those who willfully engage in much that a peaceable, fully secular state will permit (e.g., euthanasia and direct abortion on demand) stand in danger of hell's eternal fires. As a Texan, I puzzle whether these are kindled with mesquite, live oak, or trash cedar, but this is a question to be answered on the Last Day by the Almighty. Though I acknowledge that there is no secular moral authority that can be justified in general secular terms to forbid the sale of heroin, the availability of direct abortion, the marketing of for profit euthanatization services, or the provision of commercial surrogacy, I firmly hold none of these to be good. These are great moral evils. But their evil cannot be grasped in purely secular terms. To be pro choice in general secular terms is to understand God's tragic relationship to Eden. To be free is to be free to choose very wrongly. (xi)

I hesitate to assert the superiority of theology to philosophy, but I must begin by noting that there are some things theologians know that philosophers cannot know. Any theologian would know that God stokes the fires of hell with trash cedar. God would never use the beauty of a live oak tree or the determination of the mesquite to fire hell. Moreover, there is the further question of the place of fire in hell, since I prefer to believe that Dante is right to think that ice, not fire, ensures the absolute loneliness that makes hell—a loneliness that, I might add, bears an uncanny resemblance to Engelhardt's society of strangers. But these are not matters he should be expected to know.

The problem resides quite simply in Engelhardt's language. Listen again—"one should join a religion and be careful to choose the right one." The issue involves the presumptions, peculiar to a liberal culture, that shape the language of "choice." Of course, from a secular point of view one may describe someone's becoming a Christian or a Unification-ist as a matter of choice, but that is not how those becoming Christian are taught to understand what is or has happened to them. To be baptized in Christ's death and resurrection is *to be made* part of a people, part of God's life, rendering the language of choice facile.

Notice, by contrast, that Engelhardt did not use the language of "choice" to characterize what it means for him to be a Texan. He knows that such language is surely a distortion of the great and good reality that comes from finding one's life constituted by such a land and people. Along with me, Engelhardt never knew a time when he did not know how to "talk right." Of course, being born amid the riches of being Texan does not mean that one can take such a gift for granted. We must learn the skills necessary to make what we are ours, but such skills are only in-telligible because we know that being Texan first comes as gift, not as choice.

I am aware that I may be making far too much of Engelhardt's lan-guage of choice. He does say that "only by grace" is he a "born-again Texan Orthodox Catholic." Yet the issue does not turn finally on the choice of words, though what words we use is all important, but rather on the narratives and the material conditions that such narratives pre-sume. My worry about Engelhardt's second edition is that the narrative that shapes the position of the second edition is insufficiently determined by his Christian convictions. It is that way because his account of Chris-tianity remains far too "voluntary." As a result, Christians are robbed of the resources we need to resist the subtle temptations of Engelhardt's "peaceable society"—a society, I believe, that is designed to render the Christian worship of God puerile.

Engelhardt, good Christian that he is, certainly does not desire that re-sult. He explicitly claims that the

> libertarian character of a defensible general secular morality is not antago-nistic to the moralities of concrete moral communities whose peaceable commitments may be far from libertarian (e.g., the communism of monas-teries). The arguments in *The Foundations of Bioethics* are not opposed to such sentiments within particular, peaceable, moral communities. Strictly, with respect to such sentiments, the arguments are neutral. (x)

In the next section I will explore whether Engelhardt's "peaceable soci-ety," built as it is on the ruins of the Enlightenment project, is really so be-nign, but first I need to develop what I find problematic about his under-standing of Christianity and its relation to the kind of society he depicts.

When I was asked to contribute a blurb for the first edition of the *Foundations*, I wrote the following: "As a Christian theologian, I welcome Engelhardt's profound account of what a secular ethic in medicine should entail. It will show Christians why good pagans have seen the church as a threat to the peace of polytheistic and secular societies, while those who take a 'secular point of view' will find its full implications explored in the book."[4] Actually that is not what I first sent to the publisher. My first blurb read: "If you want to know why the pagans rightly thought they should kill the Christians, read this book." The publishers thought that was a little too direct.

I think the point is still valid, however. Nor have the changes in the second edition made me change my mind. Pagans understood (as Engelhardt well understands) that the great problem with Christians is that we have no use for tolerance. We are not going to validate a public polytheism even if it buys us a "peace" (which, when translated, is just another way of saying "we are not being physically killed at the moment"). The God we worship as Christians wants it all. "Render unto God the things that are God's and unto Caesar the things that are Caesar's" is not what Caesar wants to hear. Caesar also wants it all—particularly, when Caesar has become "democratic."

For example, Engelhardt says that the position put forth in the *Foundations* requires the "privatization" of all particularistic convictions (viii). Accordingly, the moral life must be lived in two dimensions: (1) that of a secular ethic that strives to be contentless and thus is able to span numerous moral communities and (2) the particular moral community within which one can achieve a content-full understanding of the good life (78). Lutherans have long had a theology to underwrite such a division, but neither Engelhardt nor I am persuaded by the Lutheran distinction between orders of creation and redemption, between law and Gospel. Given the results of this century, moreover, most Christians find such a distinction questionable at best, since we now know the horror against which it proved powerless to resist.

The issue, then, is not the misuse of such a distinction, but the distortion of Christian convictions implicit in it. For when Christians allow their faith to be privatized, we soon discover that we can no longer maintain the disciplines necessary to sustain the church as a disciplined polity capable of calling into question "the public." Of course, Engelhardt can respond that is not his problem, since such a result is not entailed by his religious convictions. I think, however, that he cannot avoid the issue so easily, as can be seen from the language of "choice" I highlighted above. The great challenge before Christians in Engelhardt's world, and I believe it is in fact the world in which we exist, is how our lives as Christians can be as involuntarily constituted as being Texan. To be Christian means that we must be embedded in practices so materially constitutive of our communities that we are not tempted to describe our lives in the language offered by the world, that is, the language of choice. Only then will Christians be able to challenge an all too tolerant world that celebrates many gods as alternatives to the One God who alone is worthy of worship.

Note that my concern is not to try to reconstitute Christendom or advocate Christian "rule" in late Enlightenment societies like the one called America. Rather, the issue is service to our non-Christian brother and sister. If, for example, we believe abortion is sin that injures not only child and mother but our very ability to be parents, then we must find ways to help one another, Christian and non-Christian alike, not to be subject to the terror of that alternative. What alternatives to abortion might look like will differ from context to context, but Christians surely cannot promise those committed to a peaceable society that our alternative will appear "peaceable" because such views are allegedly only our private opinion.

Thus, we owe it to our non-Christian sister and brother to try to help them live lives that are as life-giving as that which God has made possible for us to live. Excluding violent alternatives from the common life of a society is not a bad thing. I certainly wish for the Pentagon not to exist. I work for it not to exist. Of course, that work must always be a witness that we hope others will find compelling, but I certainly do not assume that such witness might not take publicly defensible forms that make, for example, military funding more difficult. From my perspective you cannot put enough bureaucratic controls on military spending to ensure that "we the people" are not ripped off.

To be sure, Engelhardt may respond that the kind of peaceable society he thinks necessary is one that will allow just the kind of witness I want Christians to make. I doubt that. But to show why, I will need to look more closely at Engelhardt's "peace." Before I do so, however, I want at least to mention one issue that I suspect lies at the bottom of some of my deepest dis-ease with Engelhardt. Engelhardt assumes that witness is what you need when your position cannot be "rationally" defended. I, in contrast, assume that witness is one of the most determinative forms of rationality.

At several points Engelhardt observes that Roman Catholicism made the mistake of trying to provide rational grounds for being Catholic. He suggests that prior to the Reformation the Christian West envisaged a single authoritative point of view available, not only through grace, but also through rational argument (68). According to Engelhardt, this vision led Western Christianity, and in particular Catholicism, to undermine its own roots by trying to establish by reason what only faith can show (94).[5]

I am not unsympathetic with Engelhardt's argument at this point. I have argued in a somewhat similar fashion that attempts to base Christian morality on some kinds of natural law theory can lead to violence.[6]

Yet I think Engelhardt owes us a fuller account of reason than he has supplied if we are to understand his position as well as knowing what might be wrong with it. To suggest that it is a mistake to base faith on reason depends on what you mean by reason. Certainly Aquinas did not think knowing God as Trinity was of the same status as knowing God exists, but neither did he think that belief in the Trinity lacked rational warrant. Aquinas assumed that theology was faith seeking understanding, but faith did not name the necessity of an irrational starting point. Faith, rather, is that which is established by the most trustworthy witnesses.

In *Bioethics and Secular Humanism* Engelhardt contends that a "rational perspective is that which can be defended on the basis of general principles. If one rejects a rational perspective for the resolution of controversies, one can still appeal to force, prayer, inducements, and seduction. But one will not be able to explain why any of these alternative approaches is correct without giving reasons on its behalf."[7] Christians believe we can give "reasons on behalf" of that which we believe, reasons that should not only be persuasive, but understood as true. To be sure, such "reason giving" is a complex activity requiring the transformation of our lives through location in the Christian tradition. However, as MacIntyre has helped us see, any account of rationality cannot be otherwise.[8] I am aware that Engelhardt may well disagree with MacIntyre at this point, but at least I think it is clear that Engelhardt owes us a more developed account of rationality.

The Violence of Engelhardt's "Peace"

I am a pacifist, so it is hard for me to be against peace. Nonetheless, it is important to remember that not all peace is peace and, in particular, not all peace is the peace of Christ. I am not at all convinced that the peaceable society Engelhardt desires exists, can exist, or, if it did exist, would be peaceable. What I fear is that what Engelhardt gives us is not peace, but order. He observes that "until a general conversion to the Faith or to a particular ideology, or to a generally imposed orthodoxy, one will need to search for common grounds to bind rational peaceable individuals and to direct health care decisions" (35).[9] One of the goals of ethics is to find a way to avoid the use of force for resolving moral controversies or, when that is not possible, to determine when and how to limit the use of force (67).

Engelhardt wisely refers to the fundamental principle necessary for such a project no longer as the "principle of autonomy" but rather as the "principle of permission" (xi). This change rightly indicates that the "peaceable society" Engelhardt desires can only "be derived from the concurrence of individuals. Because the only morally authorized social structures under such circumstances are those established with the permission of the individuals involved, the majority that binds moral strangers has by default an unavoidable libertarian character. However, this is not out of any value attributed to freedom or individual choice. The plausible scope of societal moral authority is limited because of plausible limits of the consent to be governed by others" (x).

I admire what I can only describe as Engelhardt's monkish intellectual austerity, an austerity that governs the development of the contours of his peaceable society. I have my doubts whether he can in fact show that the principle of permission constitutes the "core" of the morality of mutual respect (117), if for no other reason than that such an account seems too close to Kant for someone who has disavowed the Kantian deduction. That is not, however, my main worry about Engelhardt's understanding of the peaceable society. Rather, my central concern is Engelhardt's presumption that "peace" is in fact institutionalized through democracy. I contest Engelhardt's claim that the principle of permission provides only an "empty process" for generating the moral authority to sustain a minimum ethic of praise and blame (109).

Engelhardt claims that liberal democracies are

> morally neutral by default. They cannot acquire the authorization to establish a particular moral vision, religion, or ideology. After all, given the failure of reason to discover the rational, canonical, content-full moral vision, establishing a morality or ideology as a government's concrete morality or moral vision has no more secular moral plausibility or authority than would the establishment of a particular religion. Limited democracies are therefore morally committed to not being committed to a particular vision of the good; they are committed rather to being the social structure through which, and with the protection of which, individuals and communities can pursue their own and divergent visions of the good. (120)

All I ask of Engelhardt is to name just one such "social structure" that actually exemplifies his "neutral public square." When it comes to government, nature abhors a vacuum, and if the secular square is alleged to be empty you can be sure that that claim is itself an ideology for a quite particular set of interests.

Engelhardt may mean for his peaceable society to be a thought experiment, a utopian creation to enrich our imaginations. I would certainly not want to disparage the importance of utopian schemes, but I do not think that is what Engelhardt is about. He seems to believe that the liberal democracies of the West approximate, and thus partly and imper-

fectly actualize, his libertarian ideal. If they do, however, they are anything but benign. More important, even as a thought experiment, Engelhardt's "peace" remains far too coercive.

Engelhardt has read Foucault but has chosen to ignore Foucault's understanding of power. The supervisory strategies necessary to sustain
Engelhardt's "peace" are simply coercion relabeled "freedom." For example, people whom we call tribal cannot help but find the necessity of
being an individual (in order to be part of Engelhardt's peaceable
arrangements) a form of violence. Tolerance, which Engelhardt identifies
as the primary cardinal virtue of the morality of mutual respect, cannot
help but kill (419). People are, to be sure, quite literally killed in the name
of tolerance, but it is equally the case that tolerance kills the soul.

It is to Engelhardt's credit that he understands that his peaceable society must produce character types whose primary virtue is their moral
vacuity.[10] Yuppies become the prophetic vanguard of the "coming world-
wide secularity in public policy" because they see themselves as bound to
no parochial, history-bound tradition, belonging as they do to no one or
no place. That Engelhardt—at least the Engelhardt who supports a peaceable society of the kind described in the second edition—should find such
people desirable should not be surprising. They are, after all, exactly the
kind of people he needs to supply the bureaucracies that control the lives
of those who continue to persist in more determinative ways of life.

I cannot help but think Engelhardt's world, like other liberal accounts
of social cooperation, can only be imagined because he presumes continuing Christian habits and institutions. For example, I do not see how he
can account for why some people believe that they ought to care for other
people simply because those others happen to fall ill. Why should those
who constitute Engelhardt's peaceable society, who, moreover, embody
the virtues of that society, think it important to set aside some people to
do nothing with their lives except to be present to and care for the sick?
He says that his social world can only supply "a general abstract understanding of what it means to be a physician or nurse" (294). Any more
determinative conception must come from within a particular community of physicians and nurses. Yet why would the latter (i.e., a particular
community of physicians and nurses) understand themselves to be in the
same practice as the former (i.e., those who constitute Engelhardt's
peaceable society)? Indeed, given his own analysis of the variability of
what "ill," "health," "disease," and so forth can mean, there is no reason
to assume that they would even be acting in the same world of illness or
health.[11]

Engelhardt suggests that physicians are "often cast into a role analogous to those of bureaucrats in a large-scale nation. They must come to
terms with the moral commitments and views of individuals from various moral communities while preserving the moral fabric of a peaceable,

secular, pluralistic society. It is for this reason that Hegel identified civil servants as the universal class (in contrast to this, Marx assigned the role of the universal class to the workers). Civil servants are committed to the general realization of freedom in the nation according to Hegel. Letter carriers must deliver mail to all on their routes and not discriminate against some on the grounds of their political commitments. To ensure this takes place, one may need bureaucratic rules that clearly establish in general what will be done, for whom, and under what circumstances. Physicians and other health care professionals are often in the position of civil servants in that they must make clear to patients what will be done for them, to them, and under what circumstance" (293–294). Accordingly, patients and physicians who meet one another as strangers will need to know what safeguards are present to protect the patient as well as what services the physician is committed to providing.

Engelhardt's yuppies may well become such civil servants, but I see no reason why Christians would imitate them in their own "civil service." Even more important, I do not think Christians as patients could or should trust their lives to such civil servants. Indeed, what seems missing from Engelhardt's account of the kind of medicine envisioned in his peaceable society is how to account for trust. His whole project seems to be an attempt to substitute exchange for trust, all the while presuming the continued existence of the habits of trust. I see no reason to believe that such habits of trust would persist in these circumstances. In other words, I see no grounds for believing that the kind of trust that has traditionally made medicine what it is would continue in a world based more on exchange than on gift.

The language of exchange, moreover, introduces the most profound violence that I think is presupposed in Engelhardt's peaceable society. Engelhardt is way ahead of the game insofar as he knows that ethics, and in particular bioethics, cannot be separated from politics. (Or perhaps more accurately put, bioethics *is* a politics.) But missing from his account of the peaceable society, missing from his account of democracy, is economics. Such an omission, moreover, is not innocent if you believe, as I do, that nothing is more violent than the capitalist market.[12] But it is exactly such a market that Engelhardt seems to presuppose as central to his peaceable society. I am, of course, aware that such a market dominates all our lives in the modern West. What is important for those of us who are Christians in such economies, however, is not to call good the fact that we currently feel we have no alternative to that market.

O.K., If You Are So Smart, What Alternative Do You Have?

I realize that the kind of criticism I have made of Engelhardt's account of the peaceable society must appear unfair. It seems unfair because with the best will in the world Engelhardt is striving to help us find an alternative to what he fears is the coming violence. If you do not like his alternative, it seems that you must be expected to provide an alternative of your own. Yet I do not have an alternative to offer to Engelhardt's peace. At least I do not have an alternative to offer *at the theoretical level* of Engelhardt's proposal.

Our task, as Christians, is not to offer such theoretical alternatives, but rather to be an alternative. Christians provided such an alternative when they thought it a good thing to construct houses of hospitality for people who would have otherwise died alone. Christians provided such alternatives when they did not kill their children who were born deformed. Christians provided such alternatives when as patients they exemplified the virtue of patience by not asking physicians to do more than the physicians could or should. Without such fundamental practices, practices that those who are not Christian can imitate, theoretical constructions of peaceable societies of the sort developed by Engelhardt can too easily give Christians the misleading impression that we know more than we do and, even worse, the presumption that we can do more than we can.

I fear that we Christians must be content to live out our lives in the world as we find it and as we make it. It is a world, I fear, that descriptively resembles Engelhardt's peaceable society. Our task as Christians is not to make such a world more terrible than it has a tendency to be, but to survive in and for such a world—not because survival is itself a virtue, but because we have been called by God for whom our survival is a witness and a sign of God's grace. That is finally why, as much as I would have found it an attractive possibility, I could not have written the second edition of *The Foundations of Bioethics*.

Notes

1. Wolff's review appeared in the *New Republic* 196 (May 25, 1987), p. 38.

2. All references to the second edition of *The Foundations of Bioethics* (New York: Oxford University Press, 1996) will appear in parentheses in the text.

3. That is, of course, one of the purposes of my *Suffering Presence* (Notre Dame: University of Notre Dame Press, 1986).

4. Engelhardt rightly observes that the failure of the modern moral philosophical project "returns us to the polytheism and skepticism of ancient times with a remembrance of the philosophical monotheism and Faith that fashioned the West" (11). Secular people too often assume that once Christianity is rendered irrelevant, the world will be free of the gods. The truth is exactly the reverse, as we see in our own time how the defeat of Christianity occasions, not the death, but the rebirth, of the gods. The problem with the secular, in other words, is that it has such a difficult time remaining secular.

5. Engelhardt footnotes Michael Buckley's *At the Origins of Modern Atheism* in support of this point. I am not sure that Buckley's argument is the same as Engel-

hardt's. It was not Aquinas that produced the rationalism that in turn gave us modern atheism, but later Scholastic developments. Everything depends on what you take reason to be.

6. Stanley Hauerwas, *The Peaceable Kingdom* (Notre Dame: University of Notre Dame Press, 1988), pp. 50–71.

7. H. Tristram Engelhardt, *Bioethics and Secular Humanism: The Search for a Common Morality* (Philadelphia: Trinity Press International, 1991), p. 16.

8. MacIntyre has developed this account most fully in *Whose Justice? Which Rationality?* (Notre Dame: University of Notre Dame Press, 1988) and *Three Rival Versions of Moral Enquiry: Encyclopedia, Genealogy, and Tradition* (Notre Dame: University of Notre Dame Press, 1990). Crucial to understanding MacIntyre's position is his claim in *Whose Justice? Which Rationality?* that the "concept of tradition constituted and tradition-constitutive rational enquiry cannot be elucidated apart from its exemplifications" (p. 10). Too often criticisms of MacIntyre try to separate his account of rationality from the story he tells, but the whole force of his position is to deny such a dissociation can be made. "Tradition" does not name a new epistemological option to that of the encyclopedist and the genealogist, but rather is an attempt to show why you cannot begin with epistemology in developing an account of rationality. In other words, MacIntyre is developing philosophically the theological claim of what faith seeking understanding looks like.

9. Who is this "one" that takes up this project? Is it a Christian? One of the troubling aspects of Engelhardt's position is its historical abstractness.

10. Engelhardt, *Bioethics and Secular Humanism*, pp. 35–40.

11. Engelhardt observes that "a traditional Roman Catholic community is likely to have understandings of health, disease, disorder, deviance, and disability quite different from those of a community of secularized cosmopolitans. Their different constructions of medical reality can then be embedded in alternative health care systems, which carry with them quite different understandings of what should count as a disease to be treated and of what treatment expenses should be sustained by the community" (227). What Engelhardt needs to justify is why, given his account, he thinks he can still speak of "medical reality" and "health care systems" as if they are simply "there."

12. See, for example, Alasdair MacIntyre, *Marxism and Christianity*, 2nd ed. (London: Duckworth, 1995), especially the new introduction. MacIntyre observes that in premodern societies markets were auxiliary to production, but in "the markets of modern capitalism prices are often imposed by factors external to a particular market: those, for example, whose livelihood has been made subject to international market forces by their becoming exclusively producers for some product for which there was, but is no longer, international demand, will find themselves compelled to accept imposed low prices or even the bankruptcy of their economy. Market relationships in contemporary capitalism are for the most part relations imposed both on labor and on small producers, rather than in any sense freely chosen" (xii).

8 *How Christian Ethics Became Medical Ethics: The Case of Paul Ramsey*

A Case

Tom Beauchamp and James Childress have just finished preparing the fourth edition of their enormously successful *Principles of Biomedical Ethics* (1994). It occurred to me that someone ought to attend to the various redactions of that book, as we might learn much, not only about their own changes of mind, but about the history of recent medical ethics. So I asked Beauchamp and Childress if I might look at their files to see what shaped and reshaped their revisions. Being old friends they graciously accepted my offer.

In the process I discovered a document that I think is quite important. It is a case that they considered for inclusion in the famous appendix to their book, which is simply called "Cases." Why they chose not to include that case or, put pejoratively, why they may have suppressed the case, I expect to be a matter of discussion for many years. I suspect they were considering the case as a way to spark a consideration of the principle of justice and they may have decided the case was too ambiguous; yet I think their refusal to use the case involves deeper questions than simply editorial relevance. Here is the case that bore the number 666.

* * *

An elderly, but obviously quite active man burst into a psychiatrist's office late one afternoon without an appointment. He seemed quite normal in appearance, though his ample sideburns made him appear a bit odd— he looked like an academic left over from the nineteenth century. He said he had to talk with someone, since he suspected that his colleagues no longer listened to or could understand his arguments. He confessed he had little faith in psychiatry, but since psychiatrists were paid to listen he thought he might as well try one. This particular psychiatrist recalled that before the advent of psychotropics she actually used to talk to patients, so she decided to go along. Besides, she had nothing better to do.

It was not immediately clear what was bothering the patient. Indeed, it did not seem to occur to the patient that he had become a patient. The psychiatrist in fact was a bit concerned whether the patient was stable, since there were some odd speech patterns accompanied by equally repetitive physical movements. For example, the patient kept saying "You know" while pushing his finger into the psychiatrist's chest. There were also the constant "Hrumps," which the patient made as he massaged his left chest with his right hand. He did all this while keeping his ever-present pipe going at full blast.

After some time, the psychiatrist began to suspect that she had a case of serious paranoia on her hands. It seems the patient complained that no matter how hard he tried, few knew how to read rightly his many books. In effect, he said he was suffering from the dread disease of chronic misinterpretation. For instance, no matter how often he emphasized that he wrote as a Christian ethicist, people kept trying to turn him into one of the originators of the field of medical ethics.

He confessed that he had no brief against those who wanted to be medical ethicists, but his game was much larger—namely, ensuring the moral survival of Christian civilization. After all, that civilization is the result of the Christian commitment embodied in such concepts as covenant-fidelity, *hesed,* and agape. Such concepts often appear in the language of justice, duty, and fairness, but in fact they are theological concepts through and through.

For example, some had insisted on interpreting him in a Kantian manner, in particular an undisciplined thinker at Duke, simply because his book was called *The Patient as Person.* By "person," however, he certainly did not mean any Kantian account of person, since that kind of individualism is exactly what he was trying to counter. Moreover, he did not himself title the book. It was the people at Yale that did that. It must have been a liberal plot.

What is more, he claimed, most could not understand the relation between his views on war and the work he was doing in medical ethics. They thought his support of limited war to be inconsistent with his opposition to abortion. How could they fail to see that at the heart of both was his commitment to the inviolability of the individual? It is the neighbor who comes in the form of individual human beings, after all, that must be at the center of the Christian moral project.

The psychiatrist, after listening to these complaints, began to wonder what kind of diagnosis was appropriate. Was this really a case of chronic misinterpretation? The psychiatrist, of course, distrusted self-diagnosis, but there did seem to be a pattern emerging that might support such an account. Paranoia could not be excluded. In the absence of any strong evidence one way or the other, and feeling that the patient desperately needed calming, the psychiatrist, who had done a unit of CPE (Christian Pastoral Education) and discovered she had sadistic tendencies and that she ought to enjoy such desires, suggested that in the next week the patient read all of Karl Barth's *Church Dogmatics* and come back for a regular appointment.

*   *   *

Beauchamp and Childress ask provocatively at the end of the case, "Why is this case interesting?"

Christian Ethics and Medical Ethics

While I cannot pretend to explain why I think this case interesting, I do want to try to situate Ramsey's work in medical ethics, not only within his overall project but also in the history of Christian ethics in this country. Yet my object is not to provide a better understanding of Ramsey, but rather to understand a bit better how Ramsey fits into the larger story of how and why Christian ethicists have become so fascinated with medical ethics.

I am currently working on a book that attempts to tell the story of Christian ethics as an academic discipline in America. The book asks the dramatic question, "How did a tradition that began with a book called *Christianizing the Social Order*[1] [Rauschenbusch 1912] end with a book called *Can Ethics Be Christian?*" (Gustafson 1975). Gustafson describes his own sense of unease with the latter book, noting that he worked on the book for years "with the nagging sense that most persons who answer in an unambiguous affirmative would not be interested in my supporting argument, that a few fellow professional persons might be interested enough to look at it, and that for those who believe the answer is negative the question itself is not sufficiently important to bother about" (Gustafson 1978:392). I suspect that most of us concerned with Christian ethics and its relation to medical ethics are haunted by such an unease—"Who really cares?"

Of course, Christian ethicists rushed into medical ethics for many reasons, not the least of which was (and is) money and power. I sometimes point out to my students that people now go to Europe to see the great cathedrals, wondering to themselves as they view these magnificent structures, "What kind of people would build such things? After all, you might well be dead before the foundation even was complete." Someday I think people may well come to see major medical centers, like the one we have at Duke, and ask the same sort of question: "What kind of people would build such things?" If these future "tourists" are astute, they will think those who constructed such medical complexes certainly must have been afraid of death.

So medical ethicists, being the good priests they are, went to where the power is in liberal societies—medical schools. Kings and princes once surrounded themselves with priests for legitimation. Likewise, politicians today surround themselves with social scientists to give those they rule the impression that they really know what is going on and can plan accordingly.[2] Physicians, in an increasingly secular society, surround themselves with medical ethicists. God no longer exists, the sacred universe of values has replaced God, and, allegedly, ethicists think about values and decisions that involve values.

Such an analysis may sound cynical, but I do not mean for it to be so interpreted. I simply assume such a development was inevitable, given the character of our world. Nor do I mean to denigrate the good work of medical ethicists, many of whom often take a quite critical stance toward the practices of those they serve. Yet the very terms of their analysis (autonomy, nonmaleficence, justice, and so on) are primarily legitimating categories for a medicine shaped by a liberal culture. For example, it is by no means clear to me that informed consent necessarily should play the part attributed to it in most literature in medical ethics.[3] Given the Christian assumption that we are called to be of service to one another, I see no reason why some might not be drafted to be of help to others, for example, to share blood without their consent. Indeed, as I will show, Ramsey made such a suggestion.

That money and power have attracted Christian thinkers to medicine, however, is not the story I want to tell. Rather, I want to direct attention to what might be called the internal story of Christian ethics in order to understand how a tradition that began by trying to Christianize the social order now works very hard to show that being Christian does not unduly bias how we do medical ethics. Christian ethicists at one time wanted to rule, but now we seek to show we can be of help to the doctor. How did this happen?

I take my cue in this regard from Gustafson's wonderful article, "Theology Confronts Technology and the Life Sciences" (Gustafson 1978). He begins by noting how clear it is to those who read *The Hastings Center Report*, *Theological Studies*, and many other journals,

> that persons with theological training are writing a great deal about technology and the life sciences. . . . Whether theology is thereby in interaction with these areas, however, is less clear. For some writers the theological authorization for the ethical principles and procedures they use is explicit; this is clearly the case for the most prolific and polemical of the Protestants, Paul Ramsey. For others, writing as "ethicists," the relation of their moral discourse to any specific theological principles, or even to a definable religious

outlook is opaque. Indeed, in response to a query from a friend (who is a distinguished philosopher) about how the term "ethicist" has come about, I responded in a pejorative way, "An ethicist is a former theologian, who does not have the professional credentials of a moral philosopher." (386)

Gustafson continues by observing that much of the writing in the field of medical ethics is now done by people who desire to be known as "religious ethicists," if only to show they are distinguishable from philosophers. Yet it is by no means clear to what the adjective "religious" refers. It surely does not refer to anything as specific as Jewish or even Protestant or Catholic; for if it did, the writers would use the proper designation. Gustafson commends Ramsey for his 1974 declaration, "I always write as the ethicist I am, namely a Christian ethicist, and not as some hypothetical common denominator" (Gustafson 1978).

I, too, think Ramsey is to be commended for his candor. I am not convinced, however, that his execution matched his candor. For example, I always kidded him that all the theology in *The Patient as Person* was contained in the preface. He did not find that remark humorous. He refused to let the more theological parts of *Ethics at the Edges of Life* be edited out explicitly to rebut the criticism that *The Patient as Person* was insufficiently theological.[4] Yet the issue is not simply a matter of *quantity*, but rather the *kind* of theology that Ramsey represented. Despite his conservative reputation both in theology and politics, I will try to show that Ramsey remained, ironically like Reinhold Niebuhr, a theologian in the great tradition of Protestant liberalism.[5] Moreover, as a representative of that tradition, he had insufficient resources to show how Christian practice might make a difference for understanding, let alone forming, the practice of medicine.

Ramsey in many ways was the last great representative of the Protestant social gospel. He could not, of course, call for a christianizing of the social order in the way Walter Rauschenbusch did. Reinhold Niebuhr had forever blocked that alternative. Indeed, Ramsey did not have to call for a christianizing, since he assumed that he was already part of a society that was well christianized. Whereas Rauschenbusch could speak of saved and unsaved institutions, identifying the former with political democracy and suggesting that the economic order still needed saving, Ramsey, living in a different era and with a different outlook, would no longer speak of institutions being saved. Although Ramsey did not echo Rauschenbusch's call, he certainly shared with his predecessor the conviction that Christianity had formed something called Western civilization, which continued to bear the marks of the Gospel. It was no accident, given that presumption, that medicine became a crucial practice that allowed Ramsey to develop that perspective. The church may no longer have social power, but at least we still have medicine.

One way to think about these matters is to reflect on what one conceives the subject of ethics to be. The social gospelers wanted ethics to encompass all life: economics, politics, and family. For Reinhold Niebuhr the attention of the Christian ethicist was focused less on economics (now that would be left to economists) than on politics and international politics in particular. Indeed, Ramsey's attempt to discipline some of the utilitarian presumptions of Niebuhr's realism can be read in deep continuity with Niebuhr's fascination with the world of international politics. But the problem with the focus on politics, international politics especially, is that it is just too messy. Medical ethics, in contrast, offers an opportunity for the kind of problems that could be casuistically displayed, ✓ thereby giving the sense that we just may know what we are doing when we do ethics. Moreover, medical ethics (or better, the practice of medi- · cine) exemplifies for Ramsey the moral commitments that lie at the heart of Western civilization and that animate, or at least should animate, our politics and economics.

Ramsey's Understanding of the Place of Christian Ethics

I am aware that these are large themes that require further nuance, but let me try to suggest, by calling attention to how his medical ethics fits within his overall project, how this reading of Ramsey makes sense. Ramsey's basic theological position was set out in *Basic Christian Ethics* (Ramsey 1950, 1993). He seldom returned to such theological questions, since he assumed that what he said in this early work was right and needed no rethinking. However, he did write a quite candid essay about basic methodological issues entitled "Tradition and Reflection in Christian Life" (Ramsey 1982). In this article he confesses the following puzzlement:

> Puzzlement is too weak a word. Disorientation is a better word, since I thrash about not knowing what to say to the present situation in the churches. For some time now the demise of the "Constantinian era" has been *triumphantly* proclaimed. We no longer live in "Christendom"; this fact is said to be abundantly clear. But why any Christian would cite this fact with joy I do not know. Still that is not the heart of my puzzlement. My quandary is in attempting to understand how those who triumphantly proclaim the end of the Christian age can then still have the audacity to address pronouncements and counsel to governments. That was appropriate with the Constantinian era, not beyond if we are beyond. Those who still address counsel to governments must believe *either* that a remnant of the Christian age remains on which they count when testifying before Congress *or* that in so doing they do so as only one among many other voices in a society that for the foreseeable future is irredeemably secular. (1982:46-56)[6]

I confess that I love this quote, not only because it is so quintessentially Ramsey in terms of its style, but also because it is so candid regarding his Constantianism. There is, moreover, a wonderful footnote to the last sentence in which Ramsey identifies himself as one who still believes that something remains of the Christian age, a remnant that makes it possible for him to give counsel to government.

> It is in this sense that I continue to try to do "public ethics." In this endeavor I have recently been put on notice that I may be wrong by a distinguished philosopher [MacIntyre], who wrote: "But any biblical position, whether Jewish or Christian, is going to be at odds, so it seems, with the dominant secular standpoints of our culture; alliances between the theologians and the secular thinker are going to be limited to specific points or easily fractured by disagreements elsewhere. The modern secular world may provide fewer allies than Ramsey believes." . . . At the same time I continue to try to do "church ethics" in hope that the day may come when the dominant secular viewpoints on morality will be extended from the church of Jesus Christ. (Ramsey 1982:47)

Ramsey became increasingly convinced, at least if we are to believe some of his remarks in *Speak Up for Just War and Pacifism,* that the church might be forced to assume a sect-like stance (Ramsey 1988). Yet he thought such a position was a matter of necessity rather than anything that Christians should want. For example, in a letter Ramsey responded to my suggestion that his casuistry presumes that the notion of the inviolability of each life exists in our civilization because our civilization is Christian:

> There are, of course, stretches in what we may dignify by calling my "special ethics" where the Christian word to be heard is not resounding in every paragraph. Call this Christian "casuistry" if you will—but not for the reason you state. Your grounds for my endeavor to do public ethics is partially true, as an appeal to *past* Christian influences perhaps not yet altogether lost. Doubtless I may hope against hope that some among the "hearers" may strengthen their adherence to the best of past culture; or maybe search among their premises and find that they have no breastplate of righteousness with which to gird the irreplaceability and unmeldability of every human soul. But I, the author, have not left Christian premises behind when I go on to do special ethics. You may *disagree* with the way I go about doing special ethics theologically, there where you say that my "dramatic and significant assertions" are only "assertions" for which no adequate theological warrant is supplied. I think everyone of them is adequately warranted, and *directly* by the "giftedness" of life. I judge that simple warrant to be enough. You may want me at this point to pause and retell the whole Christian story. But then we disagree more in style than in substance, for I never left that behind. . . . My foundational work is not [the humanist's] nor are [the humanist's] mine. But I do believe that while Christianity ought always to be will-

ing to be a sect whenever necessary, there is always at work a culture-form-
ing impulse as well. When, therefore, I say I am disinterested in finding out
whether the King is clothed, naked or wears a simple jock strap, I mean to
say that Christian special ethics would still come to the conclusions I do.
(Ramsey 1990:318–319)[7]

Indeed it was in medicine that Ramsey found institutionalized the kind
of moral presuppositions and practices that should be characteristic of
Western civilization. Though he feared that we were in danger of having
"a medical profession without a moral philosophy in a society without
one either" (1970),[8] it is nonetheless medicine, at least Ramsey's reading
of medicine, that carries the Christian commitment to care for the neighbor as ensouled body. Therefore, the commitment of the physician to care
for the patient preceding all other moral and social considerations provided Ramsey with a practice he sorely needed to sustain Christian ethics
as a discipline in service to the world.

This move, of course, involved two questionable presuppositions: (1)
that Christians do or should attribute to the neighbor the significance
Ramsey claims to find in the Gospel and (2) that medicine is or should be
shaped by Ramsey's understanding of covenant fidelity. I will explore
both these questions, for by doing so I think we will discover some of the
reasons that Christian ethics has become medical ethics. Moreover, by
looking into these matters, I also hope to substantiate my claim that Ramsey remained embedded in the habits of mind characteristic of liberal
Protestantism as well as political liberalism.

Ramsey's Ethics

It is well known that Rauschenbusch thought Jesus was but the continuation of prophetic insight, since the prophets stood for a justice that was
independent of cultic practice and religious dogma. What is important is
not the religious beliefs but the ethical upshot. Ramsey was obviously
considerably more sophisticated theologically than Rauschenbusch, as
well as more personally theologically orthodox, but his understanding of
the significance of covenant fidelity is structurally quite similar to
Rauschenbusch's understanding of the relation of theology and ethics.

For example, Ramsey, in a manner not unlike Rauschenbusch, thought
the source of Christian love to be Jesus' preaching of the kingdom of
God. But this presented a problem for Ramsey, at least when he was
working on *Basic Christian Ethics*. Under the influence of Schweitzer,
Ramsey assumed that the role of the kingdom in Jesus' teaching could
not be separated from Jesus' eschatological expectations. "This has to be
said and said forthrightly: few contemporary Christians accept the kind
of kingdom-expectation Jesus considered of central importance, and

right they do not" (1993:35–36).[9] But if the role of the kingdom is central as a source for Christian love, and the kingdom is inseparably linked to an eschatology we can no longer accept, how can we continue to argue for the role of the kingdom as a source of Christian love?

Ramsey addressed the question by rejecting the avenue taken by Rauschenbusch and the Social Gospel, an avenue that aligned with the inevitability of progress. In vintage Ramseyan polemical prose, he writes, "Of course, it may be contended that apocalypticism is a better myth than the idea of progress prevalent since the eighteenth century, and New Testament eschatology at least permits a man to recognize a catastrophe when he sees one rather than dying in his procrustean bed of development with his illusion on" (1993:36). Yet that further complicates his problem, for he had agreed with Rauschenbusch, in "A Theology of Social Action," that "we are correct, most especially, in no longer thinking as Jesus thought about the immediate end of the 'this present age' and the coming of the kingdom of God. One of the main foundations and incentives for social action among us is the need for social control and some sort of restraint of evil to take the place left vacant by our rejection of Jesus' 'eschatological' expectation" (Ramsey 1946:4). How could Ramsey reject the eschatology and still maintain Jesus' emphasis on the kingdom's presence? He resolves this dilemma by claiming that the essence of Jesus' teaching about the kingdom, that is, "disinterested love for the neighbor," was independent of its origin in Jesus apocalypticism and stood on its own. In a passage that sounds as if it came from Bultmann's *Jesus Christ and Mythology* (1958), Ramsey says the following:

> The origin and history of Christian love may be interesting and important in its own right, but to suppose that factors determining the origins of this conception have anything to do with its value, or affect its truth to any degree one way or another, is an instance of the "genetic fallacy" so prevalent in post-evolutionary thought. Indeed, precisely from the utter removal of all other considerations, Jesus' ethic gained an absolute validity transcending limitation to this or that place or time or civilization. Precisely because all neighbors were apocalyptically removed from view except this single chance individual who might be hostile or friendly, beloved child or total stranger, Christian love gained unqualified lack of concern for either preferential interests or preferential duties, becoming an attitude unconditionally required of men in spite of hostility, in spite also of friendliness, on the neighbor's part. (Ramsey 1970:41–42)

In short, Ramsey demythologizes apocalyptic and discovers disinterested love, which, though not exactly Kant, is at least in Kant's ballpark.

I need not tell you this became the center of his work for the rest of his life. We are always living in the end time when we face the needs of the neighbor. The unwillingness to subordinate the care of the neighbor to any other ends, even the ends of the survival of the human species, is the moral equivalent to living apocalyptically. Ramsey later recants his dismissal of Jesus' eschatology, but he never rethinks the structural presuppositions that come from his original account of neighbor love as absolute disinterestedness.

For example, in *Nine Modern Moralists,* in the midst of his discussion of Edmund Cahn and the ethics of the lifeboat, which in many ways was the basis for his later thinking on medical ethics, he seconds Cahn's judgment that the crisis in the lifeboat was apocalyptic in character. The lifeboat crisis, like Jesus' apocalyptic message, made null and void all earthly possessions, family ties, and distinctions of every conceivable kind. Accordingly, it embodies the ethics of the Gospel that transcends the generic duty of self-preservation. Love-transformed natural law thus requires that all should wait and die together rather than that some lives be saved (Ramsey 1962).[10]

Ramsey notes that this was the burden of Jesus' teaching that calls for an exodus from the natural order of existence to that made possible by the immediate presence of God.

> His ethics is not understandable apart from the presence of God's kingdom. It was not, as Schweitzer supposed, the imminent *coming* of the kingdom which produced Jesus' teachings as an "interim ethic." It was rather the *presence* of the kingdom which produced his unlimited estimate of what one man owes another in prompt and radical service; and at the same time it was His living in the presence of God which rendered negligible the fixed relationships among men in this present age. His message does not stand or fall with his conception about the quick end of the world. It would be better to reverse this proposition and say that this expectation about the future sprang rather from Jesus' conviction about God and from Jesus' existence in His presence. Jesus and the prophets were so overwhelmed by their sense of the sovereign majesty and utter faithfulness of God, the legal systems and the customary or natural moralities of this world were already liquidated before their eyes. Natural self-preservation was suspended, as also were the rules about Sabbath observance, if they stood in the way of manifesting the concrete response of serving the slightest need of the neighbor. (Ramsey 1962:248)

Ramsey adds a footnote to this passage in which he suggests that this paragraph significantly changes the emphasis, but not the "substance of my interpretation of the relation between eschatology and ethics in Jesus' teachings in *Basic Christian Ethics*, Chapter 1" (1962). I think that is certainly right, as we see that now Jesus' eschatology is interpreted as requiring us to act rightly though the heavens fall. Ramsey assumed that this was love-transformed justice that went beyond natural law and was now instantiated in the laws and practices of Western society. Indeed, I cannot help but think that Ramsey's fascination with the law, which often resulted in painstaking and pain-inducing discussion of minutiae of the law, was the working out of his conviction that the Gospel had transformed the *jus gentium*, making it necessary for the Christian ethicist to look to the law for the outworking of the Christian commitment to neighbor love.

Though Ramsey's account of neighbor love seemed to imply the protection of life as a necessary condition for our civilization, he never underwrote a survivalist ethic. Indeed, in his discussion of abortion in *War and the Christian Conscience*, he argues that a fetus in conflict-of-life cases should rightly be thought capable of sacrifice.

> The fetus is not only a man, with a right to life, but something of a Christian man who would not willingly exercise this right to the detriment of another, at least not when this abstract right is of no advantage to him. Indeed, we should assume that if a fetus is capable of bearing rights he is also capable of exercising them in a charitable manner; and at the least this means that his own right to life should not be held on to in vain, to the detriment of that of another. (Ramsey 1961:182–183)

It is an interesting question why Ramsey did not extend this line of reasoning to questions concerning experimentation on incompetents.

But why should this understanding of the ethics of the Gospel be called Protestant liberalism? Quite simply, because it allowed Ramsey to think that the nicer issues of theology, such as trinitarian and ecclesiological issues, were largely tangential to ethics. Once neighbor love had been discovered, the ethicist could get on with the casuistry necessary for the working out of this commitment in Western civilization without any further attention to Trinity or ecclesiology or Christology. As Ramsey puts it in *Basic Christian Ethics*, the problem is how Jesus' ethic of neighbor love can be transposed to a nonapocalyptic setting:

> What possible bearing can an ethic which specifies to the full what a man should do in relation to a single neighbor, an ethic which reveals with no qualification at all what the reign of "righteousness" means in regard to man, what bearing can this possibly have upon moral action in a world where *there is always more than one neighbor* and indeed a whole cluster of claims and responsibilities to be considered? (Ramsey 1993:42)

I am not accusing Ramsey of the kind of reduction so characteristic of much of Protestant liberal theology, for example, that Christ means love of the neighbor. Rather, his position accepts, in a sophisticated way to be sure, the presumption that the Gospel has a moral upshot. The Christian essence can therefore be known without the frills. That essence, moreover, has a kind of transhistorical validity because it is but an expression of the character of human existence.

Given this account of the "Christian thing," it should not be surprising that Ramsey would discover in medicine exactly the Christian commitment to the care of the neighbor. Nor is it surprising that the theology necessary for the work to be done in medical ethics could be stated in the preface to *The Patient as Person*. All that is required is to assert that medicine manifests one of the covenants into which we are born.[11] Medical care, in effect, is a love-transformed institution that is part of the Christian jus gentium. The major task for medical ethics is to reconcile the welfare of the individual with the welfare of mankind when both must be served (Ramsey 1970:xiv).

Ramsey, of course, thought this commitment was under attack by atomistic individualism. Such an individualism erodes every bond of life with life, in particular the bonds into which we enter (spousal) and those into which we are born (filial). Moreover, the Cartesian dualism, that is, the strong distinction between body and soul so characteristic of modernity, creates the assumption that the quality of life can be separate from our bodily existence. Our individualism and Cartesianism combine to underwrite the Baconian project, "that is, the pervasive notion that, for every problem produced by technology used for the relief of the human condition, there will be an as-yet-distant technical solution" (Ramsey 1978).

It is not surprising, therefore, that Ramsey shaped *The Patient as Person* around the problem of experimentation on children. Medical ethics is but the working out of the "ethics of consent." Experimentation raises the basic issues of fidelity between man and man.

> Consent expresses or establishes this relationship, and the requirement of consent sustains it. Fidelity is the bond between consenting man and consenting man in these procedures. The principle of an informed consent is the cardinal *canon of loyalty* joining men together in medical practice and investigation. In this requirement, faithfulness among men—the faithfulness that is normative for all the covenants or moral bonds of life with life—gains specification for the primary relations peculiar to medical practice. (Ramsey 1970:5)

It is not necessary for the story I am trying to tell to trace the ways in which Ramsey worked out this principle in matters of implied or proxy consent. What I hope is clear, however, is how Ramsey quite persuasively constructed medicine and medical ethics in terms of his understanding of the difference Christ has made. The irony is that it is unclear whether one needs Jesus' preaching of the kingdom for such an ethic. Yet, like a doctor, who is more likely to find the diseases she has been trained to find,

Ramsey made the primary moral issue in medical ethics the issue for which his ethics was designed. He thereby made medicine one of the fundamental carriers of his understanding of Christian civilization.

Ramsey's account of the ethos of medicine in *The Patient as Person* is so persuasive that it is easy to miss what he fails to treat. For example, there is no discussion of the aims of medicine, what health or illness means or how either is determined, or the meaning and place of pain and suffering. Nor does he broach such issues as the economic and political presumptions that do or should sustain medicine. That he did not deal with such matters can be a carping criticism, since no one can deal with every aspect of a reality as complex as modern medicine. But the issue is not just that Ramsey did not deal with such issues, but that he could not, given his account of what our ethics should be.

I do not mean to suggest that such considerations are absent entirely from Ramsey's presentation of medical ethics. For example, his concern to free medicine from the secular understanding of death as unmitigated disaster is an indication that he sensed such issues mattered (1970:269). Yet deciding how to distribute medical resources in a society determined by such a view of death is, according to Ramsey, virtually impossible. Indeed, he confesses he does not know how to answer questions concerning the determination of priorities within medical procedures or between medical procedures and other social priorities (1970:269). He calls for more thought to be given to the setting of medical and social priorities, but observes that

> the expectation that this can be achieved is finally totalitarian, or else can only have a leveling or reductionist effect on the practice of medicine and on the whole human enterprise. We may perhaps know when priorities are decidedly out of joint; but no one knows exactly what are the joints. Civilization is simply not an arrangement of human activities in a set hierarchical order. A society is largely an unfocused meshing of human pursuits. (1970:275)

This view of society is, of course, the view created by the great liberal theorists, who assumed that no teleological account, either of the universe or of society, was intelligible. Freedom is all that is left in such a world, but it is a freedom governed by no purpose. Correlatively, consent is all we have to protect us from one another's arbitrary desires. The ethics of such social orders can be utilitarian or deontological, but both only reinforce and legitimate the more determinative social presuppositions. No doubt in some of his moods Ramsey resisted these presuppositions, but his account of neighbor love gave him insufficient resources to name or challenge this world.

I find it hard to see how it could be otherwise, given Ramsey's Constantinian commitments. Medicine, at least his account of medicine, confirmed his presumption that agape was in fact instantiated in Western culture. In effect, medicine became Ramsey's church, as the commitment of doctors to patients remained more faithful to the ethic of Jesus than did the commitment of Christians, who were constantly tempted to utopian dreams fueled by utilitarian presumptions.

Thus, Ramsey's account of medicine is essentially conservative. Like most liberals, he did not seek to call into question the ends of medicine. Ends, other than the care of the patient, were simply not in the purview of ethics. Medicine, like the state, particularly the democratic state, was simply assumed to be the embodiment of love-transformed natural law. In like manner, medicine was constituted by the deontological commitment he thought was at the heart of the Gospel as well as our civilization. I am aware that Ramsey's position is more complex than the description "deontological" can comprehend, but I find it hard to see how Ramsey takes us beyond what Milbank has identified as deontological liberalism (Milbank 1989). That such is the case should not be surprising, given the tradition of Christian ethics in which Ramsey stood. Christian ethics was destined to become medical ethics. After all, medicine was and is our last public.

Medical Ethics After Ramsey

Where has all this gotten us? Not very far, I am afraid. However, I hope it helps us understand why Ramsey, in spite of his strong declarations to be working as a Christian ethicist, prepared the way for the developments that Gustafson laments—that is, the subordination of theological ethics to medical ethics. If the social gospel prepared the way for the Christian social ethicist to become a social scientist with a difference, in many ways the more orthodox Ramsey prepared the way for the Christian ethicist to become a medical ethicist with a difference. The difference was the vague theological presumptions that do no serious intellectual work other than explaining, perhaps, the motivations of the ethicist. As a result, Christian ethicists continue to leave the world as they found it. Why they might conceive of their task differently is a story for another day.

Notes

This essay was originally prepared for presentation at the twenty-fifth anniversary celebration of the Institute of Religion in Houston, Texas. An earlier version of this chapter appeared in *Christian Bioethics* (March 1995). Reprinted by permission.

1. *Christianizing the Social Order* was Walter Rauschenbusch's second book. The first was *Christianity and the Social Crisis* (1907). The title of the second book sug-

gests the extraordinary presumption that the social order could actually be "Christianized."

2. Alasdair MacIntyre's account of the role of the expert in *After Virtue* rightly argues that "predictability" becomes the legitimating category for rule in modern social orders. The distinction between "fact" and "value" is not epistemologically required but rather is produced by the necessity to create social scientists that can ensure outcomes. The only difficulty, as MacIntyre argues, is that fortune cannot be eliminated from human affairs (MacIntyre 1984:93–108).

3. I do not mean to suggest that informed consent is unimportant, but I think the account of autonomy that is used to shape accounts of informed consent distorts its use in medicine. For my attempt to provide a quite different account of informed consent based on friendship, see my *Suffering Presence: Theological Reflections on Medicine, the Mentally Handicapped and the Church* (1986).

4. In the preface to *Ethics at the Edges of Life* Ramsey emphasizes: "I do not hesitate to write as a Christian ethicist. No more did I hesitate in my first major book on medical ethics to invoke ultimate appeal to scripture or theology and to warrants such as righteousness, faithfulness, canons of loyalty, the awesome sanctity of human life, humankind in the image of God, holy ground, hesed (steadfast covenant love), agape (or "charity"), as these standards are understood in the religions of our culture, Judaism and Christianity" (Ramsey 1978:xiii). He continues, "I go too far in apology. Such a reader will not find most of the following analysis to be parochially limited to a religious outlook. This is true for two reasons. In the first place, the Judeo-Christian tradition decisively influenced the origin and shape of medical ethics down to our own times. Unless an author absurdly proposes an entirely new ethics, he is bound to use ethical principles derived from our past religious culture. In short, medical ethics nearly to date is a concrete case of Christian 'casuistry'— that is, it consists of the outlooks of the predominant Western religions brought down to cases and used to determine their resolution. . . . Whether medical ethics needs religious foundation, and whether it will be misshapen without it, awaits demonstration—or, more likely, the test of time. I do not undertake to argue the point. The humanist no more than I should want our opposite positions tested at such fateful costs. I do say, however, that the notion that an individual human life is absolutely unique, inviolable, irreplaceable, noninterchangeable, not substitutable, and not meldable with other lives is a notion that exists in our civilization because it is Christian; and that idea is so fundamental in the edifice of Western law and morals that it cannot be removed without bringing the whole house down. In the second place, whether our moral outlooks are inspired by a humanistic vision of life or by a religious perspective, there may be a convergence between these points of departure on the plane of special moral problems" (xiv).

5. Protestant liberal theology comes in many shapes and sizes. By suggesting that Ramsey remained a Protestant liberal, I am primarily locating his conversation partners, i.e., the Niebuhrs. Ramsey's theological views were in many ways quite "conservative," but the structure of his own work assumed the results of Protestant liberalism. He, of course, read and appreciated Barth, but apart from employing the Barthian distinction between the external and internal covenant in *Christian Ethics and the Sit-In* (Ramsey 1961), Ramsey never struggled with the methodological implications of Barth's work.

6. Ramsey returned to these considerations in *Speak Up for Just War or Pacifism*, where he even suggested that "the hour cometh, and now is, when the practices accepted within Methodist hospitals may require the removal of the name 'Methodist' from them—if we are, with our physicians and health-care professionals, resolved to be the church of Jesus Christ" (Ramsey 1988:145).

7. My account of Ramsey's position owes much to D. Stephen Long's work. A revised and expanded version of his dissertation has just been published under the title *Tragedy, Tradition, and Transformism: The Ethics of Paul Ramsey*. I am indebted to Dr. Long for his criticism of this essay (Long 1993).

8. In a later essay, "The Nature of Medical Ethics," he put the matter even more strongly: "In an age, however, when ancient landmarks have been removed, and we are tying to do the unthinkable, namely, build a civilization with an agreed civil tradition and upon the absence of a moral consensus, everyone needs to be an ethicist to the extent of his capacity for reflection and his desire to be and to know that he is a reasonable person" (Ramsey 1973:15).

9. *Basic Christian Ethics* was originally published in 1950. This new edition contains a foreword by Stephen Long and me.

10. In many ways *Nine Modern Moralists* is Ramsey's best book. See, for example, Scott Davis, "'Et Quod Vis Fac': Paul Ramsey and Augustinian Ethics," for a wonderful account of the significance of this book (Davis 1991).

11. In his fine article on Ramsey, "Paul Ramsey's Task: Some Methodological Clarifications and Questions," Paul Camenisch notes that Ramsey is not clear about the origin, authority, and the content of the covenants under which we live. He suggests that Ramsey vacillates between the view that the covenants originate at the will of the agents and the notion that the covenants operate outside the agent's will and are obligatory in themselves. I think Ramsey never thought this ambiguity needed resolution, since he thought the crucial issue was the creation of a livable social order that respected the individual (Camenisch 1974).

References

Beauchamp, T., and Childress, J. 1994. *Principles of Biomedical Ethics*. New York: Oxford University Press.

Bultmann, R. 1958. *Jesus Christ and Mythology*. New York: Charles Scribner's Sons.

Camenisch, P. 1974. "Paul Ramsey's Task: Some Methodological Clarification and Questions." In *Love and Society: Essays in the Ethics of Paul*, ed. Ramsey J. Johnson and D. Smith, 67–90. Missoula, Mont.: Scholars Press.

Davis, S. 1991. "'Et Quod Vis Fac': Paul Ramsey and Augustinian Ethics." *Journal of Religious Ethics* 19, 2 (Fall).

Gustafson, J. 1975. *Can Ethics Be Christian?* Chicago: University of Chicago Press.

_____. 1978. "Theology Confronts Technology and the Life Sciences." *Commonweal* 105 (June 16): 386–392.

Hauerwas, S. 1986. *Suffering Presence: Theological Reflections on Medicine, the Mentally Handicapped, and the Church*. Notre Dame, Ind.: University of Notre Dame Press.

Long, D. Stephen. 1993. *Tragedy, Tradition and Transformism: The Ethics of Paul Ramsey*. Boulder, Colo.: Westview Press.

MacIntyre, A. 1984. *After Virtue*. Notre Dame, Ind.: University of Notre Dame Press.

Milbank, J. 1989. "Between Purgation and Illumination: A Critique of the Theology of Right." In *Christ, Ethics and Tragedy: Essays in Honor of Donald MacKinnon*, ed. Kenneth Surin, 161–196. Cambridge: Cambridge University Press.

Ramsey, P. 1946. "A Theory of Social Action." *Social Action* 23, 2 (October).

_____. 1961. *War and the Christian Conscience: How Shall Modern War Be Conducted Justly?* Durham, N.C.: Duke University Press.

_____. 1962. *Nine Modern Moralists*. Englewood Cliffs, N.J.: Prentice-Hall.

_____. 1970. *The Patient as Person*. New Haven: Yale University Press.

_____. 1973. "The Nature of Medical Ethics." In *The Teaching of Medical Ethics*, ed. R. Veatch, W. Gayline, C. Morgan. Hastings-on-Hudson, N.Y.: Hastings Institute Publications.

_____. 1978. *Ethics at the Edges of Life*. New Haven: Yale University Press.

_____. 1982. "Tradition and Reflection in Christian Life" *Perkins Journal of Theology* 25, 2 (Winter-Spring).

_____. 1988. *Speak Up for Just War and Pacifism*. University Park: Pennsylvania State University Press.

_____. 1990. Letter to Hauerwas. In D. Steven Long, "Whittling Off the Rough Edges: Paul Ramsey's Use of Just War Norms as Theory." Ph.D. Dissertation, Duke University, Durham, N.C.

_____. 1993. [1950]. *Basic Christian Ethics*. Louisville, Ky.: Westminster/John Knox Press.

Rauschenbusch, W. 1907. *Christianity and the Social Crisis*. New York: Macmillan.

_____. 1912. *Christianizing the Social Order*. New York: Macmillan.

PART TWO

"Re-Turning": Gaining an Orientation, Gathering Resources

9

How to Go On When You Know You Are Going to Be Misunderstood, or How Paul Holmer Ruined My Life, or Making Sense of Paul Holmer

N[O ESSAY SHOULD HAVE THREE TITLES]{.smallcaps}, particularly a paper as short as this one, but I could not resist. Each title suggests the importance of Paul Holmer for my own work, so I decided to use all of them. Moreover, the titles are interconnected. Paul Holmer knew how to go on even when no one understood the importance, in Wittgenstein, of knowing how to go on. I did not set out to imitate the misunderstandings Holmer generated, but in many ways it has worked out that way exactly because of what he has taught me. What he has taught me is that you do not need a theory to know how to go on, and indeed, the chances are that if you have a theory, you probably will *not* know how to go on. In short, he has taught me how to make sense of being a Christian in a manner that has forever ruined my life. Accordingly, I want to use this opportunity to suggest why Paul Holmer as a teacher and a writer has been so important for me and for many others as well.

Holmer may well find it surprising, if not disturbing, to discover that he has had such an influence on me. After all, Holmer knew me only as a divinity school student. He did not serve on my doctoral committee. In my first year at Yale Divinity School, I took his course on Kierkegaard and, subsequently, his two-semester course called "Philosophical Theology." In the latter, if I remember correctly, we read Wittgenstein's *Blue and Brown Books* and *Philosophical Investigations* in the first and second semesters respectively. Despite the name of the course, I do not remember that we did any "philosophical theology."

I became a student of Holmer through these courses even though at the time I did not know that I was becoming one. Of course, it is not clear that he ever wanted to cultivate a following or surround himself with students, especially ones like me. Indeed, I have no idea how one could go about becoming one of Holmer's students, since he made it impossible for any student to think he championed a "position" that the student might either accept or reject. Instead, what one learned from Holmer was a kind of attention that comes from knowing when to be quiet or, alternatively, knowing when nothing more can be said.

That Holmer espouses no position is, I suspect, the reason that some may think he lacks influence. Even though he radically altered my life, I do not think there is a footnote anywhere in my work that reads "as we have learned from Paul Holmer." That is not so peculiar as it may at first appear. After all, footnoting Holmer would be just as odd as footnoting Wittgenstein to the effect that the latter allegedly has a "theory about meaning as use." At the very least, I owe Paul Holmer much for his saving me from the presumption that Wittgenstein had any theory about meaning, or anything else for that matter. In this regard, Holmer has been wonderfully successful, like Wittgenstein, in avoiding a following. Testimony to that fact is that we have not as yet seen, for example, a paper in the *Bulletin of the Annual Meeting of the American Academy of Religion* called "Paul Holmer: A Postmodernist Prior to Postmodernism."

Not only was I not a student of Paul Holmer, I seem to remember that our relationship did not start off all that well. I had come to divinity school, not to study for the ministry, but to investigate whether Christianity could be made to conform to the challenges of modernity. I wanted to know if one could be both intellectually clever and a Christian. In short, I was a "smart-ass." Accordingly, I thought my task was to determine how religious claims could be made true by finding a better theory. Such theories, I assumed, would be supplied by philosophy. I was a perfect exemplification of the kind of person Holmer describes in *Theology and the Scientific Study of Religion,* namely, one who confuses an interest in being a Christian with an interest about Christian things (*TSSR,* 16).[1] I recall that we had the following exchange numerous times.

HOLMER: "There's a distinction to be drawn; learning about the things of the faith is not the same as learning to be faithful. But, if that seems too patent, it might be said that theology is the learning *of* faith, not the learning *about* faith. Thus the distinction is drawn with the help of two prepositions, *of* and *about*." (*TSSR,* 12)

HAUERWAS: But where do I find this language "of"?

HOLMER: You read the Bible.

HAUERWAS: But some people tell me to read this part of the Bible and other people tell me to read that part of the Bible.

HOLMER: Well, you need to read a larger context.

HAUERWAS: But some people tell me that this is the larger context, and other people tell me that that is the larger context. What do I do then?

HOLMER: You need to ask your pastor.

HAUERWAS: Some people tell me I should ask this pastor and other people tell me I should ask that pastor. How do I know which pastor to ask?

HOLMER: Stanley, are you sure you are praying enough? And by the way, what is it that you're afraid of?

Slowly but surely I began to understand why prayer might make a difference. In the class on Kierkegaard, I had dimly caught Kierkegaard's insistence that it is not so much a question of what Christians believe as how they believe. As Holmer puts it in *Theology and the Scientific Study of Religion*, "It is a moot question not only *what* people believe but also *how* they believe; for theological believing is largely a matter of how, not what" (*TSSR*, 89). But I confess I thought this emphasis on the "how" might entail being religious and at that time that was the last thing I desired!

Yet Holmer was also slowly changing my idea of what it meant to be religious. He did so by forcing us to read Wittgenstein.[2] I was learning that to become "religious is, in part, a matter of learning a new language" (*TSSR*, 163). Of course, to learn that is only to be placed at the beginning; for we must be de-schooled from the presumption, fostered by much of modern theology, that there is something wrong with first-order religious speech. That means that we must get over the presumption that if our religious language is not working, we must find some way to translate it into another language. I began to understand that if you needed to translate religious language, something had gone wrong—not with the language but with the speaker. Holmer once again captures this well:

> When Christians speak of Jesus as the truth, of the Christian life as the true life, of the Bible as God's truth, they surely do not intend to say that becoming a Christian is a matter of learning true sentences. . . . Truth in the religious sense is not a quality of sentences at all. Religion and Christianity very clearly seek to make men true subjects. Religious truth is not connotative—it is denotative, indicating always that that quality which men can aspire to, for objective truths about that quality are not that quality. There can be no substitute for being the truth, no matter what the quantity of the truth we may possess.[3]

Of course, Holmer's statement does not mean that questions of truth do not matter; instead, it is a reminder that people, not sentences, make truthful claims. Our claims, moreover, are shaped by the way we have learned to speak, and our speech is constituted by concepts that are capacities.[4] What it means to be a self is therefore more like the naming of a set of skills than it is a "what," which should not be surprising once we remember that the self is not so much a name as a relation.

Big words like "God," "sin," and "salvation" are likewise best thought of as capacities, that is, achievements. That means, as Holmer says in *Making Christian Sense*, "Most of us have hardly any concept of God at all."[5] All this began to make me understand why Holmer kept inquiring whether I was praying enough. Indeed, it made me wonder whether I actually ought to go to church for, as he reminds us, "the use of religious language requires participation in the religious life and this involves exposure to the community of believers" (*TSSR*, 109). I suspect that he might now think the word "exposure" far too weak.

Nevertheless, if he is right that theological work is unintelligible when divorced from the practices of the church, what are the implications for how and where theology is done? Some might think Holmer has used powerful philosophical therapies to underwrite a kind of confessionalism. That is another way of saying that he has become a fideistic, sectarian tribalist. But that surely does not follow. Holmer is not in any way committed to the view that Christians can believe just anything they want. Indeed, he would not know what such a description of Christian practices would mean, since to be a Christian requires training in a very definite set of "beliefs." Furthermore, part of the problem is the very language of belief itself; too often beliefs sound like "things" toward which I can assume an attitude. That is why, following McClendon, I resorted to the language of convictions as a reminder that any belief that matters is never something different from who I am.[6]

Yet the presumption persists that Holmer is one of the sources of what is frequently called "Yale fideism." Such a position, it is alleged, attempts to insulate Christian convictions from philosophical and scientific challenge. Not only that, but the Christian convictions so protected are of the most conservative brand. That nothing Holmer has said would entail such characterizations only seems to invite, from those intent on espousing the virtues of "theory," the idea that he must be trying to protect Christian practice from external challenge. That such accusations persist raises the question of how one is to go on in the face of such persistent misunderstanding.

One of the ways I think Holmer has tried to go on is by helping us forget certain kinds of questions—questions like "How can we determine the meaning of God language?" To be sure, such questions are assumed fundamental if theology is to be a respectable academic subject matter. Yet he refuses to privilege such questions, particularly in the abstract, because to try to answer such questions abstractly can only distort the character of theology.

In contrast, I think Holmer has tried to remind us that theology is the attempt to display the kind of lives necessary if we are to speak well of God. But how can that be taught as a subject? Indeed, if you think of theology as assembling a series of reminders about our speech, then it is not at all clear what it would mean for such a discipline to be "systematic." What work is left for the theologian to do, for example, if the concept of God is learned through the telling of the stories of the Old and New Testaments (*TSSR*, 45)?

I have long wondered if my answer to the question, What work is left for the theologian? is different from Holmer's. Of course, such a question may be misshapen, but I ask it as a way to press him to tell me more about the relation between the "what" and the "how." Holmer is right: The "what" can never be abstracted from the "how." But the relation is surely complex. For instance, I take it to be one of the most momentous decisions by Christians about the "what" to include the Old Testament as Christian Scripture. That is not simply a "result" we can assume. We must certainly regard it as gift, but a gift that must be constantly reclaimed if the church is to live faithfully. The Christian attitude toward and persecution of the Jews through history is an indication that we have not faithfully renegotiated that "what." I am not suggesting that Holmer lacks resources to consider this kind of question, but I remain unclear about what the sort of work that some Christian communities call "doctrine" does or should do.[7]

Using the phrase "some Christian communities" is, of course, to put the question (or questions) in another way. Holmer often seems to presume that there is agreement among Christians concerning the "what." He is right to do so because I think a phrase like "the Christian tradition" does name the ongoing consensus we rightly call catholic. Yet I am not sure Holmer shares that presumption—he is just so Protestant. In short, I wish that I more fully understood the ways in which what I learned from him help me better negotiate doctrinal and ecclesiological issues.

Of course, my way of trying to "have" a position—that is, a place to explore such questions while at the same time being paid for such explorations—was to become an "ethicist." I still remember being confronted by Holmer on his learning that I was planning to do a Ph.D. in Christian Ethics at Yale. He made it very clear to me that there was no such subject and that to the extent that I was successful in pursuing such a subject, I was going to waste my life. What was I to do, since I had decided to go in that direction because of what I had learned from him and, I should also add, from Julian Hartt?

I had decided to become an ethicist, ugly as the word is, because Holmer had convinced me that Kierkegaard had rediscovered "the pragmatic significance of the person of Jesus Christ" (*TSSR*, 203). I thought that "doing ethics" was a way to explicate the practical significance of learning to talk well as a Christian. I assumed, moreover, that ethics was a way to explore the truthful character of Christian speech, or better, how

Christian speech requires us to develop the skills to be truthful. At the very least, ethics seemed to name the investigation of how we were to live.

In order to pursue this task, I was forced to provide a different account of "ethics" than that supplied by the prevailing Kantian (and liberal) paradigms. I had the good luck to be at Yale, where the influence of H. Richard Niebuhr persisted.[8] I was not particularly taken with Niebuhr's "radical monotheism," impressed as I was by Barth, but I did learn from Niebuhr (and Gustafson) that history and the communities that constituted memory matter morally. So focused, I discovered the significance of Aristotle's account of virtue, believing as I did that the virtues named those habits (qualities) necessary for us to be agents of memory. It was long after I left Yale that I even became aware that Holmer had begun to teach a course on the virtues. I should like to think that is an example of "great minds thinking alike," but I suspect the discovery of the importance of the virtues for understanding and living morally was the result of following hints in Wittgenstein and his followers, such as Anscombe.

I confess I had no idea that these motifs—virtue, narrative, memory, vision, and description—would force me to be so . . . well—Christian! I have, accordingly, always felt something of a fraud. I certainly do not think of myself as much of a Christian, but then the very way I have been taught to think means that it is not all that important how I (or anyone else) think or feel about who I am. More important is that we make our lives available and answerable to those whose lives are more faithful than our thoughts.

Such words sound like very bad advice to many. Questions multiply, such as, How do you know you are in the right community? We are not in just one community, I am told, but our lives are constituted by multiple communities and narratives. Does that not need to be acknowledged? Moreover, how are we to test the truth of the many narratives that claim us? When all is said and done, one can be asked, Are you not a "confessionalist" who simply prefers Christianity?

Though my questioners and critics will not believe it, I have assiduously and conscientiously tried to respond to such interrogations. My responses are, I fear, seldom satisfying because I find that often I cannot respond in a manner that legitimates the presuppositions behind their questions. For example, I wrote "A Tale of Two Stories: On Being a Christian and a Texan" as a kind of response to the observation that we are never constituted by just one story.[9] There I tried concretely to show how two (at least) narratives could come into conflict for the Christian and how such a conflict could be adjudicated and, more important, lived. Yet as far as I know, this essay stilled no questions, since my "answer" did not show how such conflicts could, in principle, be resolved. What can I say? I simply know of no way in which that can be done "in principle."

Nor do I know how one knows "in principle" that one is in the right community. What I am sure about is that it is not by some "choice." For any significant participation in a community like the church, "choice" is a far too misleading description. Again, I tried to address questions about communities in essays like "On Taking Religion Seriously: The Challenge of Jonestown."[10] Once more, I must report a complete lack of success. I realize this lack is partly my fault, as most do not think questions of truth are rightfully considered in discussions concerning Jonestown or even suicide. But that is where I think questions regarding the nature of communities, truth, and why it makes all the difference how and what God we worship are unavoidably interrelated. It is my contention, in other words, that a tradition without the description "suicide" (or worse, without the prohibition of suicide) can be neither truthful nor good. Of course, a community with such a description may be perverse in other ways or use the description perversely, but such judgments can be made only within practices of sufficient narrative thickness and complexity of which suicide is one.

Those are some of the ways I have tried to work, "to do ethics," as a cover for theological reflection. Yet I have to acknowledge that Holmer was right. I have not been able to get away with it! In spite of my best efforts, certain "predictable" but misleading questions continue to be asked, such as What is the relationship between theology and ethics? No matter how many times you suggest to those who raise such queries that the very presumption that there must be a relationship between being religious and being moral reproduces a mistake, the question returns. I would like to blame Holmer for at least some of my woes. He is partly responsible for the fact that I have had to endure this continuing misunderstanding—but then it is not really his fault that I tried, by becoming an ethicist, to make an end run around the establishment and got caught!

If Holmer is partially responsible for my continued frustrations, it is because he has borne plenty of his own. After all, he has had to live with his own forms of being misunderstood, so why should I expect to do any better? Holmer has a way of saying simple things simply, so that we miss their significance. Take, for example, his suggestion, quoted above, that most of us have hardly any concept of God. Such a claim cannot help but appear mystifying to those schooled on apologetic strategies designed to make "religion" an unavoidable aspect of the human condition. However, rightly understanding that claim requires, according to Holmer, a sense of participation in a community that transforms our lives, lives that would be unintelligible if the God we worship were not to exist. Yet most people want their God (or gods) to be available with mediation.

One might expect that Holmer would therefore take a quite critical perspective on most forms of Protestant liberal theology. Yet he has charitable things to say, for instance, about Rudolf Bultmann. He notes that in one place Bultmann seems to be saying that the language of the Bible is not the language of science—which is surely a good thing to say. But when Bultmann goes on to remark that biblical language is mythological, Holmer observes that that is not only not a good thing to say but it is an unnecessary thing to say. "It is not really necessary nor illuminating to say this" (*TSSR*, 191). Think about that: Such claims are not "necessary"— which is another way of saying they are simply not "illuminating."

What a wonderfully exact way to put the matter! In order to understand biblical language, we do not need to engage in speculation about what is "myth." We do not need to try to figure out whether Jesus' resurrection is a historical or semihistorical claim, and so on. It is not as if we are trying to avoid appropriate questions: Rather, Holmer reminds us that nothing is more misleading than to try to answer a misshapen question. That, I take it, is part of the reason it is so hard to make sense of him. He wants to force us to do the hard work that makes it possible to put simple things simply.

I cannot pretend that I have learned that lesson well. I am still possessed by more theories than are good for me. Yet I should like to think that the lessons I learned from Holmer about simplicity have, over the years, become habits. The significance of habits is, to be sure, another lesson I have learned from him. This is a lesson, I might add, that has everything to do with why prayer and theology cannot be separated.

Such a lesson may make it hard for anyone who would seek to make theology just another subject in the curriculum of the modern university. Although there are many who have yet to learn this hard lesson and who thus persist in so misconstruing theology, that is no great loss. For Holmer's lessons make being a theologian a happy task. Whatever "center" there may be to my work, it has in some small way something to do with his reminder, echoing Guardini: namely, that faith is extraordinarily complex.

> By saying that faith is not merely this or that, Guardini has succeeded in convincing his readers that it is both this and that and much more besides. To remit the beliefs by retaining the morality, as did Matthew Arnold and so many others who wanted to be up to date, appears to be a bit of fatuousness on the part of the learned. To admit the beliefs and to talk of the ways of God while living the pedestrian ways of men is the faithlessness of the faithful. Faith is, even for modern men, a new kind of integrity. Because it is integrity it is also rare. Faith is no more out of date than is integrity. Guardini's diatribe against the world as well as the church is to the effect that this integrity is no longer properly discerned to be what it is. Because men are replete with the diversity of powers and drives there is a continuing case for the ordering of men. Guardini is bold enough to assert that the new life in Christ is a kind of wholeness and unity which is not of men but of God. (*TSSR*, 112)

Just as Holmer has taught us to see how crazy we would be to live in the world without the virtues,[11] so some of us shaped by him have tried to show how we would be crazy not to live our lives as Christians. The little success we have had in that endeavor owes everything to Paul Holmer, who continues to remind us that nothing is more destructive for Christian witness than the pedestrian ways many of us who would be Christian live and think.

Notes

1. Paul Holmer, *Theology and the Scientific Study of Religion* (Minneapolis: T. S. Denison, 1961). Page references to this work will appear in the text preceded by *TSSR*.

2. I make no pretense to being a Wittgensteinian scholar, but I cannot (nor would I even want to) disown the influence Wittgenstein has had on my work. I find, however, that I am often at odds with those who claim to be using Wittgenstein in theology. He is often used to support what I can describe only as a kind of "linguistic idealism of constructivism," which I find to be diametrically opposed to his spirit. In this respect, I find Cora Diamond's account of Wittgenstein in *The Realistic Spirit: Wittgenstein, Philosophy, and the Mind* (Cambridge: MIT Press, 1995) much closer to my way of reading Wittgenstein. Raymond Gaita notes that one of Wittgenstein's central lessons is to warn us "against a false sense of depth and against a false sense of appearances." *Good and Evil: An Absolute Conception* (London: Macmillan, 1991), p. 169.

3. Paul Holmer, "Christianity and the Truth," *Lutheran Quarterly* 9, 1 (February 1957): 40.

4. Richard Rollefson, "Thinking with Kierkegaard and Wittgenstein: The Philosophical Theology of Paul L. Holmer" (Ph.D. Diss., Graduate Theological Union, 1994), p. 38.

5. Paul Holmer, *Making Christian Sense* (Philadelphia: Westminster Press, 1984), p. 118.

6. I am referring to James William McClendon and James M. Smith, *Convictions: Defusing Religious Relativism*, rev. ed. (Valley Forge, Pa.: Trinity Press International, 1994).

7. David Keck wonderfully exhibits my attitude toward doctrine. He notes two reasons for revering doctrine: "First, as a historian, I am astounded by its endurance through the centuries. Many impressive thoughts have not survived, and many that have, have lost all power today. Second, and more personally, I am thankful for doctrine because I believe that only through the faithful transmission of the church's traditional teaching is it possible for me to have hope for my mother; for my father, her primary caregiver; and for the rest of the world which suffers from sunrise to sunset. Hence, as I use the term, orthodoxy is not only about doctrine or guiding principles; it also denotes a kind of existence to be desired in itself. Orthodoxy is a longing to align one's own life and memories with the life and memories of the church." *Forgetting Whose We Are: Alzheimer's Disease and the Love of God* (Nashville: Abingdon, 1996), p. 82.

8. H. R. Niebuhr died the year before I arrived at Yale to begin what was then called a B.D.

9. That essay is the first chapter of my *Christian Existence Today: Essays on Church, World, and Living in Between* (Durham: Labyrinth Press, 1988), pp. 25–46. *Christian Existence Today* is now published by Baker Books.

10. That essay appears in my *Against the Nations: War and Survival in a Liberal Society* (Notre Dame: University of Notre Dame Press, 1992), pp. 91–107. *Against the Nations* was first published by Winston Press in 1985. I am indebted to Rev. Dr. Samuel Wells for reminding me what I was trying to do in that essay. See his "How the Church Performs the Jesus Story: Improvising on the Theological Ethics of Stanley Hauerwas" (Ph.D. Thesis, University of Durham, England, 1995), pp. 78–81.

11. Holmer, *Making Christian Sense*, p. 72.

PART THREE

"Journeying On": Life on the Road,
or the Long Journey Homeward

10 *Murdochian Muddles: Can We Get Through Them If God Does Not Exist?*

On Stealing from Murdoch

"I can only choose within the world I can *see,* in the moral sense of 'see' which implies that clear vision is a result of moral imagination and moral effort" (*S,* 37).[1] How I love that sentence from Iris Murdoch's *The Sovereignty of Good.* Actually, that is to put the matter in a misleading fashion. Not only do I love that sentence, I have made a career out of that sentence. Indeed, I sometimes wonder if I have ever said anything of importance that was not stolen from Dame Iris. That I have stolen much from Murdoch is without question, but the question I wish to investigate in this essay is whether I have, as a Christian theologian, been wise in having done so. The issue can be nicely put by reading Vernon Bourke's review of my book *Vision and Virtue: Essays in Christian Ethical Reflection.*[2] The review is but a paragraph long and I cite the whole so you can get its full flavor:

> The articles gathered here have been published before in various theological journals. Hauerwas studied at Southwestern University and is now director of graduate studies in theology at Notre Dame. His point of view seems to be non-denominationally Christian: when he speaks of "the church," he means all of Christendom. Ranging over a broad field, the essays pay some attention to the general character of truly Christian ethics but show most interest in specific problems such as abortion, euthanasia, treatment of the retarded, and pacifism. On these issues Hauerwas displays wide reading (chiefly in liberal Protestant and left-wing Catholic moralists) and an open mind. Indeed his mind is so open that his own views are rarely apparent. On abortion, for instance, he criticizes Callahan, Ramsey, and Grisez, says the conceptus may be viewed as human, but then concludes that other accounts are possible. There is a latent anti-intellectualism running throughout. Hauerwas is not convinced that human understanding can solve the difficult moral problems. The "vision" mentioned in the title and at various

points owes a good deal to Iris Murdoch's estheticism. How an avowed atheist, like Miss Murdoch, can contribute to Christian ethics is an enigma.[3]

I confess that when I read this review, now almost twenty years ago, I thought this guy had to be crazy. Of course a Christian theologian can use an atheist[4]—particularly one as subtle as Miss Murdoch. Bourke had apparently never read Murdoch and therefore had no appreciation for her intriguing account of the ontological argument. Moreover, Aquinas used Aristotle in his work, which provides good precedence for theologians' using in their own work thinkers who were not Christian theists.

I thought that the differences between Murdoch and me had little to do with her atheism. Instead, my disagreements with her, if in fact they existed, had much more to do with her Platonism versus my Aristotelian propensities. I confess I was not anxious then or later to explore that difference, but I suspected it also had something to do with her attraction to and my dislike of mysticism. Quite simply, I thought the difference between us could be stated as follows: Whereas Dame Iris contends that "we develop language in the context of looking" (*S*, 33), I was convinced (and I thought I had learned this from Wittgenstein) that we can only see what we have been trained to see through learning to say.[5]

Yet even in that respect I was not sure how different our views were, since she emphasized that truthful seeing, that is, seeing that is able to combine "just modes of judgment and the ability to connect with an increased perception of detail," comes to those formed by the virtue of honesty (*S*, 96). No doubt, as Murdoch so ably depicts in many of her novels, such honest seeing often must be forced on us, sunk as we are in our fantasies. Nonetheless, a training in any skill has the potential to transform our imagination so that we can see more truthfully. To be sure, Murdoch's virtues never seem as "habitual" as we Aristotelians think they need to be, but that seems like a minor matter.[6]

Yet now, after twenty years of stealing from Dame Iris, I am not as convinced as I once was that Bourke's "enigma" deserves little, if any, scrutiny. When I first read Miss Murdoch, I was so impressed that her enemies were also my enemies that I may have failed to appreciate the fact that having common enemies does not necessarily make one friends. For example, in *The Sovereignty of Good* she quite rightly observes that Hume and Kant, each in his own way, abhor history (26). I took that to be an opening for Christian theological discourse. Now I am not so sure that I was right. As I will try to show, because we Christians are truly convinced of our creatureliness, we are more "historical" than Dame Iris believes is wise.[7] The redemption that Christians believe God has offered is not a "mystical" possibility, but one that is made possible only because of and through the Jews.

I realized, upon reaching the next to last page of *Metaphysics as a Guide to Morals*, that I would have to interrogate my adherence to Dame Iris's work. What bothered me was not her suggestion that "we need a theology which can continue without God" (*M*, 511). Such a claim comes as no surprise for those familiar with her work. Rather, what bothered me there, but also earlier in the book, was her positive appreciation of Paul Tillich's work. Her friend Tillich is my sworn enemy—thus the impetus to investigate the "enigma."

I wish to be clear about how I am approaching this task. My primary purpose is not to criticize Murdoch. My intention, rather, is to explore Murdoch's account of why she believes that we can no longer believe in the Christian God. I do so in order to test the extent to which her rich insights can be appropriated by those of us who work as Christian theologians. I hope this will be a particularly useful exercise, as I am normally willing, under severe distress, to expose my own metaphysical and ontological claims.[8] I begin, then, by affirming Murdoch's claim that "metaphysical systems have consequences" (*M*, 197). Indeed, showing how her metaphysics and ethics are interrelated is, I believe, a helpful way of underlining the difference the Christian account of creation ex nihilo makes for the Christian moral life.

In order not to keep you in suspense, I will state my argument baldly. Murdoch's account of the moral life cannot be appropriated uncritically by Christian theologians for the simple reason that her understanding of the "muddles" that constitute our lives is correlative to a metaphysics that we as Christians cannot accept. Christians believe that our lives are at once more captured by sin and yet sustained by a hope that, given Murdoch's account of the world, cannot help but appear false.[9] Moreover, Christian understanding of sin and hope is correlative to an account of creation that sustains a teleological vision of the world and our place in it.[10] Accordingly, Christians ask more of ourselves and our world than, I think, Murdoch can believe is warranted.

The problem with this comparative procedure, of course, is that there is no news in it. Miss Murdoch has always been admirably candid concerning her impatience with (and hence has little use for) religious myths—in particular, those associated with Christianity. She has always been, with some qualification, on the side of those intent on demythologizing Christian discourse. So it will not come as any great surprise to discover that Murdoch does not believe that the Jews are God's promised people or that Christ's resurrection inaugurates the end time. Yet I hope to show that Christians are not simply left with "so you believe this and I believe that." Instead, we are left with the very character of our lives, which, I would argue, gives us a basis for thinking that Christians might be creatures with purposes that we ourselves did not create.

Murdoch on Christianity and God

Miss Murdoch's reflections on Christianity are intricate and, I believe, in-terrelated in an intricate manner. I, therefore, need to display her views about Christianity in the hope of making sure that I am not misrepresent-ing her. Miss Murdoch simply begins with the observation that in our age the influence of what might be called orthodox Christianity is waning rapidly (*S*, 75). She offers us no extended account of why this may be, but calls our attention to Don Cupitt's observation that humankind is just now emerging from its "mythological childhood." Accordingly, religion has to come to terms with autonomy (*M*, 452).[11]

Her account, in this respect, is not unlike that of Charles Taylor in *Sources of the Self*.[12] What Taylor helps us see is that most people simply do not decide to stop believing in God as Trinity or in creation ex nihilo. Rather, they gradually or suddenly realize that the "sources" that once made such beliefs intelligible are no longer in place. One may still "be-lieve" such things, but they simply do not matter any more. That is an-other way of saying that the practices that made such matters an integral part of life are no longer existent. Indeed, exactly because these practices have atrophied or have vanished altogether, some insist that holding such beliefs as beliefs, particularly if they are held sincerely or enthusias-tically, is so important.

I think this kind of atheism is what Dame Iris is suggesting when she asks rhetorically, "Do not a large number of those who go to church *al-ready think* in a new non-literal way without bothering about theology and metaphysics?" (*M*, 458–459). The answer is obviously "Yes." But the far more interesting question is "Why?" Unfortunately, Murdoch does not provide thick accounts of how this came about, although she does of-fer the following observation:

> The Cartesian era is coming to an end. Wittgenstein said that he was ending it. In moral philosophy it may appear that the Kantian era is coming to an end. Theology not only reflects these problems but is forced to struggle with them in ways which bring it closer to philosophy now than it has been for some time. This is so in spite of, and partly in reaction to, the fact that in a materialistic technological society, theology might be expected to be increas-ingly isolated from general trends of thought. (*M*, 38–39)

The story of how theological claims are made to bear the burden of proof in light of certain social and intellectual developments is obviously complex, but I think the broad outlines of Murdoch's position are clear. What is especially interesting is that the very developments that have made traditional Christian theological claims unintelligible are also im-plicated in the legitimation of precisely those accounts of the moral life

Murdoch finds so disastrous. That is, the peculiar combination of behaviorist, existentialist, and utilitarian accounts of the moral life Murdoch so trenchantly criticizes in *The Sovereignty of Good* (*S*, 4–15) is produced by the same forces that have made Christianity unintelligible to itself.

Therefore, Murdoch's case against Christianity is not that fewer and fewer people in the modern West still believe or, perhaps more accurately put, that even if they wanted to be Christian, they would have no idea what that would mean. Her position is considerably stronger. She wants in fact to replace Christianity because she believes she has a better alternative. Murdoch thinks that her alternative is friendly to Christianity. She even describes herself as a "neo-Christian or Buddhist Christian or Christian fellow traveller" who believes that

> Christianity can continue without a personal God or a risen Christ, without beliefs in supernatural places and happenings, such as heaven and life after death, but retaining the mystical figure of Christ occupying a place analogous to that of Buddha: a Christ who can console and save, but who is to be found as a living force within each human soul and not in some supernatural elsewhere. Such a continuity would preserve and renew the Christian tradition as it has always hitherto, somehow or other, been preserved and renewed. It has always changed itself into something that can be generally believed.[13] (*M*, 419)

I have, of course, been spending a good part of my life trying to make Christianity hard to be "generally believed." Therefore, when Dame Iris offers to help Christians redescribe their convictions in a "naturalistic" fashion, I am less than convinced. For example, she notes that "the idea of another's suffering as redemptive is certainly intelligible. Christians may tend to connect it with Christ and see lesser human efforts as an *imitatio Christi*, but redemption can exist without God" (*M*, 131). I have no doubt that such a redemption does exist, but I also think that redemption so understood has little to do with the redemption found in Christ's cross and resurrection. To be sure, such a counterassertion requires spelling out, but at this point I only wish to suggest that Murdoch's attempt to "save" Christianity involves a substitution of one religion for another. What is worrisome about Dame Iris, in other words, is not that she is an atheist, but that she is too religious.

For Murdoch, religion is about "the change of being attendant upon our deepest and highest concern with morality" (*M*, 183). She suggests, for instance, that we cannot live without the exercise of prayer. "But, someone may say, what can we do now that there is no God? This does not affect what is mystical. The loss of prayer, through the loss of belief in God, is a great loss. However, a *general* answer is a practice of meditation: a withdrawal, through some disciplined quietness, into the great chamber of the soul. Just sitting quiet will help. Teach it to children" (*M*, 73). Or perhaps better, learn it from children, who have the extraordinary capacity to see this single blade of grass or this rock in all of its particularity. Such is the attitude of prayer.[14]

Prayer is an attention to God that is a form of love. "God was (or is) a *single perfect transcendent non-representable and necessarily real object of attention*" (*S*, 55). It is the task of moral philosophy to retain such a central concept, that is, the good, without that concept's offering us false consolation of a premature unity. For the great enemy of the moral life is "personal fantasy: the tissue of self-aggrandizing and consoling wishes and dreams which prevents one from seeing what is there outside one" (*S*, 59). That is why art is so crucial. For by experiencing the transcendence of the beautiful, we are called out of our fantasies (*S*, 60). Art can be the occasion for training us to see this or that rock, or this or that person, free from the fantasies of who they should be for "us."

Our muddles are the result of our self-absorption. Those that people Iris Murdoch's novels always seem to love the wrong person or get caught in nets of illusion. That they (and we along with them) are so caught reflects our condition, a condition rightly described by Freud (though Murdoch says she is no Freudian) and equivalent to the doctrine of original sin. The psyche is but "an egocentric system of quasi-mechanical energy, largely determined by its own individual history, whose natural attachments are sexual, ambiguous, and hard for the subject to understand or control. Introspection reveals only the deep tissue of ambivalent motive, and fantasy is a stronger force than reason. Objectivity and unselfishness are not natural to human beings" (*S*, 51).

It does no good, as most of modern moral philosophy presumes, to try to will our way out of our illusions, for such "willing" simply mires us deeper in fantasies of freedom. What is needed is a violent jolting. Such a jolting can come from a near drowning in a sea cave or from the presence of an avatar whose mysteriousness cannot be explained. The trick, of course, is to accept without explanation the gift of dislocation provided by the avatar. To be able so to live is to begin to live virtuously.

This all too brief summary of Iris Murdoch's understanding of morality helps locate her greatest objection to Christianity. The problem with Christianity is not the mythological character of its belief, but its tendency, like other totalizing metaphysical theories, to destroy the contingent. By "equating reality with integration in system, and degrees of reality with degrees of integration, and by implying that 'ultimately' or 'really' there is only one system," one loses the contingent character of the particular, which is also the source as well as the necessity of mysticism (*M*, 196).

The purification of virtue, characteristic of the mystic, derives from the mystic's refusal to be consoled. What must be acknowledged, in other words, is that morality has no point. Kant rightly insisted on the purposiveness of art without purpose, finality without end.

> The "true saint" believes in "God" but not as a super-person who satisfies all our ordinary desires "in the end." (There is no end, there is no reward.) This has also to do with time, how we live it. It is a religious position where the concept of God is in place, indeed, in a fundamental sense, defined. A proper understanding of contingency apprehends chance and its horrors, not as fate, but as an aspect of death, of the frailty and unreality of the ego and the emptiness of worldly desires. So, our evil part is condemned "not to suffering but to death." (I expressed this once in an aphorism: the false god punishes, the true god slays.) (*M*, 106–107)

The problem with much art and religious myth is that they have the effect, and it is an intended effect, of concealing the fact of death and the absolute contingency of existence, which is a correlative of death (*M*, 139). Even tragedy can console, but only if, while drawing on death, it breaks the ego and thus destroys the illusory whole of the unified self (*M*, 104). "Almost anything that consoles us is a fake" (*S*, 59), including the presumption that we are consoled by the knowledge that anything that consoles us is a fake.

Murdoch is admirably clear that her morality is a metaphysics, though she might prefer to say that metaphysics is a guide to her morality. Just as the mystics have understood that God cannot be pictured, that in the end everything, including God, must be given up, so too the good cannot be depicted. She employs the language of the ontological argument to argue that God (the Good) cannot simply be one thing among others, but exists of necessity (*M*, 470). Hence, the ontological argument becomes the metaphysical expression of the pointless character of morality.

Such a "proof" cannot be a proof exactly, but only a "clear assertion of faith" made on the basis of a certain kind of experience. Such an experience is the

> authority of the Good [which] seems to us something necessary because the realism (ability to perceive reality) required for goodness is a kind of intellectual ability to perceive what is true, which is automatically at the same time a suppression of self. *The necessity of the good is then an aspect of the kind of necessity involved in any technique for exhibiting fact.* In thus treating realism, whether of artist or of agent, as a moral achievement, there is of course a further assumption to be made in the fields of morals: that true vision occasions right conduct. This could be uttered simply as an enlightening tautology: but I think it can in fact be supported by appeals to experience. The more the separateness and differentness of other people is realized, and the fact seen that another man has needs and wishes as demanding as one's own, the harder it becomes to treat a person as a thing. That it is realism which makes great art great remains too as a kind of proof. (*S*, 66)

Our experience of the Good is derived, not from high or general ways of understanding, but from the experience present in its most minute relations and within our perceptions of the minutest things (stones, spoons, leaves, scraps of rubbish, tiny gestures, and so on) and the capacity they create for being deeper, more benevolent, more just (*M,* 474). The myth that best exhibits the ontology of our experience of the Good is that of the Demiurge. In contrast to accounts of creation ex nihilo, the Demiurge creates the cosmos with love toward the forms. In creating, the Demiurge makes use of necessity to which we must submit, as well as understand and use, if we are to be both good and happy.

This creation myth, the myth of the Demiurge,

> represents in the most elegant way the redemption of all particular things which are, although made of contingent stuff, touched and handled by the divine. The contingent can become spiritually significant, even beautiful, as in art, as in Simone Weil's idea of the beauty of the world as an image of obedience. Plato's myths are the redemption of art. This is an aspect of the return to the Cave, where illusions are not only rejected but understood. (*M,* 477)

The Demiurge is the paradigmatic artist making beauty out of necessity. The Demiurge teaches us that we must finally learn to love our death, or better, see our death as necessary for us to love.

In the light of this creation myth, we can see better why the ontological argument binds together Murdoch's metaphysics and ethics. The argument displays the necessary nonexistence of God.

> No existing thing could be what we have meant by God. Any existing God would be less than God. An existent God would be an idol or a demon. (This is near to Kant's thinking.) God does not and cannot exist and is *constantly* experienced and pictured. That is, it is real as an Idea, and is *also* incarnate in knowledge and work and love. This is the true idea of incarnation, and is not something obscure. We *experience* both the reality of perfection and its distance away, and this leads us to place our idea of it outside the world of existent being as something of a different unique and special sort. (*M,* 508)

Creation ex Nihilo, Sin, and Hope

That Murdoch rightly describes her account of morality as entailing the myth of the Demiurge should give pause to Christians who have been influenced by her work, not the least myself. Indeed, I wonder whether we Christians should even refrain from reading her novels, since they so powerfully form our imagination, urging us to see our lives in her terms. She is, after all, quite right. Art has "helped us to *believe,* not only in Christ and the Trinity, but in the Good Samaritan, the Prodigal Son, innumerable saints and a whole cast of famous and well-loved scenes and persons" (*M*, 82). Whether it is good for the Christian imagination to have that art renarrated in a manner that may make the Christian understanding of creation unintelligible for us is therefore no mere idle issue.[15]

Before such questions can be explored, however, I need at least to attempt to suggest why Christians rightly embrace the doctrine of creation ex nihilo and what difference it makes for understanding our ontological and moral commitments. It will be apparent that in trying to make this case, I remain in Murdoch's debt. For without Murdoch's defense of the ontological argument, I suspect I would have never understood the significance of Aquinas's rejection of that argument.

Aquinas's comment on the ontological argument is quite interesting. He begins by noting that not everyone who hears the word "God" understands it to signify that than which nothing greater can be thought. Yet even if everyone so understood the word, "it does not follow that he understands that what the word signifies exists actually, but only that it exists in the intellect. Nor can it be argued that it actually exists, unless it be admitted that there actually exists something that than which nothing greater can be thought. And this is what is not admitted by those who hold that God does not exist"[16] (*ST*, la. 2. 1. ad. 1). He then goes on to observe that whereas it is self-evident that truth in general exists, the existence of a First Truth is not self-evident to us.

Aquinas's objection to the ontological argument is not that existence cannot be a predicate (Kant), but rather that the intellect cannot have a priori knowledge of God's nature. Any Being whose essence is existence cannot be known through the idea of such a being, but rather through arguments from its effects. If God's existence is to be "proved," therefore, it must be through an examination of God's effects. I have no intention to explore how Aquinas's "five ways" should be interpreted in the light of this presumption.[17] More interesting for the case I am trying to make is why Aquinas must take this stance, given his understanding of the gratuity of God's creation.

In this regard, I am following David Burrell's contention that Aquinas's "proofs" are rightly understood against the background of the doctrine of creation ex nihilo. Burrell argues that creation ex nihilo for Aquinas (and Maimonides) is not in itself derived from a reading of Genesis, but rather

> the notion of absolute beginning was a sign of the difference between believers in scripture and neoplatonist advocates of eternal emanation, rather than itself marking that difference. Creation *ex nihilo* underscored the fact that the very existence of such a dependent universe did not belong to the nature of divinity but represented a free initiative on God's part, for if the universe were without beginning, it would be more natural to think of it as the necessary concomitant of its creator.[18]

Creation ex nihilo is the correlate of the Jewish and Christian view that the existence of all that is, is the result of a free decision of God. Exactly what was at stake was the issue of the necessity with which the universe "emanated from the One," and the consequent necessity characteristic of the universe itself. "It is the freedom of divinity to act, in creating and in revealing, which constitutes the nub of the notion of creator which both Maimonides and Aquinas consider to be the deliverance of the scriptures. And if that freedom means primarily that the act of creating is a spontaneous and gracious one, then the God who so creates is fulfilling no natural need and has nothing to gain thereby."[19]

In the same article, Aquinas argues that the world offers no grounds for demonstrating that it was once new. "For the principle for demonstrating an object is its definition. Now the specific nature of each and every object abstracts from the here and now, which is why universals are described as being everywhere and always (Aristotle). Hence it cannot be demonstrated that man, or heaven, or a stone did not always exist" (*ST*, 1.46.2). Nor can creation be demonstrated through efficient causation. The will of God can only be investigated through those things God must will of necessity, but what God wills about creatures is not among these. That the world began to exist is therefore an object of faith and not of demonstration or science. The article concludes appropriately with the following warning: "And it is useful to consider this, lest anyone should bring forward reasons that are not cogent, so as to give occasion to unbelievers to laugh, thinking that on such reasons we believe things that are of faith."

Reinhard Hütter nicely sums up Christian thinking on creation, and I think Aquinas's as well, by suggesting that

> "ex nihilo" has to be understood as a graceful, contingent and finite gift of God who was not in need of the world. There is no lack or insufficiency in God that needs the creating of the world to overcome it. Creation is the overflow of God's abundant love as reflected in the inner life of the triune God. "Ex nihilo" is a strictly theological predication of God. It secures God's transcendence over against the world.[20]

From the perspective of creation ex nihilo, Murdoch's account of necessity and contingency is reversed. The task, therefore, is not to see the particular as necessary, but to see the contingent as just that—contingent—or more accurately, in Christian language, as created. For the whole point is that the world, and our existence in the world, does not have to exist, but it and we do. The task is not to see the purposelessness in the sheer existence of the contingent, but rather to see the contingent as "gift" whose purpose is to praise the creator.[21] Such a task does not mean that the otherness of the contingent is obliterated by its place in a larger purpose, but that its contingency can be enjoyed because God so enjoys God's creation.[22]

That all God has created praises God as creator does not obliterate the otherness of other creatures, but rather helps us see our own "otherness" in God's other creatures.

> The "others" are other to us inasmuch as we are other to them. Respect of and care for all of God's creatures is the primary means of doxological acknowledgment of God the Creator in creation. The very plurality of cultures, traditions, languages, and species is to be welcomed as the wealth of created otherness. Creation *"ex nihilo"* undercuts uniform secularity, in which consumer subjects and objects are exploited and from which God is utterly absent.[23]

In contrast to Murdoch's account of the absolute pointlessness of existence, Christians believe that God means for all creation to worship God. Such a "purpose," however, does not mean that all that we do is guaranteed to "come out all right." "Purpose," understood doxologically, can only be displayed by a narrative that is subject to constant retelling, given the contingent character of our existence. We do not know what will happen next, but more important, we do not even know how we will need to retell "what happened," since the past, no less than the future, must remain open to renarration. The "purpose" that sustains the Christian is eschatological because we believe that creation names not just a beginning but God's continuing providential care of creation. Creation for us is not only "in the beginning" but continuing, ongoing.

We are, no doubt, possessed and blinded by the "fat relentless ego" so wonderfully depicted by Murdoch. That we are so afflicted, moreover, results in muddles from which we cannot, by a sheer act of will, free ourselves. The problem with Murdoch's muddles is not simply that we lack the resources to be free of them if God does not exist, but that the full reality of such muddles remains unarticulated in a world without God. For the Christian, "sin" names the training we must undergo to discover that our lives are possessed by powers, by narratives, whose purpose it is to hide from us the fact that we are creatures of a gracious God. Such "knowledge" does not come "naturally," but rather from being made part of a community with practices that offer the transformation and reordering of our lives and relationships. Prayer is certainly one of those practices, but Christians begin their prayers with "Our Father," a practice that goes on to instruct us to seek forgiveness and reconciliation with God and our neighbor. Only through such a reconciliation do we believe we can fully acknowledge our contingency and particularity.

Christian salvation, then, is not "mystical," but comes through the ordinary. Murdoch rightly calls attention to the wisdom of "ordinary people," who know that prayer can induce a better quality of consciousness and provide an energy for good action otherwise unavailable (*S*, 83). But "ordinary people" called Christian also know that they must learn to pray together in communities that will teach them to pray rightly. Prayer, after all, is not a self-authenticating "spiritual exercise," but a practice that becomes intelligible only as we learn to acknowledge our existence as forgiven creatures. Murdoch's world is finally too lonely for those of us called Christian, those of us who believe that we were created to be friends with God and, consequently, with one another and even our-selves. No doubt the Christian story, like any significant story, can be used and is often used to offer false consolation. But as Murdoch demon-strates, often in her novels, our hedge against false consolation, against self-deception, cannot be found in ourselves. We cannot will our way out of our fantasies. Our only escape must come to us externally. Christians believe that God supplies such "externality" by making available to us friendships and practices correctly embodied in a community called church. A people who know their salvation and have been secured through Jesus' cross and resurrection are, accordingly, required to live by resisting the false consolations of this world.

Where Does This Leave Us?

All I have done is contrast what I take to be the metaphysical and moral implications of the Christian account of creation with Murdoch's under-standing of the purposelessness of our existence. I wish I knew better how to engage her in argument. There are surely metaphysical issues that would be worth pursuing—such as why necessity is not a charac-teristic of God or why goodness is a predicate of God and can only be displayed by analogy.[24] Yet how that is or should be done has been made difficult by Murdoch because she rightly refuses to separate meta-physics and morality. So it is finally not a question of how to character-ize "what is" but how "what is" reflects, and also determines, what we are or should be. That she insists on such a close interconnection be-tween metaphysics and morality is at least part of the reason why Iris Murdoch is such a challenge to those of us who understand ourselves to be Christians.

There are, moreover, as I indicated at the beginning, issues in what might be called moral psychology that would be useful to explore. The "inner" character of our lives is much more dependent on the habitua-tion made possible by a community's practices than Murdoch seems to acknowledge. This can now be seen, not simply as a point of moral psy-chology, but as an observation about the way in which our embedded-ness as historic beings reflects a much stronger sense of our creatureliness—at least as suggested by the Christian understanding. Miss Murdoch and Christians alike believe that we must be trained to see. But I suspect the kind of training that distinguishes the two will be quite different.

However, I think that the deepest difficulty Christians have in knowing what an argument with Murdoch might look like is that we simply lack the imaginative power. Our greatest difficulty as Christians is we have lost the "sources," the practices, that are necessary to sustain our conviction that God is the origination and end of our existence. Murdoch surely offers, particularly through her novels, a re-imagining of our existence that powerfully reflects "the way we live now." Even more than her philosophy, her novels present a temptation to Christians because inasmuch as we allow ourselves to be trained through them, we lose our ability to imagine any other world.

Any response to Miss Murdoch, and it is a response that we rightly owe to her wisdom about such matters, will come from other artists—for example, Walker Percy or Flannery O'Connor—who have the imagination to create a world of hope. Yet such artists, as Murdoch has taught us, depend on quite ordinary people who have learned to live well against the odds. If Christians are to survive (or deserve to survive) in a world that has no capacity to acknowledge our created status, they will do so only because our communities are still capable of producing and locating those among us whose lives are "living prayers."

Notes

An earlier version of this chapter appeared in Maria Antonaccio and William Schweiker, eds., *Iris Murdoch and the Search for Human Goodness*, Chicago: The University of Chicago Press, 1996. Copyright © 1996 by the University of Chicago. All rights reserved. Reprinted by permission.

I am indebted to Dr. James Fodor, Dr. Reinhard Hütter, and Mr. Scott Saye for their good criticism of the initial draft of this essay

1. Iris Murdoch, *The Sovereignty of Good* (New York: Routledge and Kegan Paul, 1970). All page numbers will appear in parentheses, preceded by an *"S."* I will use the same system for Dame Murdoch's *Metaphysics as a Guide to Morals* (New York: Penguin Press, 1993), indicating this book by *"M."*

2. *Vision and Virtue* was originally published in 1974 by Fides Press of Notre Dame, Indiana. The University of Notre Dame Press edition was published in 1981. The book contains my essay "The Significance of Vision: Toward an Esthetic Ethic," in which I discuss Murdoch's work. Lawrence Blum has more recently shown the continuing power of Murdoch's account of morality in *Moral Perception and Particularity* (Cambridge: Cambridge University Press, 1994).

3. Bourke's review appeared in *Review for Religious* 34, 2 (1975): 328.

4. "Atheism," of course, is as ambiguous a term as "theism." I am simply accepting Murdoch's self-description, but I thereby do not mean to imply that her "atheism" is the same as Aristotle's. More important, I am not sure that it is appropriate to describe Aristotle as an atheist, though he took a critical attitude toward aspects of Greek theology. Murdoch's atheism is obviously more interesting for the Christian, since she believes she is denying the God Christians worship. I am not sure, however, that she in fact is denying the God we Christians know as Trinity, since she seems to think that God's existence and transcendence (what she identifies as supernaturalism) are more basic to Christians than God being Trinity. That she does so is, I fear, the result of distortions in Christian practice and thought.

5. Murdoch's views on the relation between thought and language are most developed in her early article, "Thinking and Language," *Proceedings of the Aristotelian Society,* Supplementary Volume, 25 (1951): 25–34. I believe she has continued to support the views set forth there that, in effect, argue that language and thought are not coextensive. Although I am sympathetic with her critique of the crude behaviorism that was the target of her argument, I do not think the views about language and thought presented there are nearly complex enough. I associate her views about language with her "mysticism" insofar as the former may be necessary to sustain her account of the ineffability of certain types of experience.

6. One of the troubling features of Murdoch's appeal to the virtues is the lack of a moral psychology in which they might be rooted. As a result, we have little idea how she might justify her way of treating the virtues. That is to say, she does not tell the reader how the virtues are individuated or how they are interrelated. One suspects she may, like Plato, assume the unity, if not the "oneness," of the virtues. Accordingly, we have little sense from her work how the virtues are acquired through habit.

7. The issue can be put more strongly, inasmuch as Murdoch at times seems to suggest that we are "saved" just to the extent we are free of history—a "solution" that she equally displays, particularly in her novels, as impossible. I cannot work out here, or probably anywhere, the relation between the Christian understanding of creation and history, but it at least involves the claim that given our created status, we should not be surprised that we only know ourselves as creatures through a narrative. For an attempt of mine to develop these suggestions, see *The Peaceable Kingdom: A Primer in Christian Ethics* (Notre Dame: University of Notre Dame Press, 1983), pp. 24–34.

8. My reticence about metaphysics is a correlate of my attempt to resist reductionistic accounts of theological claims so common in modern theology. Obviously, Christian conviction entails metaphysical claims—such as all that is, is finite—but one does not first get one's metaphysics straight and then go to theology. Rather, metaphysical claims are best exhibited as embedded in, not as the "background" of, our behaviors. This applies not only in Christian theology but also in any endeavor.

9. The extent to which the characters in Murdoch's novels make sense only insofar as they are sustained by hope would make a fascinating study. On the matters of hope she seems philosophically closer to Stoicism than Christianity; yet imaginatively living as we do at the end of fading Christian practices, hope is hard to give up, even for Murdoch.

10. These issues are not unrelated to the issues raised above about habituation, since sin is not a "natural" category. Sin, rather, is an achievement. You must be trained to be a sinner, which means that you must have your life embedded in a narrative through which those sins can be named. I develop these suggestions in *After Christendom?* (Nashville: Abingdon Press, 1991), pp. 93–111.

11. I find it surprising that Murdoch should underwrite Cupitt's account of autonomy, since she is so critical of Kant elsewhere in her work.

12. Charles Taylor, *Sources of the Self: The Making of Modern Identity* (Cambridge: Harvard University Press, 1989).

13. Even though Murdoch suggests elsewhere that that which consoles cannot be true, she also recognizes the need for consolation. What remains unclear on her account, however, is how one might negotiate these contrary positions. I sometimes suspect that she, like some other Platonists, assumes that some must bear the philosophical burden of refusing to be consoled in order that most people can be contented with stories that are less than true.

14. Children often play crucial roles in Murdoch's novels, insofar as they exhibit an "innocent seeing," which she equates with the mystical. Children do not need to unlearn the connections we adults impose on the world, the "necessities" that domesticate the contingent. To be able to see the sheer givenness of this rock or tree in its givenness is to be on the way to being good. Murdoch seems to think that such goodness is lost through our growing up. We lose our ability to see the contingent because of our desire to control the world.

15. Censorship of art and literature should not be associated, as it often is in liberal cultures, with denying to some the right to see or read certain works of art. The serious issue, rather, is *how* these paintings or works of art are to be read in relation to other works.

16. I am using the edition of the *Summa Theologica* translated by the Fathers of the English Dominican Province. Pagination of the *Summa* will appear in the text.

17. For an extraordinary account of Aquinas's understanding of our knowledge of God, see Eugene Rogers, *Thomas Aquinas and Karl Barth: Sacred Doctrine and the Natural Knowledge of God* (Notre Dame: University of Notre Dame Press, 1995).

18. David Burrell, C.S.C., *Freedom and Creation in Three Traditions* (Notre Dame: University of Notre Dame Press, 1993), pp. 7–8.

19. Ibid., p. 9.

20. Reinhard Hütter, "Creation ex Nihilo: Promise of the Gift," *Currents in Theology and Mission* 19, 2 (1992): 92.

21. The language of gift requires considerable theological analysis that I cannot provide here. For an example of the kind of display that I think is required, see John Milbank's "Can a Gift Be Given? Prolegomena to a Future Trinitarian Metaphysic," *Modern Theology* 11, 1 (January 1995):119–161. For a quite different account, see Jacques Derrida, *The Gift of Death*, trans. David Mills (Chicago: University of Chicago Press, 1995).

22. I find puzzling the current enthusiasm for contingency among contemporary philosophers, such as Richard Rorty in his *Contingency, Irony and Solidarity* (Cambridge: Cambridge University Press, 1989). Rorty suggests that "our language and our culture are as much a contingency, as much a result of thousands

of small mutations finding niches (and millions of others finding no niches), as are the orchids and the anthropoids" (p. 16), that is, contingency is just another word for randomness. That, of course, is fine but why not simply use "randomness," since contingency invites the question "Contingent in relation to what?" I am not arguing that the word "contingent" implies a metaphysics that assumes creation or at least the finite character of the world, but that those who use the word often trade on presumptions that they have not adequately examined.

23. Hütter, "Creation ex Nihilo," p. 96.

24. These matters are, of course, interrelated. Since the contingent characters of our own as well as the world's existence is that of creature, we can only "know" God's character analogically.

11 *Reading James McClendon Takes Practice: Lessons in the Craft of Theology*

Learning to Read with McClendon

No reading or writing is innocent. As readers we often share so many habits with the authors we read that we tend to forget that reading is a soul-making activity.[1] But we must attend carefully to the work of good writers, for as we read their work, they often require us to form new habits, and in the process, we find that they have changed our lives. I believe James McClendon to be such a writer. Yet he is deceptively so.

By calling him deceptive, I do not mean that he intentionally tries to deceive us. I mean, rather, that over the past thirty years or so he has become such a master of his craft that we can easily miss the peculiarity of what he has done. McClendon has brought voices as disparate as Alasdair MacIntyre, Jonathan Edwards, Erasmus of Rotterdam, and Dorothy Day into his theological conversation concerning the baptist tradition and postmodernism, a conversation formative of his vision of the church. McClendon's *Doctrine: Systematic Theology,*[2] the long-awaited companion to his *Ethics: Systematic Theology,*[3] continues those far-ranging conversations in ways that produce, in spite of their originality, an elegant synthesis of baptist faith that goes down smoothly. But "originality" is not something McClendon wishes to claim as a theologian, since he writes to illuminate convictions without which theology itself would be impossible. As he notes:

> However, not too much originality should be claimed for the present work. Its stance reflects a wider conceptual shift from a strictly modern understanding in which all knowledge is supposed to rest upon some universally available foundations, to an understanding some have labeled postmodern, in which claims to knowledge are less breathtaking or absolute, but are more integrally tied to the actual tasks at hand. (*Doctrine*, 455)

But to do theology that is tied to "actual tasks at hand," that is, to practices, is no easy matter, since there are no readily available paradigms to guide the way.[4] Yet McClendon, like a skilled dancer whose movement is so beautiful that we forget the strength and training that such skill presupposes, has crafted a theology that appears almost effortless in its presentation. Because of the dexterity and finesse of his craft, we can miss the hard theological work that has gone into his imaginative reconstruction of what we used to call "systematic theology." What I shall do is to try to assemble a set of reminders that, I hope, will expose some of that effort so that we might become better readers of McClendon's theological proposal. The purpose, of course, is not for us to become better readers of McClendon, since McClendon's theological project is itself an exercise in helping us become better readers of the Gospel. Good writers therefore try to force those of us who read them to attend to what we read, for in so doing they demand of us the formation of new habits, which thereby changes our lives.

In other words, McClendon wants us to read with and perhaps even at times against him, not simply to read him. The practice of Christian doctrine requires the exercise of our selves in living and thinking as Christians. For our thinking can be no idle speculation; it is intrinsic to our living as members of the church whose purpose is nothing less than the worship of God. The theologian, therefore, is not trying to provide a "meaning" for theological concepts that no longer seem to do any work. Rather, doctrine—teaching—itself is a practice intrinsic to the worship of the church, and vice versa.

Thus, McClendon candidly acknowledges that he must claim his theology to be an exemplification of the practice called teaching, which is integral to the church's very being. The material content and the form of presentation of the content cannot be separated. McClendon therefore seeks, not to provide us with more information, but rather to help us live more faithfully as Christians through learning to read with him. As he puts it:

> To put the point linguistically, the surface grammar of doctrinal theology may take various shapes: first-person confessions, historical descriptions of church teaching, axioms or theses derived from an organizing principle, biblical exegesis, rhetorical ukases. Yet its deep structure is that of a grammar of persuasion seeking assent: It says, "This is what your present convictions appear (on such and such evidence) to be: this is what (for such and such reasons) they appear to mean. Would it be better, then (for considerations here presented) to transform these present convictions *thus?*" In such a servant's question, such a "thus?" all theology's first-person confessions, all its axioms and principles, all its arguments find their reason for being. (*Doctrine*, 47)[5]

The first response of most readers, trained as we are on the disciplinary habits of the Enlightenment, is to think, "He means that it is all just rhetoric." To that, I hope, McClendon will reply, "Of course, but why use the 'just'?" Teaching is practice that cannot help but seek to change lives. The teaching goal of the church is to "indoctrinate." Accordingly, McClendon does not want us "just" to understand him. He—or at least the church he serves—wants our souls by shaping them through the persuasive practices of doctrinal reflection and articulation.

By suggesting that I want to assemble a set of reminders for reading McClendon, I do not mean I take as my task to "explain" McClendon's *Doctrine.* That would make me like the critics who think that they can say better the poet's poem through their criticism than the poet's poem can. They may well be able to tell us why the poem is bad or good, but that does not mean that their criticism can replace the poem. I do not seek to replace McClendon's "poem." If anything, I seek to help us see why the language and form of his *Doctrine* is integral to the practice of soul formation through reading.

In doing so, I hope that I can preserve something of the wildness of McClendon's presentation. For, as I will try to show below, one of the things I like so much about his teaching concerning the church's teaching is how systematic he is in being unsystematic. Accordingly, he is able to teach without domesticating that which he teaches. If you believe, for instance, that the cosmos is under the rule of God, then our world (that is, the world of predictability and order we think necessary for everyday life) must be pictured differently. Hans Hut, a sixteenth-century anabaptist missionary who was martyred because of his eschatological preaching, McClendon claims as a "paradigm case of the baptist vision ('then is now') applied in a time of crisis" (*Doctrine,* 95), precisely because Hut understood how wild the world under God's rule is. It is hard to remember that you are living in the end times when you are buying groceries for another week's dinners.

So McClendon must persuade us, if we are to become good readers, to give up our need to control the world. We must instead believe that truthfulness, not war and violence, is the way the world acquires a history befitting its ordering to God's kingdom. "Thus," as he puts it, "in the last, best sense of the word 'history,' war and its violence turn out to be anti-historical" (*Doctrine,* 99). That is theological redescription with a vengeance. Moreover, if McClendon is right about such a redescription, we cannot help but fear becoming good readers of him. For seen through his description, the world of war appears even more dangerous for those who would be truthful worshipers of God.

On a more mundane level, I think it important to note that McClendon also writes to disorient his readers' expectations about the "discipline" of theology. Those that would seek to make their mark in theology usually seek to supersede other prominent players in the field. To be sure, McClendon betrays an intimate knowledge of such players—the Schleiermachers, the Barths, the Pannenbergs—but he does not make much of that. Rather, he identifies his community of reference with such figures as Rauschenbusch, Mullins, Conner, and Harkness. Keeping this kind of company is not the way to establish yourself in the theological mainstream, much less find respectability in the academy.

In this respect, it is interesting to reflect on McClendon's project in relation to Van Harvey's analysis in "The Intellectual Marginality of American Theology."[6] Harvey notes that the marginalization of theology is often attributed to the hostility of the scientific ethos of the modern university. Whereas no doubt such developments have contributed to a loss of status for theology, Harvey argues that the more proximate and determinative cause has more to do with developments internal to theology itself.

In particular, he suggests that it was the specialization of theology in the German context that led to theology's demise. Kant (and Schleiermacher), for example, argued that the faculties of medicine, law, and theology were justified within the university, not because they were sciences, but because of their service to the state. Harvey points out that this solution, however, contained a fateful ambiguity that only became fully apparent when the fourfold curriculum—scripture, church history, dogmatics, and practical disciplines—was transferred to the American scene. "The same argument that served to justify theology in the German university in the nineteenth century can now be used to justify the exclusion of theology from the American university and the establishment of separate divinity schools under the aegis of denomination and churches."[7] In an attempt to save theology as a university discipline, the methods of theological study became more and more specialized in order to meet the demands of being a science; thus each method has its professional societies, journals, and the like.[8]

But as Harvey points out, Protestant liberal theology's strategy of becoming a "metaphysics for believers," or a phenomenology of the collective consciousness of a determinative religious community, made it increasingly difficult to locate the "expertise" that distinguished the theologian and theology. "One might still justify New Testament studies or church history because both are historical sciences, but what could be the justification for the clarification and systematization of the utterances of the Christian self-consciousness except the purpose of training leaders of the Christian churches?"[9]

The irony of this situation, according to Harvey, is that insofar as theology was and is institutionalized primarily as a subject matter for the professionalized clergy, it is seen as having no relevance to the laity. Protestant theologians may argue that their theology is for the laity, but in fact they conceive of theology in technical and academic terms often determined by other disciplines. The result is that their theology is intelligible primarily to other academics.

> Consequently, the great majority of divinity students, unless they are headed for an advanced degree in theology, find such academic theology to be at best an irrelevance and at worst an impediment to their careers, because the reward system of the church system in no way encourages their mastery of it. Members of the clergy rarely function as educators or theologians in their congregations; hence, whatever theology was learned is regarded, after five or so years, much like the calculus one learned in college. Theologians, in contrast, accept the view that the important problems in theology are technical issues that can be handled only by academics trained to deal with the discourse of other academics, such as those in philosophy.[10]

Theologians, ironically, become nonpractioners who are paid to train ministerial practitioners by educating them in matters seen as peripheral to the practice.

Against this background one can appreciate McClendon's extraordinary attempt to reshape the demographics of the readers of theology. He defies the specialization of contemporary theology precisely insofar as he refuses to leave scripture or church history to the scholars. Even more, he assumes that theology cannot be separated from practice (in the same way we cannot forget that his *Doctrine* follows from his *Ethics*). Christian practices, and the specific practice of the church in its teaching, are at the heart of this work, and therefore McClendon must challenge the reading habits of many of us who have learned "systematic theology" exactly as a way to free theology from practice.

What is not to be forgotten, however, is that the challenge that McClendon is making to theology as a system, as well as to theology as a specialization of the seminary curriculum, is more than just an "academic" matter—though it is fascinating to explore the implications of McClendon's *Doctrine* for the restructuring of seminary curricula and practices. What McClendon is challenging more fundamentally is the presumption that theology can be true to the teaching of the church and at the same time be of service to the state. So, in making us readers of a theology that exists only to be of service to the teaching office of the church, McClendon is asking us to become part of the narrative that places us "outside" the system of powers that has in the past legitimated systematic theology as well as the structure of our seminary curricula. What is more, he forces us to consider why this strategy is not just another "position" for our consideration. Indeed, I am tempted to suggest that on the fly leaf of the book should be written: *Warning to Those Schooled in Academic Theology—This Book, If Taken Seriously, Could Be Dangerous to Your Career.*

On Beginning When There Is No Place to Begin

Nowhere is McClendon's challenge to the reader more apparent than in how he begins. I have already noted that he begins doing theology not in his *Doctrine* but in his *Ethics*. But even that can be deceiving, as that book is also subtitled *Systematic Theology* (volume 1). At the very least we know something odd is going on when we see a book called *Ethics* with so much space given to the resurrection. Resurrection, according to McClendon, requires that our lives be based on miracle. That is not good news for most people trained in "ethics," a field that assumes that moral behavior depends on excluding the unexpected.

The way McClendon develops his ethics means the book cannot stand as a prolegomena for his *Doctrine*. Nor does the first chapter of the *Doctrine*, even though it is titled "What Is Doctrine?" act as a prolegomena. McClendon simply does not seem to have learned the lesson that most of us learned in graduate school, namely, that modern theology should primarily deal with *how* to do theology (i.e., "method") in case one ever gets around to doing any. Thus, much of modern theology consists more in theologians writing books on other theologians than in theologians doing any theology.

There is, of course, a way that McClendon might be read as trying to provide a prolegomena insofar as he resorts, again in *Doctrine*, to the "strand" analysis of the *Ethics*. I confess I have always been a bit suspicious of the usefulness of this analogy (borrowed from Wittgenstein), which says that several strands wound together produce the rope of Christian life; no one strand is the core or essence, for they only become rope when intertwined. In particular, I have thought it unwise to begin, as McClendon does in the *Ethics*, with the bodily strand. For in spite of McClendon's stress on the interdependent nature of the strands, the bodily strand can give the impression that there is a "bottom," a basis, that can provide a common starting point.

Now that the *Doctrine* is written, however, there can be no possibility of such a reading, which is but a reminder that not only must the *Doctrine* be read in the light of the *Ethics*, but the *Ethics* must now also be read in the light of the *Doctrine*. McClendon makes clear in part 1, "The Rule of God," that one can only begin with the end. As he says in his wonderful rendering of Mark 13, "Mark could truthfully render afresh the picture received from Jesus, for its force finally depended not on near and more distant perspectives or upon the needed conceptual foreshortenings, but upon the ultimate truth it related. Every version of the story was shaped by its ending" (*Doctrine*, 94).[11]

That McClendon has no place to begin comports well with the apocalyptic character of his theology. For as Wittgenstein observes in *Culture and Value*, "the truly apocalyptic view of the world is that things do *not* repeat themselves."[12] Christian theology therefore cannot have a starting point, exactly because such a starting point would try to ensure a stability to the world, to subject history to a cause-and-effect pattern that the resurrection has forever rendered problematic.

McClendon says in Chapter 7 of *Doctrine*, "The Identity of God," that for strictly "pedagogical reasons" he reverses the order of the three strands in his display of the God of the Gospel. Yet I wonder if he does not have a deeper reason. The very way he resists any starting point for presenting the teachings of the church is meant to exhibit that all existence is determined by the eschatology commensurate with Christ's resurrection. If our God is a pioneer, a trailblazer, as McClendon rightly claims, then I think our theology must equally take the risk of not "repeating" itself by trying to ensure a place to begin.

The attempt to make theology attain quasi-scientific "objectivity"— even in science attaining objectivity is more an image than an actual activity—by providing it with a firm foundation (intended or not) could not help but produce a domesticated theology. Such theology is but the mirror image of empire, inasmuch as it seeks to put everything in its place, to secure all the loose ends, in the interest of order and security. By providing a rational basis for theology, by finding the essential core to determine the meaning of all theological discourse, theology could pretend to be for anyone.

Architectonic theology is but the mirror image of Christianity as a system that "explains things." It is a theology for people who believe that faith in God is meant to put us firmly in control of our existence. It is a theology that attempts to take the surprise out of the resurrection. Accordingly, architectonic theology tends to a reductionistic display of the various loci of Christian doctrine, trying to show that insofar as the various doctrines are rational, they all "mean" the same thing. McClendon attempts no such exercise in "meaning," on the assumption that if the loci are not doing any work within the practices of the church, no amount of intellectual work can rescue them.

Nicholas Lash makes a suggestion at the beginning of *Believing Three Ways in One God: A Reading of the Apostles' Creed* that I think illumines McClendon's practice. Lash begins his book with the affirmation "Amen." He knows very well that this is a bit unusual since "Amen" conventionally comes at the end of an act of worship.

Nonetheless, we may begin with [Amen] because what it comes after is everything that went before. Theologians spend much time arguing where they should *begin*. This is a largely futile exercise because, if one thing is cer-

tain in this life, it is that none of us begins at the beginning. We find ourselves somewhere, discover something of what went before, of how things
went in order to bring about the way they are. Growing up is largely a matter of learning to take bearings. A more fruitful question than "Where
should we begin?" would almost always be "Where, then, do we stand?"[13]

McClendon acknowledges his stance in that community of constitutive
narrative practices called "church." Rather than beginning some place,
then, he must simply ask, "What must the church teach if it is really to *be*
the church?" He therefore seeks no minimal set of "teachings" that can be
rationally justified. He asks instead what we need in order to be about
the tasks of the church. We should therefore not be surprised when this
"baptist" theologian identifies as closest to his own approach those
Catholic theologians who see the authority of the magisterium deriving
from its consultation with the *consensus fidelium* (*Doctrine*, 25–26).

In this respect, McClendon's theology is not unlike a conversation that
was reported to me between friends, one of whom was contemplating
becoming a Catholic. The potential convert suggested that he was simply
moving from an outhouse to the main house, to which his friend replied
that the metaphor was all wrong. Rather, he should remember that in
God's house there are many rooms, albeit some are better furnished than
others. McClendon accordingly tries to provide us with as richly furnished a room as possible by helping us see that as Christians we need no
place to begin. Our task, then, is not to find the perfect place to begin but
to lose nothing that can help us live faithful to "the way."

The intention of McClendon's *Doctrine,* therefore, is not to end a conversation, but to begin one. Since the task of doctrinal theology is to explore what the church must teach if it is to be the church, McClendon
must always be open to fresh challenges. For example, he provides no extensive account of the role of Mary as the first-born of the new creation.
Our worship of Jesus may well be deficient if Mary is not made part of
that worship. That is to say, as Protestants, our worship may be deficient
just to the extent that we do not know how to pray to Mary. For Mary's
exclusion from Protestant worship and theology is, I suspect, not unrelated to the Protestant tendency to try to discover a "core" of the Gospel
that modern people will find "believable." Virgin births are thus rendered either expendable or symbolic. As a result, Christian theology loses
necessary connections with Israel, inasmuch as Mary is the inescapable
reminder that Jesus was born a Jew.

It is to McClendon's great credit that his "method" means that such an
objection cannot be excluded in principle. Such "teaching" may be as crucial to the display of Christian doctrine as the Christian doctrine of God.
For once one no longer assumes the existence of one and only one starting point, then the luxuriant character of Christian theology can be al-

lowed to flourish. It is no longer a question of "How little do we have to believe to be church?" but "How wonderful it is that the church has believed all this!"

On Seeing the Oddness of the Obvious: The Structure of McClendon's *Doctrine*

Just as it is easy to miss the significance of not beginning with a beginning, it is also easy for a reader to miss the significance of the way McClendon structures the teachings of the church.[14] The difficulty, of course, is determining the order of the various teachings of the church when one does not have a beginning. That McClendon begins his narrative with the "Rule of God" is surely not unrelated to his sense of the disestablishment of the church in liberal social orders. Put simply, it is not accidental that we rediscover God's rule precisely at a time that Christians are discovering that we no longer rule.

Because it has for so long seemed right to begin with the rule of God in a theology shaped by Christian teaching, we can easily miss the oddness of this move. Teaching is a form of ruling, since through teaching we are "ruled" to be faithful subjects of the One alone who has the authority to rule. Thus, McClendon's part 1 rightly depicts how the One that rules from a cross remakes us to be creatures capable of living according to such a surprising rule.

McClendon notes, "Every Christian doctrine seems to require every other for its clear presentation" (*Doctrine*, 123). That surely is the case, and that it is such is at once the glory and the frustration of theology. For on the one hand, the theologian cannot help but be haunted by the sense that everything must be said at once, and on the other, the theologian also recognizes that the very structure of our language prevents our doing so. For as McClendon reminds us time and time again, the shape of Christian convictions is that of a narrative. It is not just a "story" but a story about the storied character of our existence as creatures of a gracious creator. That every doctrine requires all others is therefore only a reminder that the theologian's task is to help the church teach the story in an orderly fashion through prayer and worship.

Like any good story, the story of God is complex. The temptation of the theologian is to reduce or "manage" that complexity by suggesting what it "really means." McClendon refuses to simplify, however, for even though he begins with the end, he never fails to remind us that the story is not done. "This is that" is a constant reminder that the telling of the tale is ongoing. It continues even now exactly because through Christ we have been made part of the end.[15] The "narrative character" of our existence therefore requires that McClendon structure the teaching of the church eschatologically.

Thus Hans Hut, not Hegel, is the paradigm of the virtue correlative to the vision of Christ's overwhelming triumph. That virtue, of course, is patience. McClendon lifts up the example of Hut as one "whose vision of Christ's overwhelming triumph in the last day was second to none, but who when he instructed his converts gave them the task, not of conquering the world with the world's weapons, but of obeying the commandments and practicing love one to another while they awaited God's own time" (*Doctrine*, 97). Such patience is not merely what we must do until we are saved. It *is* our salvation. Accordingly, McClendon's account disorders our world more determinatively than Pannenberg (or probably Moltmann) would find comfortable.

That McClendon's *Doctrine* is structured eschatologically will certainly provoke many who assume that theology must begin at the beginning—that is, with God and creation. Yet McClendon does not treat the identity of God until chapter 7. Are you not supposed to begin theology with the doctrine of the Trinity? McClendon does not do so, not because he has doubts about the Trinity as an expression necessary to Christian worship, but because God must be displayed as part of the practice of church teaching. McClendon puts the matter clearly when he notes that his task

> was to show the Christian good news as good news about God. This did not mean that pagans were offered some (or some more) "religious experiences," or that benighted ancients who lacked a morality were offered one, courtesy of the Christians. Of course, when the Gospel appears, experience changes. Of course morality changes—yet the news is greater, more radical, than "experience" or "morality" can indicate. Was it then a new *philosophy* of God? More than that, as we shall see. The God Christians know is the God of Jesus Christ, that is, the God known to them as they know the risen Christ and share the fellowship called church. Neither Christ nor Spirit is confined to the pages of the New Testament. So we searched there and beyond for the impact of Jesus Christ, and the entailed impact of God's Holy Spirit—a wider search, and one hardly begun here. The results to this point will disappoint some. Spheres of action for Jesus' God have been indicated, and names for God named, some familiar, some strange. Yet "God" has not been defined here, or God's essence described, apart from the Israel-Jesus-church story itself. (*Doctrine*, 293–294)

Here we see McClendon exposing his pedagogical intent in shaping our reading of the Gospels and correlatively shaping who we are to be as church. He does not let us begin with God, for such a God cannot be other than an abstraction—even as Trinity. Instead, he forces us to focus on learning the story through becoming servants to the rule of God found in Christ. Accordingly, he even treats sin and salvation prior to treating the identity of Christ.

I mention this point because I have to acknowledge that it makes me nervous. I worry that such an order can underwrite an anthropological account of sin and salvation that subsequently determines the meaning of Christ (rather than an account of salvation learned from Christ). McClendon is acutely aware that this is a problem. He sharply criticizes Reinhold Niebuhr for providing an account of sin that fails to see that we only come to a clear awareness of sin after we are saved from it (*Doctrine*, 124).

Raising this issue, however, helps us see the power of McClendon's execution of the structure of the church's teaching. For he does not assume that he is displaying theological language as if that language were a primitive metaphysics separate from the practices of the concrete people called church and whose very lives tell us the nature of the world. McClendon can treat salvation and sin prior to Christology precisely because there is in fact no "priority" other than the story-formed practices of the church. By doing so he reminds us that questions of Christ's identity (e.g., speculation concerning the "two natures") are in service to the church's faithful practice. In effect, the structure of his theology is to force us to remember that theology is not an end in itself. Theology is not, in other words, a speculative endeavor.

That McClendon first treats the atonement (chapter 5) before developing his Christology (chapter 6) is also a move of great significance. I take that to be an attempt to recontextualize these traditional theological topics and loci by placing them in a narrative mode appropriate to the fundamental claim, "this is that." Accordingly, he resists all accounts of "theories" of the atonement that de-eschatologize the cross. McClendon forces us, in effect, to become better readers of the Gospel so that we might see in our reading that we are ourselves already characters *in* the story. For there is no place that we can position ourselves outside of the story of Christ without distorting how God's rule rules.

I have only touched the surface of the extraordinarily subtle way in which McClendon has structured his *Doctrine*. Anyone familiar with the habits of modern theology cannot help but marvel at the imaginative way that McClendon has displayed the network of "rules and meanings" constitutive of Christian practices. It is as if one has entered a new world, and it will take us some time before we will learn all the skills necessary for the journey to which McClendon has beckoned us.

There is one move he makes, however, to which I want to call particular attention. That is partly because I think it extremely important and partly because I cannot resist doing so in a context that prides itself on its Reformed background—that is, Professor McClendon's residency, Fuller Theological Seminary. I refer, of course, to McClendon's account of creation as an eschatological doctrine. In contrast to those who assume that creation is a presupposition of the redemption that comes in Christ, Mc-Clendon rightly suggests:

> The ultimate end of creation and redemption alike is the fulfillment of God's great kingdom rule. This rule, when it shall be achieved, will mean God's glory fully shared, imparted to all, incorporating all. Then creation (the doctrine of divine origination and conservation) and salvation (the liberation of a people suited to that coming glory) and last things (the doctrine of the consummation itself) are partner doctrines in the exposition of the all-embracing rule of God. In a figure, creation and salvation are not parent and child; neither has birthed the other. Rather they are sisters, mutually interacting and supporting each other along with a third sibling, eschatology. And all this is in fulfillment of the rule of God, which (at least in the structure of this book) is the mother doctrine that includes them all. (*Doctrine*, 147–148)

Although it would be a mistake to attempt to locate the center, or "essence," of McClendon's *Doctrine*, I think no move is more important for the overall structure of his work than this. For it means that he cannot pretend to have knowledge of the good ends of God's creation abstracted from the story embodied in cross and resurrection. It obviously puts him at odds with all those who want to use the "doctrine of creation" to ground common knowledge and practice between church and world. Such a move may seem more intelligible in a "postmodern" world, but I suspect that McClendon would rather think that God has led us to rediscover the "place" that makes creation good news.

McClendon's position in this respect is, I think, quite near to that of Nicholas Lash, who in reflecting on Mark's account of Jesus in Gethsemane, says:

> I would not be wandering too far from Mark's text if I suggested that what occurs on Calvary in the death of Christ is that which happened "in the beginning" and at the Exodus: God's Word makes a world, a home for us with him. The spring festival, rather than mid-winter, once marked New Year's Day. On 25 March, according to the fifth-century calendar known as the martyrology of Jerome, "Our Lord Jesus Christ was crucified, and conceived, and the world was made." On this day God brings all things alive, *ex nihilo*. Out of nothing, by his word, he makes a world, a home. Out of the virgin's womb, Christ is conceived. Out of that world-threatening death on Calvary, life is newborn from an empty tomb. Christ's terror is God's Word's human vulnerability. But, it is just this vulnerability, this surrender, absolute relationship, which draws out of darkness finished life, forgiveness of sin.[16]

I should like to think McClendon's (and Lash's) account of creation the end of all attempts to distinguish between orders of creation and orders of redemption. I have to confess, however, I am not hopeful in this respect; not because I think their respective theological displays deficient, but because of the powerful practices that underwrite many modern accounts of the doctrine of creation. So we find ourselves again remembering McClendon's overriding presumption that doctrine itself is a practice that must be ordered, as all the practices of the church are, to the witness through worship to God's good rule.

I have not tried to compare and contrast in detail McClendon's understanding of the structure of doctrine with other theological alternatives, but it does strike me that the most instructive such comparison may well be with Karl Barth. The unsystematic character of McClendon's presentation is, I think, quite similar to Barth's actual practice. Through repetition, Barth forces his readers to attend to the story of God. I suspect that Barth knew repetition was a way to train Christian readers. Comparing in this respect McClendon's practice of forcing a slow reading with Barth's practice of repetition could be quite illuminating.

Deceiving Modesty: Can a Baptist Be a Catholic?

One of the engaging aspects of McClendon's work is its openness to the breadth of Christian tradition. Nevertheless, he not only tells us, in both the *Ethics* and the *Doctrine*, that he writes as a Baptist, but that this "baptist" identity makes a difference for what he writes. Do we have to become Baptist to be good readers of McClendon? I have a colleague who refuses to use McClendon's *Ethics* on grounds that we ought not to subject people preparing for the Methodist ministry to Baptist theology. Although I have pointed out to him that a Baptist theology that makes Dorothy Day the heroine is at least a little odd, he is not persuaded that it makes that much difference.

Can McClendon have it both ways? Can he be a Baptist yet mine, as he obviously does, the resources of the Christian tradition for the constructive development of his theology? For example, in developing his Christology, McClendon notes:

> When the identity narratives we call Gospels were first circulated, the task of interpreting them gave rise to further questions, and these to still others, until the first great post–New Testament theological debate, the ancient Christological controversy, had taken shape. It continued for centuries, and gave lasting (some said permanent) shape to Christian thought. For baptist Christians, to be sure, these controversies and conciliar decisions of the second, third, fourth, fifth and later centuries do not have the authority that they exercise in creedal communities such as the Catholic and Orthodox. Yet *all of us* are the heirs of these discussions and must take them into account in our thinking, albeit with an attentive eye toward those counted losers as well as toward the winners (for truth is not always, or even usually, allied

with the kind of power that wins fierce ecclesiastical and political wars).
(*Doctrine*, 238–239, emphasis added)

On what grounds does McClendon make "all of us" heirs of this history?
I raise this problem partly because it is also a problem for the way I do theology. I describe myself as a "High Church Mennonite," by which I mean I am a Methodist. But then I range across the Christian tradition, plundering it in ways that seem to suggest I am responsible to no one concrete tradition. I am sure one of the reasons I so operate is that by being educated at Yale I acquired the presumption that the best theology is also the most encompassing. This stance can give the impression that in trying to stand everywhere, I (and perhaps McClendon) can end up standing nowhere. Because it appears that we get to pick and choose amid the variety of the Christian tradition, we may in fact simply reproduce the liberal self. Theology, even a theology as radically ecclesial as ours, therefore becomes but an exemplification of consumer preference.

For example, in considering the continuity between past, present, and future, McClendon observes that the Catholic answer involves a theory of hierarchical succession hierarchically maintained, whereas a Protestant answer depends on each believer's having an inward and spiritual relationship to Christ. He suggests that the Baptist vision has no need to disavow either of these modes of relating Christ to the church, since both seem to require something like the other. Yet McClendon suggests that neither of them can do the work demanded, because "if it is true that the True Church is successor to the apostles, it is equally true that all those it calls heretical and false are successors as well, while (to consider the idea of spiritual authenticity as the rule) this individual way of thinking dissolves the very objectivity it proposes to establish" (*Doctrine*, 46).

He proceeds to observe that the Baptist vision allows or, more strongly put, demands a variety of Bible readings depending on time and place.

Yet the thesis of this volume is that the unity that arises by use of the vision is nevertheless sufficient to define an authentic style of communal Christian life, so that participants in such a community can know what the church must teach to be the church. . . . This is not a sectarian way, declaring all others wrong in order to be alone right. It is rather an ecumenical way, confessing the fullness of its style of Christian existence and offering it to all in the hope that in the conversation that ensues it will be adopted by all. That it has not yet been so adopted is tragically true—tragic in the persecution, suffering, and exclusion that, as *Martyrs Mirror* and other writings testify, have stalked the baptist way throughout its history. That it may nonetheless be adopted by all is only to affirm in another way Hans Frei's rules listed above: the Gospel centers in Christ; the Gospel is for all; the Gospel opens into a world of freedom. (*Doctrine*, 46)

I fervently hope that McClendon is right about this. Yet I can hear the question coming, as it often comes to Mennonite theologian John Howard Yoder (and to me), "Where is this baptist church?" It surely is not among those who bear the name Baptist! Indeed, in many ways it looks more like the Roman Catholic church than any of our other contemporary options. I see no reason in principle that McClendon would object to such a possibility. The importance of this problem is that such matters cannot be idle speculation for McClendon. His church must exist, given his understanding of what the church must teach to be the church.

I have but one suggestion in this respect. I think McClendon's ability to range over diverse traditions is not a "pick and choose" method. It is, rather, a renarration of the Christian past that is neither Catholic nor Protestant. For McClendon (and Yoder), the issue is not shaped by Reformation polemics, but rather by the faithfulness of Christians to manifest God's rule through faithful practices. Put differently, the crucial issue is not the magisterial office of Rome, but the Constantinian accommodation of the church to the powers and their demonic practices.

My hunch is that the reason some of us have a fresh appreciation for past theological practices, even when those practices were in service to a Catholic and Protestant Constantinian strategy, is that we believe those practices now offer new resources for naming and resisting the powers. A people who have learned to accept the authority of Scripture or bishops are at least on the way to learning the practice of forgiveness and reconciliation, as well as nonviolence, as part of their life in Christ. In short, I suspect that McClendon believes, or at least hopes, that God has now brought Christians to a point where we can only survive in the world by using our past differences as a source of our unity. So his *Doctrine* hopefully envisages a church that can produce readers of this extraordinary project. Like him I believe that they exist.

Notes

I am indebted to Kelly Johnson for rewriting this chapter. She not only made it more intelligible but also made the argument more precise.

1. Greg Jones puts this wonderfully in his recent review of George Hunsinger's *How to Read Karl Barth: The Shape of His Theology*, in *Modern Theology* 9, 2 (April 1993): 228–230. Jones notes that we usually acquire skills through apprenticing ourselves to a master. Without such masters we resort to manuals; for example, we use manuals for fixing kitchen sinks, learning to play golf, and so on. We are a bit surprised if we need a manual to help us read a book, but Jones argues we should not be surprised, since anyone may be able to read, but few know how to read well. I am suggesting that all theology is primarily an attempt to help us "read" well, but since, as McClendon emphasizes, worship is the preeminent

Christian practice, then our "reading" cannot be limited to texts. I am, in effect, writing a "how to" essay on a "how to" book.

2. James Wm. McClendon, *Doctrine: Systematic Theology*, vol. 2 (Nashville: Abingdon Press, 1994), hereafter *Doctrine*.

3. James Wm. McClendon, *Ethics: Systematic Theology*, vol. 1 (Nashville: Abingdon Press, 1986), hereafter *Ethics*.

4. By "practice" McClendon means "a complex series of human actions involving definite practitioners who by these means and in accordance with these rules together seek the understood end" (*Doctrine*, p. 8). It was tempting to focus my presentation on the importance of McClendon's account of practices, their relation to convictions, and the teleological ordering of practices. I suspect that when practices become demonic, they do so because they are not appropriately ordered. Whether McClendon has provided a sufficient account of the teleological order of the practices, and how that order should order the presentation of doctrines, I think will be a fascinating question for the future. Moreover, whether McClendon should be ready to endorse MacIntyre's rather surprising non-tradition-determined character of practice is also an issue for future discussion. See, for example, Phil Kenneson's criticism of MacIntyre's account in "The Reappearance of the Visible Church: An Analysis of the Production and Reproduction of Christian Identity" (Ph.D. Diss., Graduate School of Duke University, 1991), pp. 275f.

5. The language of surface and depth can be misleading. McClendon is not suggesting that "depth" is the "meaning" or substance that the "surface" does not already embody.

6. Van Harvey, "The Intellectual Marginality of American Theology," in *Religion and Twentieth-Century American Intellectual Life*, ed. Michael J. Lacey (Cambridge: Woodrow Wilson International Center for Scholars and Cambridge University Press, 1989), pp. 172–192.

7. Ibid., p. 185.

8. Hans Frei's account of the implications of the founding of the University of Berlin for theology generally supports Harvey's account. See Frei, *Types of Modern Theology* (New Haven: Yale University Press, 1992). Frei wonderfully shows why the kind of typology of theology he provides is the result of the way "knowledge" is produced by such institutions.

9. Harvey, "The Intellectual Marginality," p. 190.

10. Ibid., p. 191.

11. To say this without implying that the "end" means closure is not easily accomplished. That the end is resurrection, as McClendon helps us see, forces the church to be ever surprised by miracle.

12. Wittgenstein, *Culture and Value*, ed. G. H. von Wright, trans. P. Winch (Chicago: University of Chicago Press, 1980), 56e.

13. Nicholas Lash, *Believing Three Ways in One God: A Reading of the Apostles' Creed* (Notre Dame: University of Notre Dame Press, 1993), p. 2.

14. McClendon's work is filled with startling insights, many of which, except for the limitations of time and space, I would like to explore. I am particularly taken with chapter 10, where he makes mission central to the display of doctrine. I would especially like to dwell on his suggestion that the truth of *extra ecclesiam*

nulla salus is that the very meaning of salvation turns upon the shared life Christians take up when they came to Christ (*Doctrine*, p. 423).

15. McClendon's whole project is shaped by the avowal of "this is that," which he says is a "trope of mystical identity binding the story now to the story then, and the story then and now to God's future yet to come" (*Doctrine*, 45). I have found in my experience of teaching the *Ethics*, however, that this idea is one of the most difficult aspects of McClendon's position for contemporary seminarians. I am not sure why that is the case.

16. Lash, *Believing Three Ways in One God*, pp. 117–118.

12 Creation, Contingency, and Truthful Nonviolence: A Milbankian Reflection

Milbank's polemic against liberalism and the secular in *Theology and Social Theory* is so dramatic as to cause one to overlook the constructive theological proposals in the book.[1] I am not suggesting that the polemical thrust of *Theology and Social Theory* is separable from Milbank's theological claims, but there is a temptation among commentators, at least initially, to concentrate on the former because in that book almost no one is free from having his or her ox gored. In this essay, however, I want to call attention to the quite extraordinary manner in which Milbank interrelates reflection on the Trinity, creation, contingency, truth, and nonviolence. In particular, I want to show why Milbank's argument for the unavoidability of narrative as the form of truth reflects his understanding of creation as the ongoing nonviolent work of the God we know as Trinity.

I am interested in drawing out Milbank's understanding of these matters because his reflections help me to respond to a challenge by Robert Jenson about aspects of my own work. Jenson, as usual, goes to the heart of the matter by challenging not only me but also anyone who, like Milbank, accepts the critique of "foundational" accounts of knowledge. Many think that our willingness to assume the contingency of our own convictions means that we must abandon all attempts to claim Christian beliefs as true. Accordingly, are we not committed to the belief that any claim to truth is but a mask for power and is resolvable only on the basis of violence?

Jenson's question was provoked by the suggestion I made in *After Christendom?* that the Christian alternative to hegemonic and violent narratives that dominate liberal education, such as "Columbus discovered America," is simply that of witness.[2] In a letter appended to the book, David Toole, then a graduate student in theology, notes that the very notion of witness can be violent if that witness asserts for the other a truth that the other does not already possess. I acknowledge Toole's point, observing that this is but "a reminder that the way of nonviolence is never easy and that our language can embody . . . violence in ways we hardly [know]."

Jenson's question follows:

> Can Hauerwas's thinking finally sustain its own central claim, that the church is the world's salvation? The church cannot save the world in any of the ways the liberal church tries, and Hauerwas rightly rubs our nose in this plain fact. But *how* then is the church the world's salvation? The student has a point: every claim to speak truth does indeed exercise something that might plausibly be called "violence," if we so choose to use the language. If Hauerwas accepts this usage of "violence," he must abandon also witness as what the church can do for the world. It seems, indeed, he must end with a doctrine that the church saves the world simply by silently existing. Now even such a doctrine may be sustainable, but only by a lot of more speculative systematic theology than Hauerwas seems willing to countenance.[3]

But if the Christian witness is one of silence, then what does that do to Christ's commission to the church to make disciples of all nations? Surely such a commission requires witness to Native Americans as much as to liberal societies. Moreover, such a witness surely must entail some account of conversion from one narrative, one community, to another.[4]

Of course, I can "say" that Christians ought to witness and try to convert "Native Americans," but saying that seems more assertion than argument. I can respond to Jenson, "It all depends on what you mean by 'violence.'" "Violence," as well as "nonviolence," are context-dependent notions that require display in order to make sense. So I cannot answer Jenson's question in the abstract, since that would only reinforce the ahistorical accounts of Christian practices and convictions I am trying to counter.[5] Yet I think such a response would leave Jenson rightly dissatisfied, since it could not help but appear, like my attempt to stand neither with the "multiculturalists" nor with the "Eurocentrists," as but another "dodge."

An adequate response to Jenson therefore requires the display of material theological claims I believe Milbank has begun in *Theology and Social Theory*. Milbank provides the theological resources necessary for appeal to truth without those appeals embodying, or at least underwriting, the false universalism of secular epistemologies. He does so by helping us see the intrinsic connection between the Christian conviction that the God of Jesus Christ creates nonviolently and the necessity of those who worship that God to learn to live nonviolently in a world of violence. In effect, Milbank has taken up the task of explicating the metaphysics of a nonviolent creation in the hopes of providing a counter ontology to the pervasive metaphysics of violence embedded in Christian and non-Christian discourse.

Milbank contrasts the Christian conviction that creation is essentially nonviolent to that of the Greeks and liberalism (which Milbank suggests may have begun with the Greek distinction between religion and politics [329]), both of which assume agonistic accounts of existence. For Christians, violence is always a "secondary willed intrusion," which is known only because of a profounder peace. Such a peace is not driven to hegemonic or totalizing accounts of existence, since God's creation is the ongoing actualization of a sociality of harmonious difference displayed in the Trinity. That is why

> Christian logic is *not* deconstructable by modern secular reason; rather, it is Christianity which exposes the nonnecessity of supposing, like Nietzscheans, that difference, nontotalization and indeterminacy of meaning *necessarily* imply arbitrariness and violence. To suppose that they do is merely to subscribe to a particular encoding of reality. Christianity, by contrast, is the coding of transcendental difference as peace. (5–6)

Accordingly, Nietzsche was correct to single out Christianity for attack. He rightly saw that Christianity was the only viable alternative to his agonistic world. That does not mean that theology can "rationally" refute, à la MacIntyre,[6] the ontology of difference at the heart of Nietzschean postmodernism, but theology can help narrate why, given the creation of "the secular," Nietzsche's account of our "world," insofar as it is the world created by "liberalism," was inevitable.

Although Milbank's account of this thinker or that thinker may be open to challenge, it is my conviction that he is right in his claim that the very creation of the "secular" is implicated in an ontology of violence. Thus, liberal political and social theory is unable to imagine any society able to control violence except through counterviolence. Liberalism's "universalism," in this respect, is but the mirror image of Christian presuppositions—indeed, as Milbank tells the story, liberalism is only possible as a counternarrative to that of the church. In *Theology and Social Theory* Milbank attempts to display a counterontology to liberalism in the hope that by so doing he will force the "secular" to acknowledge its own contingency.

Many may think that such a "display" is insufficient, for how can Milbank defeat liberalism by using its own tools?[7] When Milbank says that he finally can only out-narrate liberalism, he is not giving up on a truthful witness. Rather, he is reminding us why it is that the very God to which Christians witness requires narrative display. That is why he argues that narrative is a more basic category than either explanation or understanding: unlike either of these it does not assume punctiliar facts or discrete meanings. Neither is it concerned with universal laws, nor universal truths of the spirit. Yet it is not arbitrary in the sense that one can repeat a text in just any fashion, although one can indeed do so in any number of fashions. . . . If reading texts means that we renarrate them or repeat them, and if, as we have seen, textuality is the condition of all culture, then narration—of events, structures, institutions, tendencies as well as of lives—is the final mode of comprehension of human society. (267)

Milbank argues that because narrative is more basic than explanation, there can be no genuine sociological comprehension of the inherently "inexplicable" character of Jesus of Nazareth (116).[8] Jesus' reconception of Israel through his life certainly entails a sociology but it cannot be construed sociologically—that is, Jesus cannot be accounted for by assembling "explanations." In this respect, there is a continuity between Jesus' refusal to seize power and the early church's refusal to overthrow existing structures. If the church tried to overthrow the existing structures, it would have simply become a parallel structure, a parallel "cause." Instead, the church attempted to create alternative, "local" areas of peace, charity, and justice.

That our existence is created means that insofar as "science" is possible, it can only be a "science of the particular." Accordingly, history remains theology's great ally. For it is written history that defies the universal by reminding us that lived history enacts the different. Positivist and dialectical traditions, with their corresponding forms of social science derived from the Enlightenment project, tried to defeat the "particularistic obscurantism" of Judaism and Christianity in the name of the universal.

But this challenge is at an end, for it has seen that it was itself made in terms of metaphysics, and of a "religion." In the "new era" of postmodernism the human has become subordinate to the infinitely many discourses which claim to constitute humanity, and universality can no longer pose as the identical, but can only be paradoxically invoked as the different. (260)

What drives Milbank's display of the ontological relationship between nonviolence and narrative is not the epistemology and ontology of postmodernism. Rather it is Jesus Christ, through whom we learn of God as Trinity, who is the fundamental ontological claim that must shape all other claims. Hence, though Milbank is in general agreement with Blondel, he nonetheless criticizes him for developing a general ontology. In contrast, "one ought to say that *only* because one first experiences the 'shape' of incarnation, of atonement, is one led to formulate the abstract notion of their occurrence; and only then does one construe reality in terms of the need for the perfecting offering of love" (217). Milbank is reminding us that though theology certainly makes metaphysical claims, such claims must remain disciplined by the prior theological commitments. That our existence is contingent is surely a metaphysical claim correlative of our created status. Yet any metaphysical speculation that such claims invite can never become an end in itself but must serve to remind us that finally our salvation comes from the Jews—thus the unavoidability of narrative and, correlatively, analogy, for any knowledge worth having.

These themes in Milbank's work are focused through his account of the Trinity. According to Milbank, Trinity denotes that God is the God in which nothing can be unrealized and yet in which no actualization, even an infinite one, can exhaust God's power.

> Infinite realized act and infinite unrealized power mysteriously coincide in God, and it must be this that supports the circular "life," that is more than *stasis*, of the Trinity. Yet "power-act" plays out through, and is constituted by, the Trinitarian relations: it is not that the Father is power and the Son act, for this would depersonalize their relation and make it *not* a real surface relation at all (this is why the Father-Son relation is not *just* a signified-signifier one, implying an "absence" of the Father, but also an "adjacent," figurative relation). (423)

Accordingly, the Trinity in the most concrete fashion possible witnesses to the nonviolence of God's creation. Creation is not a finished product but rather God's continuously generated ex nihilo in time. Creatures thus do not assist God in creation but participate in God's continuing creation as Trinity.[9] In this respect, one of the most interesting ways to think of *Theology and Social Theory* is to interpret it as an extended reflection on the work of the Holy Spirit. The materiality of the Spirit's work is the reason Milbank can make the astounding claim that theology must be its own social science. It must be so exactly because Christian convictions are necessary for us to locate the final causes shaping our history as God's ongoing work of creation.

Milbank is not suggesting that a Christian sociology can be deduced from the Christian doctrine of the Trinity in and of itself—because there is no doctrine of the Trinity in and of itself. A distinguishable Christian social theory is possible only because there are Christian practices. Put in terms of Christian dogmatics, Milbank's position assumes that Christian theological reflection "begins," insofar as Christian reflection has a beginning, with ecclesiology. For

> the Church stands in a narrative relationship to Jesus and the Gospels, within a story that subsumes both. This must be the case, because no *historical* story is ever over and done with. Furthermore, the New Testament itself does not preach any denial of historicity, or any disappearance of our

own personalities into the monistic truth of Christ. Quite to the contrary, Jesus's mission is seen as inseparable from his preaching of the kingdom, and inauguration of a new sort of community, the Church. Salvation is available for us after Christ because we can be incorporated in the community which he founded, and the response of this community to Christ is made possible by the response of the divine Spirit to the divine Son, from whom it receives the love that flows between the Son and the Father. The association of the Church with the response of the Spirit which arises after the Son, and yet is fully divine, shows that the new community belongs from the beginning within the new narrative manifestation of God. Hence the metanarrative is *not* just a story of Jesus, it is the continuing story of the Church, already realized in a finally exemplary way by Christ, yet still to be realized universally, in harmony with Christ and yet *differently*, by all generations of Christians. (387)

Milbank's position cannot help but challenge the narratives of the enlightenment, since it is the church that ultimately interprets and locates all other histories. As he says:

> if one takes one's salvation from the Church, if one identifies one's self as a member of the body of Christ, then inevitably one offers the most "ultimate" explanation of socio-historical processes in terms of the embracing or refusal of the specifically Christian virtues. Not to embrace such a metanarrative, or to ascribe to it a merely partial interpretive power, would undo the logic of the incarnation. For why would we claim to recognize the divine *logos* in a particular life, unless we had the sense that everything else was to be located *here*, despite the fact that this life is but one more life, itself situated along the historical *continuum*? Thus if the enlightenment makes this sort of thing impossible, it also rules out salvation to the Church as traditionally understood. (246)

Milbank, in one of his striking asides, which I think nicely suggests the power of his theology, observes that to be part of the church is to have "the moral luck to belong to the society which overcomes moral luck" (231).[10] For to belong to the church means one has become part of those "practices of perfection" that make us capable of becoming friends with one another, ourselves, and God. The "music of creation" is thus constituted and continued in the church. The music that the church has learned to sing through becoming friends of God and one another is a music for all God's creation. If the church is about "out-narrating," it can do so only to the extent that it can "out-sing" the world.[11]

Therefore, Milbank cannot offer us a theory of truth that is more determinative than the Christian witness to Trinity through song. For if we had such a theory, then we should worship that theory rather than praise the Trinity. What good are definitions of truth when such definitions can distract from that which constitutes us as truthful witnesses to God's very life? The very contingent character of a truthful witness cannot be denied if we are to witness truthfully to the truth that we are creatures of a gracious creator. That is what I think Milbank means when he claims that truth for Christianity is not correspondence but rather *participation* of the beautiful in the beauty of God (427).

I do not know if Milbank represents the kind of "speculative systematic theology" that Jenson suggests I need, but I think the relationships Milbank develops between theology and social theory help me respond to Jenson's questions. Given Milbank, it should be clear why I am not as deferential to the narratives of the Enlightenment as I am to those of the Native Americans. Put quite simply, the narratives of the Native Americans do not represent the subtle co-option of the Christian narratives in the way that those of the Enlightenment do, born as the latter are from Christianity's own life. Indeed, I think it imperative that Christians challenge the narratives of liberalism exactly because they fail to acknowledge their own violence. Of course, the confrontation between theology and "the secular" cannot be other than conflictual, as hegemonic narratives, when confronted by their hegemony, always attempt to claim that "peace" is being threatened.

Moreover, Christians seek no less to witness to and thus convert Native Americans than Enlightenment liberals. I do not think, however, that conversion means the same for each. Indeed, if conversion is the recognition of membership in a more determinative community than the one in which I first found myself, then the conversion for most liberals is going to be more dramatic than for most Native Americans. For the liberal presumption that they belong to no community, no narrative, other than the community they themselves have chosen masks the deepest violence of modernity.

Christians should try to convert Native Americans, but since I am not living among Native Americans, I have little idea what that means. I do know, however, that it should have at least meant that the Christians who first confronted Native Americans should have refrained from killing them. As part of that peaceable witness, they would have also had to ask the Sioux not to kill the Pawnee if they were to live as Christians. Native Americans might have found that quite a challenge, even a violent challenge, to their very identity. But I have no way of knowing that in principle. It depends, indeed, on what the concrete narratives and practices are that Christians confront. What I do, of course, challenge is the assumption that conversion has primarily to do with an individual's self-understanding rather than his or her being put in the context of a different community with a different set of practices. To be sure, a Navaho might become Christian and still remain a Christian Navaho. We would simply have to wait and see what the full implications of that would be across generations. I am, after all, still a Texan even though I am a Christian.

One aspect of the problem we confront as part of the Christian witness to Native Americans is how that witness can be made in the face of the extraordinary violence perpetrated on Native Americans in the name of Christianity. Jenson chides me for siding with the fashionable "multicultural" attack upon "Eurocentrism." I certainly have no wish to be "fashionable," but I am willing to take that risk in order to challenge the accommodation of the church to those narratives that underwrite murder in the name of "progress."[12] By challenging the story Enlightenment historiography tells about the triumph of Columbus, I am trying to help Christians discover how our narrative practices have been captured by a sociology that subsumes Christ and the church within a narrative in which "Western civilization" becomes the primary actor.

The more challenging theological issue is how Christians, white and Native American Christians alike, are to witness to Native Americans in the face of the violence perpetrated on them in the name of Christian "civilization." In that context I think the witness of the church might well take the form of silence through presence. Learning to live with those you have wronged may not be a bad place to begin if the salvation we believe has been made present by Christ is as materially palpable as body and blood.

Milbank notes that Augustine denied the existence of true virtue and justice in a pagan society because the pagans failed to worship the true God. Augustine argued that

> the form taken by true worship of the true God is the offering of mutual forgiveness in the community, and at one point he associates absence of the practice of forgiveness ("true sacrifice") with the absence of monotheism. In addition, thought of God the Father seems for Augustine to have been quite inseparable from the thought of heaven, our Mother, or the eternal community of all unfallen and redeemed creatures enjoying visions of the infinite Trinity. Thus, when he says that the pagans fail to "refer" all earthly *usus* to the peace of the one true God, he adjoins to this a failure of referral to the peace of the heavenly community. Without "mutual forgiveness" and social peace, says Augustine, "no one will be able to see God." The pagans were for Augustine unjust, because they did not give priority to peace and forgiveness. (409)

Missing in Milbank, however, is the concrete display of such forgiveness and reconciliation that makes God's peace present. What we need are stories, witnesses, like the one Rufus Bowman tells regarding the relationship of the Brethren, German "Dunkards," to the Indians in Morrison's Cove, Pennsylvania, during the French and Indian Wars.[13] In order to tell this story, Bowman has to draw on U. J. Jones's quite unsympathetic account of the Brethren contained in the latter's *History of the Early Settlement of the Juniata Valley*. Bowman notes that Jones was quite critical of the Brethren both for refusing to take up arms and for refusing to pay money to support those willing to take up arms, not only during the French and Indian War but also in the Revolutionary War. In the tone of "they got what they deserved," Jones describes the behavior of the "Dunkards" during an Indian raid in the midst of the Revolutionary War:

> On their first expedition they would have few scalps to grace their belts, had the Dunkards taken the advice of more sagacious people, and fled, too; this, however, they would not do. They would follow but half of Cromwell's advice; they were willing to put their "trust in God," but they would not "keep their powder dry." In short, it was a compound they did not use at all.
>
> The savages swept down through the Cove with all the ferocity with which a pack of wolves would descend from the mountain upon a flock of sheep. Some few of the Dunkards, who evidently had a latent spark of love of life, hid themselves away; but by far the most of them stood by and witnessed the butchery of wives and children, merely saying, "Gottes wille sei getan." How many Dunkard scalps they carried to Detroit cannot now be, and probably never has been clearly ascertained—not less than thirty, according to the best authority. In addition to this they loaded themselves with plunder, stole a number of horses, and under cover of night the triumphant warriors marched bravely away.[14]

Bowman notes that Jones ended his account with a brief aside, the significance of which Jones completely missed. It seems that during the massacre the Brethren repeated so often "Gottes wille sei getan" that the Indians retained a vivid recollection of them. During the war, some of the Indians who had massacred the Brethren were later captured. Interestingly enough, they were anxious to discover whether the "Gotswiltahns" still lived in the Cove. They thought "Gotswiltahns" must have been the name of that quite strange tribe.[15]

I think, finally, that such an example is what Milbank's book is all about. Without such examples Christianity makes no sense and there is no witness. It is when we lose the practices necessary to remember these people that the contingent witness that we must always make as Christians cannot help but be violent. I suspect, when all is said and done, that the Brethren of Morrison's Cove do not need Milbank. But I am sure that Milbank, and the rest of us that would do theology, need the Brethren of Morrison's Cove. They are God's witness that as God's creatures we can live nonviolently in a world of violence.

Notes

Phil Kenneson, David Matzko, and John Berkman made extremely helpful criticisms of an earlier draft of this chapter. I am in their debt.

1. John Milbank, *Theology and Social Theory: Beyond Secular Reason* (Oxford: Basil Blackwell, 1990). Page references to Milbank appear in the text and notes.

2. Robert Jenson, "Review of Stanley Hauerwas's *After Christendom?*" *First Things* 25 (August/September 1992).

3. Ibid.

4. Questions like these about *After Christendom?* have been raised by my colleague George Marsden. I am grateful to him for the serious consideration he gives my work.

5. John Berkman puts the matter this way: "Is Christian witness necessarily violent? I wonder if that is like asking is sex necessarily violent? or is sports necessarily violent? or is the master/apprentice relationship necessarily violent? or is Jesus' relationship with the disciples necessarily violent? If there cannot be peaceable varieties of witnessing, sexual relationships, ice hockey (yes! ice hockey!), vocational training and discipleship, then I do not know what it would mean to call any of these activities violent. Violence depends on there being a contrast. Now, whereas a concept like 'a peaceable axe murder' is an oxymoron, certainly 'peaceable witness' is not. It seems to me that the core uses of 'violence' cannot refer to 'witnessing,' but rather only extended senses of 'violence,' senses commonly employed in some of the deconstructive literature. Perhaps we need to ask, 'Whose violence? Which peaceableness?'" The comments were made in a letter to me. John Berkman is a former graduate student of mine who now teaches at Catholic University.

6. Milbank's relationship to MacIntyre is obviously complex. In many ways, *Theology and Social Theory* could not have been written if MacIntyre did not exist. Milbank wrote *Theology and Social Theory* prior to the publication of MacIntyre's *Three Rival Versions of Moral Inquiry*. It is my guess, however, that MacIntyre's "realism" in that work would only reinforce what Milbank takes to be his disagreement with MacIntyre. Milbank senses that his disagreements with MacIntyre finally come down to this: He approaches social theory as a theologian, whereas MacIntyre approaches it as a philosopher. The key point at issue here is the role that must be accorded to Christianity and to Christian theology. For MacIntyre, it is true, Christianity has come to matter more and more, but Milbank argues that it remains the case that MacIntyre "opposes to philosophy and practice of difference not, primarily, Christian thought and practice, but the antique understanding of virtue, with the accompaniments of Socratic dialectics, and the general link of reason to tradition. Of course, for MacIntyre, one must subscribe to some *particular* tradition, some *particular* code of virtue and here he identifies himself as an Augustinian Christian. But, all the same, the *arguments* put forward against nihilism and a philosophy of difference are made in the name of virtue, dialectics and the *notion* of tradition in general" (327).

7. There is a very serious problem about the character of Milbank's whole project as he attempts to supply a counternarrative to that of liberalism. Does he reproduce exactly the violence of liberalism by trying to write such a grand narrative of how we have gotten in our peculiar straits today? In that sense his project is not unlike MacIntyre's project in *Whose Justice? Which Rationality?* Obviously, in my own work I have tried to chip away at liberalism one piece at a time. Milbank, however, may be right that you can only counter a totalizing narrative with an-

other narrative that is equally totalizing, but I fear that in the process the Gospel cannot help but appear as just another "system" or "theory."

8. Though Milbank's Christology remains underdeveloped, I hope I am correct to think that when he does turn his attention to these matters, he will be sympathetic to the portrayal of Jesus by John Howard Yoder.

9. It is crucial to note that Milbank's account of participation is quite different than that of Gustafson. Milbank is making an ontological claim correlative to his trinitarian account of creation. Accordingly, participation is not, as it is for Gustafson, a self-validating claim about our status as humans.

10. Milbank's reflection on the notion of luck obviously draws deeply on the work of Bernard Williams and Martha Nussbaum. I think he does so profoundly, since our violence is often the attempt to render certain and necessary contingent moral commitments that we have made and for which others have paid the price—i.e., our attempt to rid our life of luck is the source of our greatest violence. The word Christians use to describe how our lives are constituted by such luck is grace. Yet grace does not remove, as the Greeks tried to remove through theory, the contingency of our existence. I have thought that it would make a fascinating comparison in this respect to juxtapose Iris Murdoch's reflections on contingency with those of Milbank. For an attempt to develop these themes, see Charlie Pinches and Hauerwas, *Christians Among the Virtues: Theological Conversations with Ancient and Modern Ethics* (Notre Dame: University of Notre Dame Press, 1997).

11. It is surely one of the most interesting moves, in a book of interesting moves, that Milbank sees the importance of Augustine's *De Musica* for the explication, not only of creation, but also of the doctrine of the Trinity. He notes the way Augustine sees in *De Musica* that all the elements of creation are not "things" but are inherently interconnected "qualities," which combine and recombine in an endless variety that reflects God's glory (pp. 424–425).

12. I confess. When I was working on the last chapter of *After Christendom?* I was worried about the use of "Columbus discovers America" as the central example in that chapter. Yet I became convinced, in spite of appearing "trendy," that there is no better example that challenges current educational practices.

13. Rufus D. Bowman, *Church of the Brethren and War, 1708–1941* (Elgin, Ill.: Brethren Publishing House, 1944), pp. 74–75. I am indebted to the Reverend Jeff Bach for calling my attention to Bowman's narrative.

14. Ibid.

15. Ibid., pp. 75–76.

13 Remaining in Babylon: Oliver O'Donovan's Defense of Christendom,

with James Fodor

On How Not to Read O'Donovan

Oliver O'Donovan's *The Desire of the Nations* is a bold, courageous, and compelling account of the challenges facing Christianity in a time when the church is on the brink of extinction in modern Western cultures. ("Extinction," when applied to the church, is another way of saying, "being totally assimilated into," or "engulfed by," modern Western cultures.) In a sense, O'Donovan's reclamation of a Christendom paradigm for reimagining our present predicament is a salutary (one might even say, prophetic) gesture. It is salutary precisely to the extent that it is so unexpected. After all, who would think of defending, at such a time as this, the idea of Christendom—that is, the notion that state legitimacy requires the legal privileging of Christianity? It almost borders on the absurd. In an era when theologians are trying to outdo one another at being novel, innovative, creative—motivated largely by a fear of being out-of-date and thus irrelevant—it is rare indeed to find someone so committed to re-animating the ancient traditions of the faith. But O'Donovan's project is no mere exercise in nostalgia, let alone the machinations of a political reactionary.

There is a subtlety and depth to O'Donovan's argument that can be lost on the casual reader, especially the reader who mistakenly assumes that whatever O'Donovan is about can be safely subsumed under current political categories and paradigms. That is clearly not the case. O'Donovan refuses the framework set by modern political theory, particularly the false dualisms that such theory fosters. His objective rather is "to push back the horizon of commonplace politics and open it up to the activity of God." Although he is willing to admit that "earthly events of liberation, rule and community-foundation provide us with partial indications of what God is doing in human history," if "we are to grasp the full meaning of political events as they pass before our eyes," "we must look to the horizon of God's redemptive purposes" (2).[1] The political theology in which O'Donovan is interested, then, is one that is distinctively, explicitly, Christian and God-centered.

In this essay we will present what we take to be the central arguments of *The Desire of the Nations*, raise some questions about the hermeneutical architectonic that governs O'Donovan's reading of Scripture, and, finally, suggest where we think we may differ. We use the phrase "may differ" because the reader will discover that there are more things on which we agree with O'Donovan than on which we disagree. In particular, we admire his refusal to retreat to the "transcendental" in an effort to secure a place for "religion" in modernity. His is a historical theology that rightly begins with the fundamental theological fact that out of all the peoples of God's good creation Israel is God's promised people. If that is not true, then the resurrection of Jesus Christ cannot be what Christians have assumed it to be, namely, God's eschatological act to renew all creation. We differ with O'Donovan to the extent that he thinks resurrection and ascension make it possible for Christians to be more than God's wandering people.

Since much of our essay will involve criticism, or at least questions, about O'Donovan's reading of Scripture, we need to make clear our admiration for his "use" of Scripture. Because he refuses the sequestering of the theological into the transcendental offered by modern political arrangements, his political theology is unreservedly scriptural in its content and orientation. Scripture provides the narrative for the church to read rightly the world in which we live. In all of this we agree and only wish we were as at home in Scripture as is O'Donovan. Indeed, in spite of their differences, O'Donovan and John Howard Yoder are allies in this last respect, since unlike most contemporary theologians they think Scripture matters. Indeed, we suspect that those who understand Yoder's work are best prepared to appreciate O'Donovan's different readings of Scripture.

"We cannot discuss the question of 'secular' government, the question from which Western political theology has too often been content to start, unless we approach it historically, from a Christology that has been displayed in narrative form as the Gospel" is the hallmark sentence of *The Desire of the Nations* (133). Accordingly, O'Donovan contends that after the ascension, nations could not not respond to Christ. In the Exile Israel learned that it must always exist under dual authority, that is, after its captivity in Babylonia Israel understood that its history is inescapably a history of two political entities that must coexist in time and space. Jesus "destabilizes" this dualism by making possible merciful judgment—or better, claiming for secular authority merciful judgment (147, 200). Such judgment is possible just to the extent that states are enabled to recognize that they cannot be the church, the recognition of which is contingent upon the latter's distinctive presence.

The history of this politics, a theological politics, is but a witness to the gratuitous character of our existence. Everything we have to say about ourselves, our history, the universe, is distorted if what we profess does not reflect the truth that God has created ex nihilo. The great heresy of modernity is the assumption that human presence in the world is suffi-cient to summon out of chaos and emptiness order and beauty. "Faith in creation means accepting the world downstream of the Arbitrary Origi-nal, justified to us in being, goodness, and order. Voluntarism, on the other hand, situates the agent at the source; it offers a mystical access to the moment of origination and leads the spirit to the rapture of pure ter-ror before the arbitrariness of its own choice" (274). The history and poli-tics that reflect such voluntariness are, for O'Donovan, a counterhistory to the politics of God.

Accordingly, O'Donovan is rightly critical of the tendency in recent theology to convert the meaning of Christ's triumph exclusively into a doctrine of history.

> A redemption that has merely the transformation of the world in view will not deal seriously with the fact that what God has done in Christ he has done for his creation and for his own sake as creator. It is not enough to un-derstand the triumph of the Kingdom as improving or perfecting a world that was, as it stood, simply inadequate. The distinct ideas of a good cre-ation on the one hand and a redeemed creation on the other are then col-lapsed into an undifferentiated ongoing activity of God, in which the lower is raised to the higher, a depressing conception of Manichaean character, sometimes dignified with the name of "continuous creation," though in fact it constitutes a denial of the decisiveness implied in the term "creation" and is really only concerned to assert continuousness. (143)

Such continuousness, which is often dressed in the high humanistic language of freedom and creativity, turns out to be a way to encourage us to accept our fate. Correlatively, our lives are robbed of joy. The church, in contrast, is *the* community of praise, of joy, precisely to the extent that it lives by pointing to the resurrection as the restoration of God's good or-der in creation. Only creatures who know that glory belongs to God alone can be glad. Indeed, their joy is possible because they do not need to do the work of God (181).

The Gospel of the life, death, and resurrection of Jesus, then, is the nar-rative that traces events back to their divine source and forward to their divine end. The Gospel cannot be a myth; it cannot be a symbol, even though mythical and symbolic aspects are clearly part of its narrative. How else can one tell the story that involves at once the being of God and earthly events? Yet in true myth the narration is form but not substance. For "truth" is more profound than the narrative, insofar as it always overruns and frustrates the narrative.[2] The Incarnation, therefore, "is not true myth, because the point to be communicated was the coming of the Kingdom, an event which could, indeed, be dated. The reason for taking the event back to its source outside this world's events is that Jesus wholly mediates the Kingdom in his personal being, and that the Kingdom has its origin in God's eternal purpose" (136).

A cursory display of these central theological presumptions points up something of the complexity, nuance, and intricacy of O'Donovan's political theology. Modern political theory, to be sure, offers us "partial indications" of our creaturely status, and therefore any easy refusal of modernity would not only be immature but also unwarranted. O'Donovan, although he clearly recognizes the dangers and limitations of modern political frameworks, concedes that no other model is available (228). In other words, O'Donovan's concern is with "the Christian political tradition as we have inherited it" (262). That means that he is committed to explicating the way in which modernity is itself a child of Christianity, albeit one that has forsaken the father's house and followed the path of the prodigal (275). Although there certainly must be a careful differentiation and "distancing" of Christianity from modernity (the two are clearly not equatable), O'Donovan recognizes that there can be no simple shrugging off or disowning of modernity either.

Just as O'Donovan cannot be situated within current political paradigms, neither can he be easily "located" within the present spectrum of theological reflections on politics. It is quite easy to see, for example, how a superficial reading might mistake O'Donovan's refusal of liberation theology (what he calls "the Southern school of political theology" [3]), combined with his endorsement of the Christendom idea (226), for a call for the reactivation and reinstitution of an antiquated political theology. To be sure, O'Donovan registers great excitement at having rediscovered "the Great Tradition of political theology" (via a close reading of Hobbes's *Leviathan:* xi, 21), a tradition that makes modern political thought pale by comparison. But this should not lead one to the facile conclusion that O'Donovan's enterprise advocates a simple return to some premodern, golden age. Although he variously describes his own project as one of "recovery" (21), "restoration" (19), "retrieval" (19), "reclamation" (46), even one of "renewal" (11), it is no static duplication or prosaic repetition of the past that he is after. Rather, what he envisions is a discerning "re-orientation" (2), an "opening up of the horizon again" (20), which will lead, he hopes, to a repetition with a contextually appropriate difference—a difference arising from and informed by the Scriptures. In the same way that the Gospel writers situate "the Palm Sunday narrative at the head of the Passion story," thereby preventing the reader from supposing that "David's rule could be, as it were, revived and reconstituted, but point us forward to its resumption in a climax of a quite different kind" (25), so too contemporary Christians must narrate God's rule in Christ in such a way as not to endorse thoughtlessly the past manifestations of Christendom but to search for ever new and more appropriate displays, as called for by the church's present circumstances.[3] Despite the care and precision of his arguments, we fear that many politically conservative readers will miss the nuance and suppleness of O'Donovan's theological craft and misconstrue his outline of a political theology as a blanket endorsement of the conventional political agenda.

O'Donovan's Hermeneutic Architectonic: First Question

In a move reminiscent of Charles Taylor, O'Donovan sees himself as engaged in a project of retrieval and "re-membering" (creating a reconfiguration by narrating again) the lost sources of a political theology. Although he clearly wants to pass beyond modernity's "suspicion and totalised criticism" and offer instead "a positive reconstruction of political thought," O'Donovan's objective is to provide the reader not simply with a theology of politics but a bona fide political theology. By restoring the "lost theological horizon" (19), which has, for the most part, been "occluded by the shadow of the modern period" (4), O'Donovan enjoins an attentive listening to a more ancient politico-theological discourse as well as a more encompassing reading of Scripture.

Perhaps the most attractive, refreshing feature of O'Donovan's hermeneutic is that it is confident and unapologetic, avowedly guided by the resources of Scripture and the Christian tradition. That is to say, O'Donovan consciously endeavors to develop a political theology that is not beholden to any "external" narrative but that "takes seriously its own authorisation in the Gospel of Jesus Christ" (21). By discerning and explicating the inner logic of the drama of God's dawning Kingdom, O'Donovan attempts to display "the one public history which is the theatre of God's saving purposes and mankind's social undertakings" (2).

The reason why the shadow cast by "late-modern liberal culture" (9) is so long and so dark, according to O'Donovan, is that the culture has ventured to separate politics and theology. However, precisely because liberal culture has lost its theological horizon, modern political theory finds itself hopelessly entangled in self-inflicted incoherence and unintelligibility.[4] Regrettably, many current theologically informed expressions of politics do not fare much better because they too tacitly endorse the same separation of theology and politics. That is another way of saying that any political theology that attempts to exert its influence on politics "through carefully guarded channels of influence that preserve a cordon sanitaire" (2) cannot help but fail. By contrast, what O'Donovan is after is a robust political theology replete with a full political and theological conceptuality and having as its preoccupation "the one history which finds its goal in Christ, 'the desire of the nations'" (2). The theologian's task, therefore, is one of articulating an understanding of the unfolding drama of God's rule without *either* capitulating to modernity's separation of religion and politics (which thereby relegates religion to a spiritual or "private," but clearly nonpolitical, realm) *or* apologizing for its own insights and agenda (which thereby makes its practitioners and its message cowering and timid instead of bold and hopeful).

> The renewed advocacy of political theology in our own time has had as its concern to break out of the cordon sanitaire. When that advocacy has been at its clearest, it has insisted that theology is political simply by responding to the dynamics of its own proper themes. Christ, salvation, the church, the Trinity: to speak about these has involved theologians in speaking of society, and has led them to formulate normative political ends. They have turned out to know something about the ends of politics, and perhaps about the means, too, without needing to be told. It is not a question of adapting to alien requirements or subscribing to external agenda, but of letting theology be true to its task and freeing it from a forced and unnatural detachment. (3)

O'Donovan's enterprise is therefore unreservedly theological. Nonetheless, he conceives of that task primarily in theoretical (or at least formal) terms. That is to say, he is essentially interested in articulating the *structure* or *design* of a political theology. He refers variously to this formal display as an architectonic, "a unifying conceptual structure" (22), a hermeneutical framework. In short, O'Donovan is in search of "the unifying hermeneutic principle" (22, cf. 27), which will lay bare "the authority structure" (93, cf. 105) of God's rule.

O'Donovan isolates three primary "terms" (36) (or "affirmations" [45]) that constitute the "exegetical framework" of his political theology. Borrowing three common Hebrew words, salvation, judgment, and possession, O'Donovan constructs an interpretative matrix, which he will later develop and extend through a rather elaborate declension, qualifying and relating these terms to various (six) "theorems" and (four) "moments." The result is a rather complex formal configuration. What remains puzzling is where the exegetical framework leaves off and the theory begins—or whether in fact they can be so easily distinguished. First, we need to consider O'Donovan's exegetical framework.

As O'Donovan puts it, "Yhwh's authority as king is established by the accomplishment of victorious deliverance, by the presence of judicial discrimination and by the continuity of a community-possession. To these three primary terms I add a fourth, which identifies the human response and acknowledgment of Yhwh's reign: praise. Around these points of reference other leading terms which concern the law, the land and the city group themselves" (36). Apparently these derivative notions are ascertained by conjoining, in differing combinations, the three primary terms. "Vindication" (land), for example, results when the notions of victory and judgment come together. Likewise, "law" results when judgment and possession meet; and "city" (Mount Zion) is produced through the combination of possession and victory. Moreover, the question of God's presence may also be modulated by this tripartite structure. That is, through conquest God's presence is "immediate"; through judgment it is "mediated"; and finally through the law it manifests itself as a "concealed immediacy" (50). All of that gives the impression that O'Donovan's exegetical matrix is too neat and symmetrical, and perhaps a bit too clever. (One wonders, for example, what becomes of covenant, a theme clearly central to O'Donovan's political theology, inasmuch as "the unique covenant of Yhwh and Israel can be seen as a point of disclosure from which the nature of *all* political authority comes into view" [45; emphasis added]).

What, then, is the cognitive status of O'Donovan's exegetical framework? Although these three primary terms (and their several permutations and combinations) are no more than "primary points of reference" and, according to O'Donovan, only "play an organizing role in the exposition of political theology" (36), and although such concepts or exegetical devices cannot themselves claim "to be directly authorised by" the scriptural text, but only serve "to comprehend the text and illuminate it by allowing one aspect to shed light upon another," O'Donovan nonetheless believes that they do something more. They provide not only "an important clue for the development of the affirmation of God's kingship in the New Testament" but also "a framework for exploring the major questions about authority posed by the Western tradition" (45). In other words, despite O'Donovan's disclaimer that his exegetical framework has little more than heuristic value, he nonetheless wants to "stretch" beyond the insights thereby gained and use them to make strong theoretical claims. This is both a curious and a puzzling move. What is the difference between exegesis and theory, and what is entailed by extending (or extrapolating) from one to the other? At certain times O'Donovan contends that his formal interpretative structure is "a purely exegetical schema" that "has no theoretical function" (133; cf. also 145, 45). At other times he appears to conflate the two, speaking of them together without apparent differentiation: "the exegetical and theoretical outline" (46).

Given the subtlety, sophistication, and care of O'Donovan's theological project, our concern over the differentiation between exegetical articulation of certain key concepts and their theoretical elaboration may sound rather pedantic. However, because O'Donovan seems preoccupied with such structural considerations in sketching his political theology (and there may indeed be some merit in displaying the formal features of God's rule), then on his own terms he owes the reader a clearer explanation of how his move from exegesis to theoretical description is warranted and whether in the end any significant difference obtains between these two practices. That is another way of asking for further elaboration on the relation between the value of his formal outline and the material specifications of the narrative articulated in his close readings of the biblical text. It is rather telling, we think, that many of the wonderful insights and observations on selected scriptural passages that O'Donovan proffers are perfectly intelligible without recourse to his tripartite exegetical/theoretical framework or his invocation of the four "moments" and the six "theorems."[5] It is not clear, in other words, in what way(s) his hermeneutical theory actually guides his readings of and commentary on biblical texts. Nor is it readily apparent how his exegesis informs his theoretical claims, that is to say, his hermeneutic architectonic.

O'Donovan's very use of "architectonic" is also revealing. It immediately suggests that what he is interested in recounting is a master narrative, a grand story on the scale of Augustine's *City of God*.[6] In this regard, his work is not unlike that of John Milbank. Both are very much concerned with ruling and God's rule. Whereas O'Donovan wants to rule morally, Milbank wants to rule intellectually. In some ways we are in deep sympathy with such aspirations. Even though the desires embodied in both O'Donovan's and Milbank's work strike a resonant chord, we are nonetheless hesitant to endorse either project without qualification. To be sure, both represent great possibilities; but they also constitute great temptations. Being all too cognizant of the sinful proclivities of the human imagination and of the seeming ineradicable human pride that reserves for political life its most virulent manifestations, we find our hope in the prospects of human rule under God to be more tempered by the eschatological "not yet" than encouraged by the eschatological "already."

We realize that our "worries" about O'Donovan's (and Milbank's) architectonic ambitions may suggest to some extent our own "anabaptist" predispositions. Yet we think our differences are a good deal more complex. For example, O'Donovan is right in asserting that "the Christendom idea," that is, the idea that secular authority is to be fashioned to serve the advancement of the Gospel, "has to be located correctly as an aspect of the church's understanding of *mission*. The church is not at liberty to withdraw from mission; nor may it undertake its mission without confident hope in success. It was the missionary imperative that compelled the church to take the conversion of the empire seriously and to seize the opportunities it offered. These were not merely opportunities for 'power.' They were opportunities for preaching the Gospel, baptising believers, curbing the violence and cruelty to empire and, perhaps most important of all, forgiving their former persecutors" (212).

Although we will express some dis-ease with this claim, or at least will want to know more about how O'Donovan thinks the state should render service to the church by facilitating its mission, we have no reason to dissent from such an account of Christendom. Of course, Christendom was part of the church's rightful missionary enterprise (223). O'Donovan faithfully notes that Christendom should not be celebrated as a story of coercion, though it was certainly that, but rather should be seen as the way in which the power of God humbled the haughty ones of the earth by harnessing them to the purpose of peace. We, like O'Donovan, are catholic Christians who believe that even in the church's unfaithfulness, it is still the church. So the violence that was accepted as part of Christendom does not mean that we must think that God abandoned the church when it became established.

We appreciate the rhetorical force of O'Donovan's question: "Does the authority of the Gospel word confer no social structure on the community which bears it?" (208). This we take to be an anti-Gnostic or anti-docetic ecclesiology with which we are in profound agreement. The Gospel will and must be enculturated. Indeed, there was never a time when the Gospel was not enculturated; hence, the question is not whether it will be embodied but whether or not such an embodiment is faithful to the Gospel (225). O'Donovan is no less insistent than Yoder (or we are) that the church serves the world when it takes seriously its own life as service to the world.

The church has to instruct the state if the state is to be humble. Along the way the church has learned various strategies to accomplish such ends, but these ways, these political doctrines, can also become a substitute for proclaiming Christ. We think O'Donovan is exactly right to suggest that when the Christian understanding of salvation history was replaced by an open-ended concept of historical development in the interest of underwriting liberal regimes, Christians not only lost any sense of what a Christian secular government might look like, but even more they undermined the intelligibility of the doctrine of the Trinity. The latter was left "high and dry on the austere sands of the *Quicunque vult* without its necessary point of reference in the Pascal triumph" (246). Accordingly, O'Donovan criticizes Jacques Maritain's proposals for a "democratic secular faith," which substitute a "democratic creed for the Gospel." The church may have to make the best of whatever political contexts it finds itself within, but "'making the best' means making the evangelical content of the doctrine clear, not veiling it in embarrassment" (219).

In these many ways we find ourselves in sympathy and concord with O'Donovan. Yet agreeing with O'Donovan's ecclesial presuppositions does not require our endorsement of, let alone our concurrence with, his "architectonic" ambitions. We will say more about this later in this essay. Suffice it to say now that when all is said and done we believe O'Donovan thinks he knows more about how the story comes out than we think can be justified—thus our sense of the necessary eschatological reservation, "not yet."[7] Put colloquially, we believe that Scripture is best read as an aid for the church to "muddle through" rather than an architectonic for rule. Our differences with O'Donovan in this respect are simple but we believe profound. Whereas O'Donovan seeks correlation with Israel, we look for analogies. Put differently, O'Donovan reads back from the loss of Christendom to the Scriptures to justify the need for the latter. We think he should read forward from Scripture, helping us see the loss of Christendom as God's positive disciplining of the church in order that we might better understand how our habitation in Babylon should proceed. In short, we think that God has placed Christians in a position where we might learn from the Jews at the very least one thing: namely, that God's people live and survive by their wits, not by being recognized or accorded official status by those who would claim to rule. Such a view, moreover, shakes the very politics of reading the Scriptures, to which we now turn.

Reading Scripture Politically: More Questions

Our reservations about O'Donovan's reading of Scripture encompass the formal character as well as the material content of his argument. Although the two are not easily separated, we will consider the formal questions first.

The formality and abstractness of O'Donovan's hermeneutical project are marked by several infelicities and puzzles. Although his language is circumspect and guarded, O'Donovan occasionally lapses into objectivist language, especially in his polemical statements. Compare, for example, his baffling reference to "the text itself" (104), and his further remarks (in a passage where he contests John Howard Yoder's reading of Matthew 18:15–20) concerning what "the text" does and does not "say" (151–152). That O'Donovan is quite confident that he knows (indeed, that anyone knows!) what "the text says" is all the more perplexing given his acknowledgment that what is currently under consideration is his own reading of the Matthean text over against that of Yoder. Apparently, by appealing to what "the text says," O'Donovan believes that one is invoking an ultimate authority, a final arbiter. What is wrongheaded about such objectivist appeals—wrongheaded, we assume, on O'Donovan's own grounds—is that they locate final authority in something called "the text itself." The assumption behind such appeals is that words on the page are thought to "contain" meaning. In this regard, it is hard to know what to make of O'Donovan's claim that authority rests in "Paul's words," not in the exegesis of Paul's words (152)—which seems to imply that one can have access to the meaning of Paul's words without actually interpreting them!

Although these kinds of hermeneutical infelicities are uncharacteristic of O'Donovan's otherwise careful work (i.e., they are not a systemic feature of his hermeneutic architectonic), they do nonetheless convey, if not widespread alarm, then at least one or two disturbing reminders of the limitations of his formal outline. First of all, these deficiencies and lapses demonstrate (unintentionally) the fact that despite O'Donovan's failure to produce a consistent hermeneutical theory, he has nevertheless advanced important theological work and insight. Second (perhaps a more charitable view), these deficiencies indicate that O'Donovan is better in his close readings of the biblical witness than in his polemical engagements.

In fairness to O'Donovan, it must be conceded that he exacts great pains in plumbing the depths and richness of the biblical texts. Indeed, his fine exegetical work constitutes some of the most rewarding and insightful aspects of his political theology.[8] We are not faulting him for his lack of narrative elaboration of the concepts he investigates or even his point of departure (his theoretical concentration on concepts rather than an exposition of narrative content). For as with any hermeneutical enterprise, what matters is not one's point of entry into the hermeneutical circle but one's manner of proceeding. At this point O'Donovan's hermeneutic methodology exhibits some confusion.

Although O'Donovan is right to argue that modern Western politics has turned its back on its theological horizons (20), which largely accounts for its present incoherence and unintelligibility, we are not convinced that "a truthful description of the political act" (20) can be accomplished on the basis of either a conceptual analysis or a formal display of the structure of a political theology.[9] Although we do appreciate the relative value of theory, we are more convinced of its ad hoc employment than of the need, as asserted in O'Donovan's work, for its systematic display before any important work in political theology can be done.

We have some of the same reservations about O'Donovan's related claim regarding the precedence of (and implicit separation between) a political theology and a political ethics. Although it may be advisable for strategic reasons to elaborate a political theology *before* one engages in a political ethics, the two are inseparable and emerge concurrently. That is to say, they must be articulated together. Although O'Donovan appreciates their indissociable character, he nonetheless betrays a somewhat confused understanding of their mutual relatedness. He notes in several places (cf. xi, 249, 286) that *The Desire of the Nations* represents only the first part of an originally planned two-part project—a political theology to which a political ethics demands to be "added" (xi). Elsewhere O'Donovan speaks of their relation not so much in terms of a sequential order (i.e., of a political ethics being "added" to a political theology) but in terms of the distinction between them as centered in a relative difference of emphasis or focus. "We wrote in chapter one of the 'political act,' the act which is authorised and carries authority, which can give moral form to a community by defining its commitment to the good in a representative performance. . . . The scope and possibilities of the political act will have to be explored, should God grant it to be, in a sequel to this work that will carry its focus from political theory to political ethics" (249). In other words, "political ethics has to carry forward into detailed deliberation the principle established by political theology: authority is reordered towards the task of judgment" (286). Here the relation between a political theology and a political ethics is not so much one of sequential order, or even relative focus, but one of increased detail and specification.

Now of course all that needs to be said about politics and ethics cannot be said simultaneously, and we do not fault O'Donovan for failing to accomplish the impossible. But we do seriously wonder what effect his decision to articulate a political theology apart from a political ethics says about the purported relation between the two. Does O'Donovan separate political theology from political ethics merely for strategic reasons, or is there something of a conceptual (or logical or methodological) precedence reflected in this chosen order of treatment? Whereas O'Donovan's own various and not always compatible descriptions of the relations between these two parts of his project indicate something less than clarity, our suspicions are further aroused, since this distinction seems to legitimate his concentration on the formal aspects of his political theology.

O'Donovan, moreover, seems to equate the delineation of the formal considerations of a political theology with the truth (or theological coherence) of the scriptural witness to God's rule. O'Donovan rightly remarks that whatever theological coherence there is to the history of God's saving actions with Israel, it must "arise from within the history and is not imposed upon it from the existing norms of our own historical period" (29). He elaborates the point more fully:

> The ancient writers themselves used . . . to express truth about the relations of things in narrative . . . [in which and through which] . . . they discerned truths about the relation of things. . . . This interconnexion of history and truth the theologian must be prepared to explore with them, not simply re-narrating Israel's history as the outcome of a purely historical enquiry, nor

simply re-reading the documents in an enterprise of literary exegesis, but finding the truth within the unfolding patterns of the history. As the structures of Israel's experience pass by us in their historical sequence (tribe, monarchy, cultural-ethnic enclave, movement of world-renewal), the concepts deployed by Israel's writers in the interpretation of those structures (peace, judgment, possession, worship) allow us to find the sequence of happenings intelligible. And from those concepts we may derive an orientation of political principle through which the legacy of Israel regulates our own political analysis and deliberation. (29)

O'Donovan is right about Christian theologians needing to devise their own political theology and orientation with an eye to the legacy of Israel as disclosed in the scriptural tradition. But it is not the concepts per se or the structures and patterns as such that are important. Rather it is the analogical extension of those concepts, patterns, and structures to new situations, situations that evince both continuity and discontinuity with the scriptural witness and the history of Judaism.[10] And one cannot make those analogical extensions by attending to formal considerations alone: Elements of form, design, sequence, structure, and pattern remain unintelligible in themselves. They only seem to display a ready intelligibility exactly because those structural features remain parasitic upon (albeit subconsciously) the particular narratives from which they have been abstracted. This tacit knowledge of and peripheral attention to the specific narrative content, though unacknowledged, lends intelligibility to the patterns and structures we purport to discern. The inattention to those tacit considerations makes O'Donovan's theoretical remarks concerning the form of political theology at best abstruse and at worst vague and diffuse.

If O'Donovan is committed to elaborating a formal, overarching interpretative matrix, a hermeneutic architectonic that would theoretically ground his political theology, then he must tell us more. How, for example, does "a unifying conceptual structure" (22) differ from (but also relate to) "the unifying hermeneutic principle" (23)? Ostensibly, hermeneutic principles and conceptual structures are not one and the same; the former may be said to constitute the "grammar" and the latter supplies the "vocabulary." But as to exactly how these principles and structures work together O'Donovan says very little. What is the relation, moreover, between principle and practice (cf. 44)? And what about O'Donovan's "hermeneutic strategies" (24)? How do they relate to his overriding hermeneutic architectonic? Are they merely useful devices, heuristic schema that can be dispensed with after they have yielded their exegetical insights, or are they much more integral and indispensable (and thus theoretically necessary) to O'Donovan's political theology? Just how "loose" is O'Donovan's system (cf. 45, 46)? Is it provisional and open-ended or is it more or less complete in its broad outline? All in all, our fear is that O'Donovan, given his highly formal account, is in danger, al-

beit for different reasons, of having the charge he leveled against the political theology of Karl Barth recoil upon himself; namely, that it is at
most "a magnificent, but incomplete, beckoning movement" (286).

If the formal display of O'Donovan's hermeneutic architectonic is
problematic, then so is his choice of themes and relative concentration on
certain scriptural concepts. Whereas O'Donovan assumes that an analysis and development of an account of the reign of God is the appropriate
point of departure, we remain open to the possibility that there may be
other images of God's care of and love for creation that might also be just
as crucial as "kingship" and "rule"—such horticultural images and descriptions as gardening and vine dressing, not to mention the profoundly
central pastoral image of shepherding (or that of the householder or the
servants who tend the estate of the absentee landlord). Do these central
scriptural images not also represent a certain politics? How are they to be
integrated into a robust political theology? To be sure, the Scriptures often speak of monarchy and kingship with reference to God's superinten-
dence of and providential guardianship over creation, and that is clearly
a fundamental category in any political theology. But even there kingship
requires a great deal of qualification, which is to say, thick narrative redescription from the vantage of a peculiar tradition. For the reign of God
among the people of Israel and in the person of Jesus is markedly unlike
the kingly rule of monarchies of the nations, displayed not only in the
manner or *mode* of that rule but also distinguished in its peculiarity and
uniqueness by its *subject* and *relations*. The anointed one (Jesus) is, after
all, both servant and messiah, victim and priest, sufferer and liberator, afflicted and physician. To be sure, the concept of divine kingship is "at
once fundamental to Israel's political self-awareness and to Jesus' proclamation of the fullness of time" (30).[11] However, we are not convinced that
kingship alone can do full justice to the providential care of God for creation as manifested in nature and in history, including our own political
history.

Ironically, O'Donovan's almost exclusive concentration on kingship
and rule for determining the meaning of "the political" undermines the
comprehensiveness suggested by his hermeneutic architectonic. Although he is right to criticize the southern school of theology for being
satisfied with a rather small stock of scriptural concepts (16; cf. also
10–11), he is in danger of falling into the same trap himself. Liberation
theology's selective focus on a rather eclectic ensemble of key themes
(e.g., Exodus, *shalom*, jubilee) is clearly not adequate to produce a full political conceptuality, let alone an adequate political theology. Although
O'Donovan's Christendom project represents something of an advancement over the one-sidedness and limited character of the southern school
of theology, it too might be said to advocate its own selective reading of

the scriptural witness, given O'Donovan's concentration on kingship to the exclusion of other scriptural concepts and images, the latter of which may not immediately spring to mind as "political" in their bearing.

Although O'Donovan recognizes that theology is a manifold witness, he also acknowledges that it must have "a unified object on which it concentrates its witness." That means that the "Gospel is one Gospel" (21). It follows that "theology needs more than scattered political images; it needs a full political conceptuality. And politics, for its part, needs a theological conceptuality. The two are concerned with the one history that finds its goal in Christ, 'the desire of the nations'" (2). In short, a political theology worth its salt is one that completely articulates "the one public history which is the theatre of God's saving purposes and mankind's social undertakings" (2). Something more than sheer eclecticism or the exegesis of a few cherished passages is required if a full political theology is to be outlined, namely, "an architectonic hermeneutic," one that would be able to locate political reflection on such pivotal events as the Exodus and the Exile within an understanding whose center of gravity is firmly located in the Gospels (22). Again, although we are in agreement with the main tenor of these claims, we see no reason (as O'Donovan does) to privilege the concept of God's rule over creation and history predominantly in monarchical terms. In short, monarchs always desire architectonics, but we believe that what is crucial is the character of the church's witness to God's rule. That is to say, because the church assumes the role of a servant to the world, such architectonic ambitions must be kept at bay.

O'Donovan Among the Prophets

The idea of keeping those ambitions at bay may seem strange, given the role of the prophets in O'Donovan's account. For in spite of his concentration on kingship and God's rule in developing his political theology, it is the prophets who act as the key to his hermeneutic.[12] Jeremiah, in particular, represents for O'Donovan the quintessential prophet. Perhaps the main reason why this exilic figure is so crucial to O'Donovan's political theology is that Jeremiah epitomizes the role of "mediatorial representative" (76), one who both mediates God to the people and represents the people to God. Insofar as Jeremiah accepts as his own the misery and despair of the people, experiencing in his body and soul the full force of God's anger and judgment, he becomes a type of Christ—"like a negative image of the role of the king" (76). As O'Donovan remarks, "The prophet has, in effect, taken over the mediatorial role, a sign that the monarchy, which was to mediate Yhwh's rule to his people, has been set aside" (77). That means that now "the sole obedience of the people is to heed prophecy" (78).

Is it accidental that O'Donovan should align so closely the work of the theologian with that of the prophet? ("Christian theology must assume the prophet's task" [12].) If so, then the theologian must, like Jeremiah, risk the painful isolation and loneliness that comes with proclaiming a seemingly antithetical and self-contradictory message, namely, one that advocates "a provocatively pro-Babylonian stance" while holding out "encouragement to *exiles*" (69; emphasis added).

Without question O'Donovan demonstrates this Jeremiah-like ability to a remarkable degree in his own Christendom project. However, by underscoring the term "exiles," we would like to remind him not only of the *status* but also of the *specific location* of his audience. Christians in Babylon are in fact resident aliens, "refugees" (79), displaced persons. And indeed part of what it means to live in Babylon is accepting the reality that in present circumstances perhaps "the only mediator of Yhwh's judgments to his people" (69) is in fact the regnant secular powers. But this message will clearly be heard with different ears depending on where exactly in modern Western cultures it is sounded. If heard in places like Britain or Europe (or even Canada and Australia), where Christianity is more or less perceived by many as a curious but largely antiquated cultural oddity, a remnant of a distant era, in such contexts a hopeful reminder of God's ultimate conquest of ungodly powers is salutary. Perhaps in these situations Christians need to be reassured that despite their current marginal status, their collective weakness and feelings of painful isolation, God's rule will prevail. But for Christians in America, who see themselves very much in control and whose strident "political" rhetoric and activism (witness the energies of the religious right, for example) prevents them from seeing themselves as "resident aliens," let alone from experiencing the painful isolation and loneliness of refugees, what is most helpful, indeed necessary, is a reminder that they too, even in America, continue to live in exile.

To be sure, American Christians also need to hear the message that God rules, that Yhwh's final restoration of his covenant people is assured. But unless American Christians understand that the way God rules is not always or even predominantly through them or through the nation in which they find themselves, then this message will only further entrench the all too plentiful ideological distortions (civil religion) that are on parade in America under the guise of the Christian faith. Jeremiah in Britain, in other words, will have a rather different tone than Jeremiah in America.

O'Donovan, reminiscent of the prophet Jeremiah, appeals to two sorts of Christian. On the one hand, he entreats those who remember (out of diverse motives and with varying degrees of accuracy) the "good old days" of Christendom. He enjoins those who are tempted toward nostalgia to leave off the self-indulgence of such illusions and engage instead in the hard work of discernment and practical judgment regarding what are the church's most appropriate political strategies. On the other hand, O'Donovan unsettles the complacent confidence of those who are "at ease" in Babylon, Christians who have become totally assimilated into the dominant liberal culture. He effectively exposes the poverty and bankruptcy of such capitulation, persuading those Christians that a mere identification of the Gospel with the liberal project is to exchange the indispensable Christological birthright of the faith for a mess of "political" porridge.[13]

Christians, like the Jews of the Exile and the Diaspora, are in a situation where the temptation to capitulate to the regnant forces of the day, to "fit in" and be "accepted" and liked by all, is virtually overwhelming. O'Donovan's "Christendom project" is intended to call us back to that sort of faithfulness (replete with a peculiar thickness of Christian practice of which we would like to see more in *The Desire of the Nations*) that renders impossible a simple coextension of Christianity with the modern Western culture. For this we are grateful and find ourselves in his debt.[14]

Our gratitude extends even further when it comes to O'Donovan's recovery of the importance of Israel and Judaism for the self-understanding of the church. But once again, as indebted as we are to O'Donovan at this point, our appreciation must be qualified by several reservations.

O'Donovan on Evil, Israel, and the Holocaust

The irony of O'Donovan according such a central place to Israel in the ongoing life of the church, and hence in developing his own political theology, is that he proceeds as if the Holocaust did not happen. Although he is right, for example, to point out the "unhappy combination" of conflicting ideas present in Barth's views about the state (cf. 213–214), O'Donovan is not fair to (certainly not appreciative enough of) the way in which Barth was struggling to articulate theologically the nature of the state in view of the rise of National Socialism and the wake of the Nazi experience. O'Donovan criticizes Barth for the latter's description of the Nazi state as "pagan" *tout court*. Although he claims to understand why Barth may have made this equation, given the rather peculiar historical circumstances out of which Barth was writing, O'Donovan implicitly discounts Barth's gestures as a signal to the church that we are living in a profoundly new era.

Without trying to defend the internal difficulties of Barth's own position, we do think that there is something crucially correct about Barth's attempt, given the Nazi experience, to describe the state in a "new post-Christendom way" (214).[15] Here, however, O'Donovan is in danger of failing to heed his own council, namely, to advance "a *history* of creation order" that is also "a history of *creation order*, a proclamation rooted in the contingency of history and at the same time a vindication of reality that affords us an authority for doing something without equally affording an authority for doing the opposite" (19). In other words, what we find odd about O'Donovan's response to Barth's views of the state is not his identification of its internal dissonances and inconsistencies, but the way in which O'Donovan proceeds as if *he himself* were not living in a post-Holocaust world, a world radically altered in light of the Nazi experience. Does O'Donovan finally take Israel's history (the history of Judaism) seriously enough, and to that extent does his understanding of the foundations of Christian morality and political theology still align itself too closely to a "natural law" view?

Although O'Donovan is clearly right in warning against any facile equation of a political theology with a theory of progress (which is marked in *The Desire of the Nations* by its code word, "providence"), he fails to do justice to the profoundly annihilative and dis-creative character of the Holocaust. Although the Holocaust defies any final rational analysis or understanding, the magnitude and character of the evil that was unleashed in that dark night marks an eruption of primordial chaos that threatens the very structures of creation.[16] There is found no intimation of this in O'Donovan. Although he may be right to indicate that a proper political theology such as the one he, following Augustine, endeavors to display, despite its strong sense of historical development, nonetheless resists an optimistic view of history and a sanguine belief in "social malleability" derived from the revolutionary traditions of the Enlightenment, it is not clear that a Christian political theology can be satisfied with the assertion that a Christian sense of history is "inherently ambiguous."[17] After all, ambiguity is the favorite word political liberals use to justify "a politics of the lesser evil."

Ambiguity is not sufficient to signal, let alone account for, the Holocaust. One wonders whether O'Donovan is indebted more to Augustine (and the Neoplatonists from which the latter drew in articulating his understanding of evil) than he is to the Hebrew prophets and especially the writers who stand in the biblical wisdom tradition. "Guided by the prophets of Israel and the seer of the Apocalypse, Augustine sees this design of God as one which is fulfilled by the growth of Rome's overweening love of glory. God's purpose is achieved by his allowing evil to wax great." In other words, according to Augustine, the growth of Rome "turns out to be a demonic history, which expresses the divine purpose only as providence, following its own hidden course," yet being put to use in the attainment of higher ends. This by no means legitimates Rome, let alone exonerates her of condemnation and judgment. Indeed, as

O'Donovan rightly points out, Augustine's problem "is not to conceive of progress within the political realm, but to distance himself from it, to retain the perspective that God brings the pretensions of the proud to naught. What appears to be civilisational progress is, in fact, on the moral and spiritual level, self-defeating."[18] But is this to say enough, especially in light of the Holocaust and in particular in the Christian complicity in that ghastly slaughter?

The irony is that despite the care and circumspection with which O'Donovan avoids the charge of advancing a supersessionist theology under the guise of history, and in spite of his emphasis on the ongoing validity of Israel for the church, he nonetheless is strangely silent on some of the most recent events in the history of God's people and their implications for Judaism's self-understanding (and therefore Christianity's political theology). May it be that O'Donovan is, after all, more at home in the world of Augustine than in the world of the late twentieth century, a world that lives not only with the ineradicable memory of the Holocaust but also very much in its shadow? If Christians are to learn who we are by attending to Israel, we will do so just to the extent that we discover again, as the Jews have done for centuries, how to live by our wits.

Learning to live by one's wits is a skill acquired by those who, as a people, have discovered how to survive without ruling. We believe that however much Christendom may have at certain times and in certain places represented the church's faithful and unfaithful witness, that day is now behind us. Wilderness, not rule, is where we presently dwell as Christians. As we know from Jesus' own temptations, wilderness means learning how to live under conditions of great testing. It means living a life that continually calls for the deployment of the "survival skills" of witness and mission and prayer. For those who think they are in control, who are convinced that they are called to rule, these skills cannot help but atrophy. O'Donovan's readings of Scripture afford great aid in the development of such skills, but in the end we believe that he offers more than we should want. It is our conviction that God is again teaching the church that, like the Jews, our first task is to learn to wait upon the Lord and by so waiting to become better and more faithful readers of Scripture.

Notes

1. Page numbers in parentheses refer to Oliver O'Donovan, *The Desire of the Nations: Rediscovering the Roots of Political Theology* (Cambridge: Cambridge University Press, 1996).

2. The example O'Donovan has in mind here is the "Christ-hymn" of Philippians 2:5–11, which, through its double use of the word "form" (Christ was in the form of God and accepted the form of a slave) expresses both aspects of Christ's mediational work: of God to mankind and of mankind to God (135). Although

O'Donovan concedes that "it would be possible to regard the narrative form of this passage merely as a device to show up this significance of double representation," and thus as myth ("a narrative which had the purpose not of reporting happenings but of disclosing permanent realities"), the truth conveyed by Philippians 2:5–11 requires an appropriate "extension" of the narrative structure in order to coordinate "in one time-space field the being of God on the one hand and the earthly events which reflect his being on the other" (135–136). As O'Donovan explains: "The reason for taking the event back to its source outside this world's events is that Jesus wholly mediates the Kingdom in his personal being, and that the Kingdom has its origin in God's eternal purpose. It fulfils all that God intended in Creation. It is necessary, then, to say not simply that the Kingdom has appeared, but that it has been waiting to appear. And as with the Kingdom, so with its mediator: Christ, too, has been in waiting" (136). O'Donovan argues, therefore, that the Gospel cannot be reduced either to history or to myth. Rather, it is "a *history* of creation order," which is also "a history of *creation order*" (19).

The intricate ways in which time and narrative, history and fiction, are interwoven constitute a main feature of the hermeneutical reflections of Paul Ricoeur, whose ongoing project provides a fuller description of the formal characteristics of narrative clearly compatible with O'Donovan's analysis. See James Fodor, *Christian Hermeneutics: Paul Ricoeur and the Refiguring of Theology* (Oxford: Clarendon Press, 1995), especially chap. 6, "Narrative, Revelation, and the Naming of God," for an account of Ricoeur's narrative analysis of the text of Scripture.

3. O'Donovan remarks, "To urge an ideal (which is best done remotely, at a distance from practical decisions) is not the same as to bring the ideal to bear upon practical decisions in concrete circumstances. Because the legacy of Christian political doctrine has to be proved afresh at every turn in engagement with political decision, it can only become useful in the context of an exploratory partnership between church and state in search of authentic political discipleship. Here, certainly, is the manna which when kept breeds worms" (220).

4. O'Donovan begins his political theology by outlining two persistent suspicions that lie at the root of the modern separation of politics from theology. The first concerns the fear that politics will corrupt morality or theology, whereas the second espouses its opposite, namely, the fear that politics will be corrupted by theologians. Both have received philosophical legitimation. As O'Donovan explains, the second of these suspicions has largely contributed to a crisis of authority in modernity to the extent that it has undermined the notion of final causality. The result is the dominance in modernity of "an acephalous idea of society" (16, 249). "In the seventeenth century philosophy came to lose confidence in the objectivity of final causes. Political communities, even when created from below, had been believed to be ordained by Providence to serve the end of earthly perfection; but now there arose a tradition of explaining societies entirely by reference to efficient causes, focussing these in a notional compact whereby each individual citizen was supposed to have surrendered sovereignty over his own person in return for certain protections. Individual agents had their ends; but objective structures only had their origins" (8). The consequence is that despite the insistence on "the autonomous self-justifying character of politics" (9), modern societies lack any unifying vision, being ruled instead by "the imperative of uni-

versal suspicion" (10). Politics, in other words, has been replaced by "social process"—another name for a nonteleological historical dialectic. Unfortunately, because engaging in this critical function proves to be all-consuming, modern politics (not to mention modern theology) has succeeded only in depriving itself of any coherent, conceptual grounds of authority. The irony is that while claiming a certain "autonomous self-justifying character" (9), all forms of modern political life invariably fall victim to "the characteristic dilemma which besets the favourite causes of liberal idealism: how to claim moral licence for themselves without licensing their opposites. Each movement of social criticism draws in its train a counter-movement, and there is no ground in logic for paying more or less respect to the one than to the other" (10). In short, teleology has been exchanged for sheer contingency—which is but another way of saying that "a politics that does not encompass the direction of society ceases to be a politics at all" (10).

The tragedy of modern politics (as well as modern political theology) is that it has rendered the notion of God's rule more or less unintelligible. Although incoherent and confused, these manifestations of political life are not entirely without hope of redemption, according to O'Donovan. Although a genuinely theological concept of authority may indeed be quite remote from "both poles of the authority-dialectic in the modern tradition: state sovereignty on the one hand, popular sovereignty on the other," they "are best understood as residual fragments of an original theological whole, which owe their opposition and their arbitrariness to the loss of their common centre of attraction" (81). Moreover, this loss of teleology (or eclipse of final causality) casts light on some of the most vile and offensive aberrations of politics in our own time. As O'Donovan puts it, "the doctrine that *we* set up political authority, as a device to secure our own essentially private, local and unpolitical purposes, has left the Western democracies in a state of pervasive moral debilitation, which, from time to time, inevitably throws up idolatrous and authoritarian reactions" (49). That is another way of saying that the impasse constructed by modern politics, on an avowedly anti-sacral basis, is itself motivated by a religious impulse, albeit a corrupted and idolatrous impulse. "For without the act of worship political authority is unbelievable, so that binding political loyalties and obligations seem to be deprived of any point" (49). An appreciation of the indispensable importance of teleology in accounting for "the persistent cultural connexion between politics and religion" (49) is therefore imperative. Indeed, attending to the question of final causality allows us "to understand why it is precisely at this point that political loyalties can go so badly wrong." For as O'Donovan remarks, "a worship of divine rule which has failed to recollect or understand the divine purpose can only be an idolatrous worship which sanctions an idolatrous politics" (49).

5. O'Donovan contends that his six "theorems" (list follows) are meant to give movement to his structure (81); they indicate something of the direction to be taken (46). (1) "Political authority arises where power, the execution of right and the perpetuation of tradition are assured together in one coordinated agency" (46). (2) "That any regime should actually come to hold authority, and should continue to hold it, is a work of divine providence in history, not a mere accomplishment of the human task of political science" (46). (3) "In acknowledging political authority, society proves its political identity" (47). (4) "The authority of a human regime

mediates divine authority in a unitary structure, but is subject to the authority of law within the community, which bears independent witness to the divine command" (65). (5) "The appropriate unifying element in international order is law rather than government" (72). (6) "The conscience of the individual members of a community is a repository of the moral understanding which shaped it, and may serve to perpetuate it in a crisis of collapsing morale or institution" (80). These theorems, however, are as much summations or succinct recapitulations of O'Donovan's conceptual analysis as they are constructive indicators of directions to be taken. Moreover, he speaks of one of these theorems as "a corollary necessary to *complete* the exegetical and theoretical outline" (46; emphasis added). This remark adds an additional element of abstruseness to O'Donovan's sketch for a political theology, but it also raises questions regarding its systematicity and relative adequacy. It is not clear, for example, if O'Donovan's outline is meant to be a provisional sketch, an open-ended, preliminary adumbration, or whether he envisions the parameters delineated as more or less comprehensive, with only the details remaining to be filled in. For example, with regard to the second theorem, we need to know how long a regime must hold power in order to be considered a work of divine providence. At first glance the theorem seems concrete, but terms such as "law" and "government" are really quite empty.

Initially, O'Donovan provides an analysis of certain key concepts that, though not directly authorized by Scripture, nevertheless perform a certain heuristic function (i.e., play a certain organizing role). But then O'Donovan finds that this is not quite adequate; hence, he must "stretch beyond" this exegetical framework in order to advance certain theoretical claims. Now it appears that in order for his outline to attain a measure of systematic fullness, it stands in need of several corollaries or "theorems," all of which are then inflected by four "moments." All that is to say, O'Donovan's hermeneutic architectonic is more intimidating and abstruse than it is clarificatory and helpful.

6. On O'Donovan's indebtedness to and affinity with Augustine's political theology, see his "Augustine's *City of God* XIX and Western Political Thought," *Dionysius* 11 (December 1987): 89–110. In order to understand (something of) O'Donovan's project, one has to be cognizant of the central importance of Augustine in his political theology. Like Augustine, O'Donovan is keen to provide a master narrative—a "synthesis" (together with a typology) of all earthly political societies that fall under the paradigm of Rome. (Babylon, of course, is seen as a type of Rome, just as the antitype—following the author of the Apocalypse—constitutes the fuller manifestation of the type.)

O'Donovan sets out to construct an outline of a general theory of society (i.e., a political theology) from the vantage point of a Christian theology of creation and history. What most captures O'Donovan about Augustine's political theology (contra modern accounts of politics) is the way in which, in Augustine's account, the progressive transformation of the social order is accomplished only through Israel and the church. (In O'Donovan's reply to his respondents at the Duke conference on New Testament and Ethics, Spring 1995, one of the first things that he remarked on was that none of his respondents had appreciated sufficiently in his political theology the place he accorded ecclesiology in the transformation of the social order. O'Donovan, of course, is very careful to differentiate the transformation of the earthly social order by the church from a progressive view of history.) O'Donovan's goal, like Augustine's, is not only to formulate a definition of political community to which Christians can subscribe, but also to sketch an outline of a political theology that would elicit from Christians a certain recognition and acknowledgment, thereby authenticating its validity. O'Donovan's project, then, is an attempt to articulate—via the idea of "Christendom"—the qualitative changes that resulted with the dawning of the Christian regime vis-à-vis the former pagan political regimes.

7. Although we wholeheartedly agree with O'Donovan's important emphasis on the eschatological/apocalyptic dimensions of political theology, and the importance of firmly rooting such a theology in a Christology whose scope is as much cosmic as it is historical, we get the sense that O'Donovan's tension, though admirably balanced, nonetheless betrays a decided proclivity for the eschatological "already" over its "not yet." We, in contrast, are a bit more tentative and inclined to stress the eschatological "not yet" (perhaps because chastened by past Christian abuses in political theology but also wizened from the experience over long years of Christian pilgrimage, of following Christ "on the way"). O'Donovan appears all too confident and self-assured about "how the story will come out." Not only is he convinced of what the proper point of departure for a political theology should be (i.e., the reign of God), but also he has some fairly strong and settled ideas about how this reign works itself out historically and hence how it "arrives" and "will arrive." We, in contrast, are more disposed—if indeed one's objective is to develop "a full political conceptuality" (2)—to affirm the importance of emphasizing many different points of departure (not excluding the reign of God, to be sure) as well as several possible points of arrival. We are not as confident as O'Donovan appears to be concerning how the story will come out. That it will come out in the resplendent glory of God's rule we have no doubt. But when and exactly how God's reign will fully manifest itself we are more agnostic. To be sure, O'Donovan also readily acknowledges, following Augustine, that all our claims to witness God's reign in so-called developments of history are in fact inherently ambiguous. O'Donovan, "Augustine's *City of God* XIX and Western Political Thought," p. 105.

8. Nonetheless, there appears to be a diminution in the extent and fullness of biblical exegesis as one moves from the preliminary drafts of O'Donovan's project (e.g., the Hulsean Lectures) to their final form in *The Desire of the Nations*.

9. Our fear is that despite O'Donovan's careful qualification of his hermeneutic architectonic (his language is guarded concerning the relative merits of a formal outline of a political theology and the subsequent need to employ practical judgment in particular circumstances), his hermeneutic remains all too formal and vague. One senses that his preoccupation with analyzing concepts—in particular, "the political act" (a tactic whose importance he credits to Paul Ramsey's work [20–21])—rather than exhibiting the richness of the narrative may in fact be more determinative of his hermeneutic architectonic than the scriptural narrative it purports to illumine. Alasdair MacIntyre's insights regarding the irreducible narrative intelligibility of human action are in order at this point. Narrative history, not isolated, abstract concepts (like "the political act") "turns out to be the basic and essential genre for the characterization of human actions." See Alasdair Mac-

Intyre, *After Virtue: A Study in Moral Theory*, 2nd ed. (Notre Dame: University of Notre Dame Press, 1984), p. 208. In other words, because a narratively intelligible action is "a more fundamental concept than that of an action as such" (*After Virtue*, p. 209), it is incumbent upon the expositor/analyst to set whatever concepts are under investigation firmly within the particular narrative in question.

To his credit, O'Donovan studiously resists the temptation to be carried away by abstractions. Compare, for example, the way in which he comes perilously close to the precipice when he moves from kingship to authority to the ontological conditions of human freedom, action and the good (30), or the way in which he skates on the very edge of something called "the total tradition of humanity" (73). Although tempted, O'Donovan refuses to move too far away from the particularity of his Christology and indulge instead in constructing some generalized anthropology.

10. See, for example, George Lindbeck's use of analogy for suggesting how Israel's story should continue to shape the church's understanding of its own story in "The Church," in *Keeping the Faith: Essays to Mark the Centenary of Lux Mundi*, ed. Geoffrey Wainwright (Philadelphia: Fortress Press, 1988), pp. 179–208. For another very suggestive account of how such analogies might work, see James Alison, *Raising Abel: The Recovery of the Eschatological Imagination* (New York: Crossroads, 1996), pp. 30–33.

11. In a remarkable turnaround, O'Donovan has largely forsaken the spatial metaphors that dominated his Hulsean Lectures and has concentrated instead on temporal imagery in *The Desire of the Nations*. That is not to say that spatial metaphors are completely absent in the latter, but they are noticeably sparse compared to the former work. However, temporal references have increased dramatically, in particular O'Donovan's penchant for the term "moment." He speaks of "atavistic moments" (8), "church moment" (192), "the Constantinian moment" (197, 198), "moments of transition" (158, 212), "moment of penetrating insight" (70), "moment of free choice" (275), "moments of self-disclosure and self-discovery" (272), "moments of unmasking" (9), "moment of obedience" (13), "moment of decision" (20, 284), "moment of disclosure" (47), "moment of revelation" (75, 124), "moment of authorisation" (161), "moment of confrontation" (137), "crisis-moments" (67, 100, 139), "fateful moment" (227), "innovative moments" (20), and the list goes on and on. O'Donovan is clearly right in recounting the Christian hope as analogous with that of the Psalmist. For both can claim that "now it is only a matter of time until the ancient promise is fulfilled" (87). Perhaps it might be more accurate to say that "now it is only a matter of *timing*," given the emphasis on *kairos* over *chronos*—the qualitative rather than the quantitative aspects of time as conveyed in the Gospel expression, "the fullness of time," echoed in O'Donovan's various descriptions of "moment."

12. See especially chap. 2, "The Revelation of God's Kingship," where references to prophecy are just as prominent as those to kingship. Rule, of course, requires agents: prophets, priests, kings, magistrates, princes, and so forth. In other words, rule has to be expressed in appropriate political forms, as the situation demands. The significance of the prophets is that they embodied God's rule at important junctures in the history of God's people, Jesus himself being the last and great prophet.

13. O'Donovan is no friend of liberalism and in particular the kind of liberalism found in the United States, that is, one that advocates an institutionalized "separation" of church and state. He nonetheless thinks that the commitment to freedom, mercy, natural right, and openness to free speech by liberal regimes at least creates conditions in which the church may work. Yet at the same time this is no John Courtney Murray–like deferral to the American system. O'Donovan, in other words, recognizes that the four aspects of U.S. liberalism have proved difficult to realize and certainly cannot be actualized unless the work Gregory began fourteen hundred years ago is resumed (270–271). The judgments required for legitimacy, that is, the kind of rule Paul justified in Romans 13, is morally impossible for societies that do not acknowledge God.

What, then, is the nature of the authority left to secular governments in the aftermath of Christ's triumph? O'Donovan provides the reader with a "fresh" reading of Romans 13, a passage that, he concedes, is among the most famous and most disputed discussions of political authority in the New Testament (147). Inasmuch as Romans 13 is set within a context that advocates "the continued significance of Israel as a social entity in God's plans for final redemption," O'Donovan is right to underscore the importance of this pericope for a reconceptualization of political authority in the Gospel era. As he words it, "St Paul's famous paragraph about the authorities arises naturally from his claim for Israel. Christ's victory, after all, is the same victory that was promised to Israel over the nations, the victory of God-filled and humanised social order over bestial and God-denying empires, a victory won for Israel on behalf of mankind. As Israel is claimed for faith, then, so the authorities are claimed for obedience to Israel, chastened and reduced to the familiar functions that were once assigned to Israel's judges" (147).

Although O'Donovan is right to emphasize the continuity between Israel and the church with regard to the rule of God, he seriously undermines his own project by positing a strict analogy between Israel and the world ("secular authority") vis-à-vis the church's reclamation of preexisting structures in the life of Israel for the church's own life. For one thing, the church's appropriation of Israel is *not* to be put on a level with the church's appropriation of the world as O'Donovan suggests: "Given that Christ has overcome the principalities and powers by his death and resurrection, what rights can they still claim? The question is parallel to the question he [Paul] has just asked and answered about Israel" (147). This analogy (or "parallel," to use O'Donovan's language) fails to do justice to the undivided, organic ties (Paul's image of "grafting" onto the root comes to mind here: See Rom. 11:17ff.) between Israel and the church, which cannot be said of the church's relation to the world. It is quite wrong to say that "as Israel is claimed for [Christian] faith . . . so the authorities are claimed for obedience to Israel" (147). For one thing, secular authorities are not "mediators" of the rule of God in the way Israel is. To be sure, secular authorities may be "vehicles" or "instruments," as was Cyrus in Israel's life, for example. But this sort of language cannot be applied to Israel without a great deal of qualification. Moreover, the danger of O'Donovan using the language of "overcoming" with reference to the church's prevailing over the principalities and powers is that it suggests a similar "overcoming" of Israel by the church, thereby relegating Israel to "the old age" (147) and tacitly endorsing a supersessionist theology, something O'Donovan elsewhere rightly disavows. In short, the connections between church and Israel are more intimate and indivisible than they can ever be between church and world. And although we think O'Donovan certainly wishes to maintain a qualitative difference between functions that Israel and the world play vis-à-vis the church, he finds himself hard-pressed to allot a privileged role to Israel, given the Christendom model with which he works.

14. We are, however, by no means convinced that O'Donovan is right in his claim, on behalf of God's reign, that Christendom is *the* necessary political experience. Secular governments do not need theories of legitimacy in order to rule. Such governments just exist. Our task as Christians is to survive such governments (not to mention theories of political legitimacy). O'Donovan thinks that the church has needs that it can allow secular authority to provide. But such an account leads one to assume that, in principle, a benign relation of complementarity exists between church and world. To presume that the secular authority has priority, even a temporal one, which the church respects or leaves intact for its own ends, begs the question of the Christendom model O'Donovan espouses.

15. A similar criticism is leveled, albeit in a secondary sense, against Yoder, whom O'Donovan also sees as unfairly characterizing in Nazi colors not so much the state but mainstream Christian tradition. As O'Donovan puts it, "Yoder's own view of the mainstream seems to have been formed in the post-Nazi era of the German speaking world" (152). We think that O'Donovan is also wrong in suggesting that Yoder cares about or requires that the state protect individual liberty (223–224). Yoder's "anabaptist" forebears would not have understood our concept of the "individual." Moreover, Yoder has written eloquently about the importance of the care of the needy and protection of the innocent as roles of the state. Yet O'Donovan is on to something when he criticizes Yoder's "voluntarism," which can too easily, particularly in modernity, underwrite rationalistic accounts of the faith.

16. See Jon D. Levenson's fascinating study, *Creation and the Persistence of Evil: The Jewish Drama of Divine Omnipotence* (San Francisco: Harper and Row, 1988).

17. There is also a sense in which the apocalyptic character of John's vision in Revelation is, despite O'Donovan's persistent reference to the work, not adequately modulated by the eschatological emphases of other biblical texts to which he appeals. We noted in the original O'Donovan manuscripts (the Hulsean Lectures) how very sparse were his references to the Book of Hebrews, which clearly represents another way of reading the Old Testament. In his Hulsean Lectures O'Donovan discussed the Book of Hebrews on four separate occasions, explicitly referring to ten specific passages, in Hebrews. In *The Desire of the Nations*, the "finished" product, there are just as many scriptural references to Hebrews (ten) but one less separate occasion in which the book is treated. In both cases, the way of reading Israel's history as espoused by the author of the Book of Hebrews is severely underrepresented.

18. O'Donovan, "Augustine's *City of God* XIX and Western Political Thought," p. 106.

14 *Remembering Martin Luther King Jr. Remembering*

Remembering King

"The Ethics of Black Power" was the first article I had published. It appeared in my college newspaper, *The Augustana Observer*, in 1969. The blond-haired and blue-eyed Swedes at Augustana College in Rock Island, Illinois, were generally supportive of "civil rights," as represented by Martin Luther King Jr., but they were not sure that "Black Power" was a good idea. I long ago lost that article, but I remember drawing on Joe Hough's analysis in *Black Power and White Protestants* to provide a Niebuhrian defense of "Black Power." Like most "good white people," I have followed the continuing struggle of African-Americans in this country, but the 1969 article remains the only time I directly addressed those issues.

I am, after all, a white southerner from the lower-middle classes who grew up embedded in the practices of segregation. Segregation was so "normal," I did not even notice that there were no black people either in the schools I attended or where I went to church. I have no idea how deeply the habits of racism are written into my life, but I know that they are not the kind of habits you simply "outgrow" or "get over." I have, therefore, refrained from pontificating on "race" because I feared that that is what it would be—pontification.

I have written about the South, which obviously involves race, but I have not written about "the struggle." Yet few churches better embody what I think faithful churches should be than the black church. Moreover, I have nothing but admiration for Martin Luther King Jr. and the movement he led. Still, for me to "use" Martin Luther King Jr., and the church that made him possible, to advance my understanding of "Christian ethics" seems wrong. That is not *my* story, though I pray that God will make that story my story, for I hope to enjoy the fellowship of the communion of the saints.[1]

Yet that is an eschatological hope, which, as much as one desires it, cannot be forced. Christian unity, Christian peace, comes as a thief in the night, making us more than we could have ever wanted. The longing for such unity should not be confused with the reality of such unity, for that reality must be forged through common memory. The way Martin Luther King Jr. is remembered by African-Americans and, in particular, in the African-American church is and should be different from the way he is remembered by "America." I fear that the celebration of Martin Luther King's birthday as a "national holiday" is the attempt to separate King from the church he served and loved.

I therefore admire Christopher Beem's industry in discovering a reference to King in one of my essays.[2] When I first read his critique, I was surprised that he had found such a reference because, for the reasons given above, I have avoided appealing to King. I was even more surprised by Beem's argument that I should choose between my admiration for King and my understanding of the relation between the church and liberalism. That is a lot to hang, to use Beem's own words, on a "somewhat incidental reference" (120).

Moreover, as Beem indicates, that reference was not generated by me. Rev. Wilson Miscamble, C.S.C., used King (and Gandhi) as an example to challenge my alleged sectarianism. Miscamble suggested that, unlike Latin American base communities, which foster social and political responsibility, "communities of character" (Hauerwas 1981)—which exist solely in the abstract—are inwardly focused and self-absorbed. As Beem notes, Miscamble then observed, "Hauerwas is quite unlike Gandhi and Martin Luther King, Jr. They advocated not only *being* nonviolent, but also actively seeking justice in the world through nonviolent resistance. Hauerwas founders in *being*. He gives us a corporate ethic of disposition but is not interested in the ethics of action" (Miscamble 1987:75). In the same paragraph in which his appeal to King and Gandhi is made, Miscamble developed his critique by attacking my claim that it is not the first task of the church to make the nation-state work. He argued that Christians must act in the world as it is, not as we would like it to be; therefore, recognizing real politics means having to choose between guns and butter.

In response to Miscamble's criticism, I simply observed that I found it odd that he should appeal to Gandhi and King in support of "political realism." My reference to Gandhi and King was an attempt to suggest, not that they would agree with my position, but rather that within the context of Miscamble's argument they would more likely be my allies than his (Hauerwas 1987:91). I certainly did not assume that I should or could appeal to King to support my position in general.[3] Even more unlikely would have been a similar use of Gandhi.

Yet I am in Beem's debt for raising the issues in the way he has. I confess that I do not find his argument logically compelling, but I like the issues he has raised concerning King's (and my) relation to liberalism. Unfortunately, I think his argument involves questionable readings of King and the civil rights movement, as well as a failure to understand the continuing problem of racism in America. Though it is less important, he has also gotten me wrong. I am, however, grateful to have this opportunity to develop my own thoughts on these matters.

On King and Liberalism

I do not pretend to have a profound understanding of King's life or thought. I have read the standard biographies and his books. Yet I think I know enough to know that Beem's portrait of King is, to put it kindly, "thin." Beem is so anxious to make King an advocate of the "ideals" of the Declaration of Independence that we lose any sense that King was, from beginning to end, a Baptist minister. My colleague Richard Lischer, in his book *The Preacher King: Martin Luther King, Jr., and the Word that Moved America*, quotes King's response to those who criticized his involvement with opposition to the war in Vietnam: "Now those who say, 'You are a civil rights leader. What are you doing speaking out? You should stay in your field.' Well, I wish you would go back and tell them for me that before I became a civil rights leader, I was a preacher of the Gospel" (Lischer 1995:314–315).

One of King's close associates in the movement, Rev. Wyatt Tee Walker, has observed that King's prominence could hide the importance of the black church for the civil rights campaign.

> The African-American Church received considerable recognition as the driving force for civil rights during the halcyon days of the movement. The high profile of Martin Luther King, Jr. sometimes obscured the institutional role of the Black Church that he personified as an ordained minister. Closer scrutiny of the Black Church's history will reveal that all thrusts for liberation and wholeness have moved on the singular impulse of religion. From the early days of slave religion to the present, and all intervening way stations of freedom struggles, the African-American Church has been the critical dynamic that gave form and direction to our thirst for political and personal liberation. (Walker 1994:2)[4]

No doubt King understood the struggle as liberation for both black and white. Yet King was clear from beginning to end that his overriding concern was the liberation made possible by the black church. Consider, for example, the end of his famous speech at Holt Street Baptist Church in 1955, the speech that in effect began the bus boycott:

And as we stand and sit here this evening, and as we prepare ourselves for what lies ahead, let us go out with a grim and bold determination that we are going to stick together. We are going to work together. Right here in Montgomery when the history books are written in the future, somebody will have to say "There lived a race of people, black people, fleecy locks and black complexion, of people who had the moral courage to stand up for their rights." And thereby they injected a new meaning into the veins of history and of civilization. And we're gonna do that. God grant that we will do it before it's too late. (King 1991:51)

In *Prophesy Deliverance! An Afro-American Revolutionary Christianity*, Cornel West locates King among those who laud the uniqueness of African-American culture and personality.[5] West describes King as a "weak exceptionalist" because King assumed that African-Americans have acquired through their historical experience a peculiar capacity to love their enemies, to endure suffering patiently, and thereby to "teach the white man how to love." "In King's broad overview, God is utilizing Afro-Americans—this community of *caritas* (other-directed love)—to bring about 'the blessed community.' He seemed confident that his nonviolent movement of predominantly Afro-Americans was part of a divine plan" (West 1982:74–75).[6]

King, as Beem documents, certainly appealed to liberal sentiments, but that is what they were, sentiments. I doubt that King had a well-developed view about "liberalism." He did not need a "theory" for his purposes. Indeed, I suspect that any such theory would have been more trouble than it was worth. Rather, he used anything that would help in the struggle. I have long thought that King, rather than Thomas Aquinas or Alan Donagan, would be the best example of the ultimate *bricoleur* described by Jeffrey Stout (Stout 1988:74–75). King brilliantly made do with "whatever [was] at hand" and in the process became America's greatest public theologian.[7] Drawing on the best of American civil religion, he forged a moral vision that remains our best resource for any future this country might have.

Nor would I argue that King simply "used" liberalism. I have no doubt that he believed, as Beem quotes him, in the "equal and inestimable value of the human personality." Yet it is also the case, as Lischer documents, that toward the end of his career, King not only became increasingly cynical about such liberal platitudes but also began to "slough" off such sentiments: "By the end of his life, the one true church in which we are *all* brothers and sisters had disappeared, its place taken by the redemptive mission of the bowed but awakened black church" (Lischer 1995:15).

One simply cannot underestimate the effect on King of the Vietnam War—which he saw as an instance of America's ongoing racism—and the Poor People's Campaign.[8] He increasingly distrusted liberalism and, according to Lischer, expressed outright disgust with American civil religion (Lischer 1995:181–182).

> By 1968 King was saying that racism is written into the heart of white America and into the documents to which African-Americans furtively appealed for protection. You can't trust your own county, he tells his people, because it isn't yours. For a group in Montgomery in 1968 he makes the astonishing comparison: "and you know what, a nation that puts as many Japanese in a concentration camp as they did in the forties . . . will put black people in a concentration camp. And I'm not interested in being in any concentration camp. I've been on the reservation too long now." (Lischer 1995:273–274)[9]

Beem may object that King's disillusionment with liberalism toward the end of his life does not undercut his case that King assumed a "cohesion" between Christian and American values. Yet I am suggesting that King's "liberalism" was always subservient to his embeddedness in the black church and the memory of his people that that church embodies. King could confidently appeal to liberal sentiments because he was a black Baptist preacher who would never be a liberal.

On Liberalism and Memory

This brings me to Beem's understanding of my understanding of "liberalism." Beem notes that I "define" liberalism as "a political philosophy committed to the proposition that a social order and corresponding mode of government can be formed on *self-interest* and *consent*." I confess that when I read Beem's quote, I thought I had probably said that. I also thought how insufficient it was as a "definition" of liberalism. I was particularly embarrassed to think I had offered it as a "definition" of liberalism, since I have strong philosophical doubts about the very idea of "definition." But I thought I was probably still making such mistakes back in 1981.

I was pleasantly surprised, however, to discover that the sentence that Beem quotes from *A Community of Character* was not offered as a definition, but came at the end of a paragraph that provides a fuller account of liberalism, an account that I think important for understanding King. There I note that America is often assumed to be a social order unlike others, since America allegedly began from "scratch." I observe that such a presumption is a profound distortion of American history, but its power is hard to deny. Liberal practice and theory, I suggest, is

> successful exactly because it supplies us [Americans] with a myth that seems to make sense of our social origins. For there is some truth to the fact that we originally existed as a people without any shared history, but came with many different kinds of histories. In the absence of any shared history

we seemed to lack anything in common that could serve as a basis for societal cooperation. Fortunately, liberalism provided a philosophical account of society designed to deal with exactly that problem: A people do not need a shared history; all they need is a system of rules that will constitute procedures for resolving disputes as they pursue their various interests. (Hauerwas 1981:78)

The next sentence constitutes the "definition" of liberalism that Beem quotes.

I hope I am not being unduly defensive in insisting on the context of the sentence that Beem alleges is my "definition" of liberalism. I do so because it is important that my critique of liberalism not be reduced, as Beem reduces it, to moralistic judgments about "enlightened self-interest," "selfishness," or "individualism."[10] Such matters matter, but they have never been at the heart of my theological critique of liberalism. Rather, my concern has always been what liberalism does to remembering as a political task. I think there is no better example of the deficiencies of liberal remembering than what is happening to the memory of Martin Luther King Jr.

It is not for me to say for African-Americans whether the celebration of a national holiday for King is good or bad, but such a celebration (also nicely exemplified in Beem's article) threatens to abstract King from King's memory of slavery and from the black church. Liberal memory makes King the great hero of the liberal ideals of "freedom of the individual" and "equality," but King did not represent "individuals." He did not seek individual freedom for African-Americans. King sought freedom for African-Americans as a people to remember slavery and the triumph over slavery offered by the black church.[11] But "America" does not want to remember that slavery (and, even less, genocide) is part of our history. Rather, we want to assume that if everyone has "civil rights," if everyone is free to be an "individual," if everyone is moderately well off, then we can say to those who are still upset about past wrongs, "Oh come on, what's a little slavery between friends?"

I know of no one who has better illuminated these matters than Stanley Fish. In his book *There's No Such Thing as Free Speech and It's a Good Thing, Too*, he gives the following account of liberalism. Fish notes that part of the successful strategy of neoconservatives against "political correctness" is to place their opposition in the position of having not only to respond to arguments but also to dispute the very vocabulary in which the issues are framed. That vocabulary is made up of words like "fairness," which ensure that those who use such words occupy the rhetorical high ground. Fish notes that such vocabulary is the speech of liberalism, which accordingly becomes the main target of the essays in his book. Fish characterizes liberal thought as that which "begins in the acknowledgment that faction, difference, and point of view are irreducible; but the liberal strategy is to devise (or attempt to devise) procedural mechanisms that are neutral with respect to point of view and therefore can serve to frame partisan debates in a nonpartisan manner" (Fish 1994:16). According to Fish, that means that liberalism involves an inherent contradiction—it denies any transcendent perspective of the kind associated with traditional Christianity (against whose dogmas liberalism defines itself), and yet it believes in the capacity of partial (in two senses) human intelligence to overcome all partialities. In "Liberalism Doesn't Exist," an essay he wrote later, Fish argues that exactly because liberalism cannot acknowledge a transcendental perspective, it "does not have at its center an adjudicative mechanism that stands apart from any particular moral and political agenda" (Fish 1994:137).

Fish illumines his attack on liberalism by providing a reading of King's "I Have a Dream" speech. He observes that liberals read the speech as a demonstration of the possibility of a nonracist society. "I have a dream that one day my four little children will not be judged by the color of their skin, but by the content of their character" sounds like good liberal rhetoric celebrating the "individual." Yet Fish argues that these words cannot be divorced from the historical occasion that produced them.[12] Though it was nearly a decade after *Brown v. Board of Education*, blacks were still being denied the vote and access to restaurants and hotels, and King was speaking to those who marched on Washington in support of the civil rights bill. By reminding us of the context of King's speech, Fish is not trying to diminish the significance of King's speech or his sincerity. Rather, Fish is reminding us of the *local* nature of King's achievement and, equally, that whatever King's intention or intentions may have been, they were also *locally* sincere. King was not saying, Fish maintains, that once Jim Crow laws are removed, the job will be done. As he notes, King later in the speech asks, "'When will you be satisfied?' and answers 'never,' not 'until justice rolls down like waters and righteousness like a mighty stream'" (Fish 1994:99). These are not the sentiments of a man who is calling for *procedural* justice, for the reign of fairness that is divorced from history. To abstract King's speech from that history, to narrate King as calling for freedom and equality in the abstract, is to put King on the side of those he was opposing. For, as Fish points out, to construe King's speech as a call for "fairness," as an injunction against any race consciousness, is the tactic now used by those who oppose affirmative action programs.[13] Those who detach King's words from the history that produced them "erase the fact of that history from the slate, and they do so, paradoxically, in order to prevent that history from being truly and deeply altered" (Fish 1994:99). That is why Fish rightly argues in another chapter, "You can only fight discrimination with discrimination" (Fish 1994:70–79).

Beem asserts that

> while the fulfillment of King's dream of full integration and equality re-
> mains woefully distant, it appears to me unassailable that the entire Ameri-
> can polity (and particularly the deep South) is more just and reflects a
> greater measure of equality then was the case prior to, say, 1955. Further, I
> believe it is equally self-evident that this change is inescapably connected to
> King's efforts within the civil rights movement. (120)

I hope that is the case, though I am not the one to make such judgments.
What I am sure about, however, is that the very terms by which such
"success" is measured are part of the problem.

Dyson observes that race relations in America are mired in a bog of tor-
tuous irony: "The passion and vision of liberals—whose intent it was to
vanquish the obvious and vile manifestations of racial animosity—have
now been co-opted by conservative intellectuals who conceal the abated
but still malicious expression of racism" (Dyson 1993:150–151). Those
who would resist racism have, according to Dyson, temporarily lost the
battle of language. "Classical liberalism and neoliberalism continue to
publish laundry lists of ancient racial indignities made fresh by today's
news. But these liberalisms are burdened by a loyalty to a form of social
analysis that obscures recognition of structural impediments to racial
progress, a failure that only promises certain defeat of its goal of full integration of blacks into American society" (Dyson 1993:151).

The term "structural impediments" sounds very much like what
Christians call the "principalities and powers." King, moreover, provided
the language and practices that Christians have been given to face those
powers. It is the language of sin and salvation embodied in the practices
of confession, reconciliation, and nonviolence. Beem rightly notes that
King believed that Christians should be socially active. So do I. The crucial question is "how?" King, as far as I am concerned, is a model of such
activism for Christians, since he refused to hide his Christian convictions
in the name of "pluralism." He fought for his people's "rights," he fought
for freedom and equality, but he never failed to remind those for whom
he fought, as well as those against whom he fought, that the fight was finally about sin and salvation. That is why King is not just the hero of the
American civil religion, he is a saint of the church.

Forgetting "Epistemology"

I have tried very hard to forget that I once thought I had to have a theory
of knowledge to know what I know. That is, I have learned that it is an
epistemological mistake and, even more important, a theological mistake, to think a "ground" must be secured to begin theological reflection.

In a similar fashion, I do not think you can or should try to develop a rational theory about rationality. You can always learn something from such theories, but what you learn is not necessarily dependent on the theory.

Beem faults me for not providing an epistemology or theory of rationality that will allow us (I assume by "us" he means "we" liberal Americans) to "develop a shared substantive conception of the good that transcends [our] metaphysical differences" (127). To which I am tempted to say, "Oh my, I am so sorry." He commends King for having an epistemology, an account of rationality that can ground universal judgments "by which all human beings, regardless of their unique histories, can come to perceive the will of God" (128). Beem thinks this epistemology coheres with the assertion of the Declaration of Independence that truths are self-evident. He even footnotes Jefferson's view that "truth is great and will prevail if left to herself."

I do not know whether King had an epistemology or an account of rationality of the sort Beem suggests, but if he did, I do not think it did him much good. What King had, as West describes it, was an extraordinary ability to mobilize and organize a very particular form of southern resistance. King was able, according to West, to maintain a delicate balance between the emerging "new" black petite bourgeoisie, black working poor, and black underclass to create a mass movement that was as unprecedented as it was unstable. "In this sense, King was an organic intellectual of the first order—a highly educated and informed thinker with organic links to ordinary folk. Despite his petit bourgeois origins, his deep roots in the black church gave him direct access to the life-worlds of the majority of black southerners" (West 1993:272–273).

In short, if you are a black Baptist preacher in the South, you probably do not need an epistemology. In fact, if you have one, it might actually get in the way. An epistemological theory is what white liberals need to reassure themselves that they are not "biased" when they support one of their favorite causes. King no doubt continued to be influenced by what he had learned at Boston University, but he well understood that truth, if left to itself, will not prevail. He knew that because he knew that Jefferson owned slaves.

What King also knew was that America is a society at least partly constituted by some people whose forebears were once slaves and by other people whose forebears owned slaves. He knew that black people bore a history of discrimination in the name of race. He knew that white people did not think they were racist. He sought to mitigate the most obvious injustices of those histories. But he also knew that such mitigations were not sufficient. The issue finally was not justice, but memory. The crucial question remains whether Americans can ever acknowledge what it means to be a slave nation. That is what Martin Luther King Jr. never forgot and what we who would follow him must remember.

Notes

An earlier version of this chapter appeared in *Journal of Religious Ethics*, 23, 1 (spring 1995): 135–148. Reprinted by permission. Copyright © 1995 Journal of Religious Ethics, Inc.; all rights reserved. Reprinted by permission.

I am obviously indebted to my colleague Richard Lischer for sharing his extraordinary knowledge and understanding of King with me. Less obvious is the debt I owe to Michael Cartwright of Allegheny College for his incisive advice about the issues raised by Christopher Beem. Dr. James Fodor and Mr. Scott Saye kindly read and critiqued this chapter.

1. My reservation about writing about King is not that white people should not write about black people. I am sure that our respective experiences have made us different, but I believe that some black people can write about whites with more insight than many white people. The issue is not whether we can understand one another's experience, but rather what one is trying to do in appropriating another's story. I am sure that no account of the white church in America can be told without attention to the black church, but I am not sure the reverse is the case. The problem is therefore an ecclesial one. Part of my reservation concerning King is the uncertainty about how his story can or should be told. How the story is told depends so much on the continuing struggle about race in America. I admire those who began the telling of King's story, but I suspect that his story, like all good stories, will require many tellings.

2. Christopher Beem, "American Liberalism and the Christian Church," *Journal of Religious Ethics* 23, 1 (Spring 1995): 119–133. Page numbers in parentheses refer to this article.

3. Beem suggests that King and I share a common commitment to the "ideal" of nonviolence because we assume that nonviolence is the "quintessential response to the Gospel message of love" (121). That may characterize King's views, but it certainly is not how I understand Christian nonviolence. Of course, King's practice of nonviolence is more important than the criticism I might have of his rationale for nonviolence.

4. See also Michael Dyson's argument that King's debt to the black church must be recognized if the movement King represented is to have any future: "The recognition that King was part of a larger tradition disallows America to escape its obligation to those King represented by relegating his thought to the fixed and static past. Instead, it forces America to critically engage and constantly examine the dynamic contemporary expressions of the thought and practices emerging from the tradition that birthed and buttressed King" (Dyson 1993:240).

5. West identifies three distinct Afro-American historical traditions in addition to the *exceptionalist* type exemplified by King: The *assimilationist* considers Afro-American culture and personality to be pathological; the *marginalist* treats the Afro-American culture as restrictive and confining; the *humanist* accents the universal human content of Afro-American cultural forms, making no sociological or onto-

logical claims about Afro-American superiority or inferiority (West 1982:70–71). Beem, in contrast to West, would seem to put King in the last category.

6. Dyson, while agreeing with West's assessment, further suggests that King's exceptionalism included belief that the moral heroism of black people would enable them to effect their destiny through the exercise of transformative moral agency. "The standards of moral excellence that King expected through disciplined participation in nonviolent demonstrations, which included rites of self-examination and purification, were of inestimable worth not only in fighting for denied social privileges and rights, but in the healthy enlargement of crucial narratives of self-esteem. King understood the virtues of 'everyday forms of resistance,' and appealed to the 'weapons of the weak' in opposing unjust social forces" (Dyson 1993:234–235).

7. For a more critical understanding of Stout's account of the *bricoleur* and, in particular, King as *bricoleur*, see Hauerwas 1994.

8. King observed that Americans applauded nonviolence as long as it served their self-interest, but when it came to the children in Vietnam, Americans quickly discovered there is a limit to nonviolence. He wrote, "They wander into towns and see thousands of children homeless without clothes running in packs on the streets like animals; they see the children degraded by our soldiers as they beg for food. They see the children selling their sisters to our soldiers, soliciting for their mothers. We have destroyed their two most cherished institutions—the family and the village. We have destroyed their land and their crops. We have corrupted their women and children and killed their men. What strange liberators we are!" (Lischer 1995:276–277).

In a 1968 address King said, "The problem is America has never lived up to [its own covenant] and the ultimate contradiction is that the men who wrote it owned slaves at the same time." Lischer observes, "In the late period of his life, he preached as if he had just stumbled upon the dirty secret of America's misery" (Lischer 1995:313).

9. James Cone has shown how King's loss of faith in America and Malcolm X's extraordinary transformation make them, in spite of their undeniable differences, necessary conversation partners not only for the future of black theology but also for the future of African-Americans in the United States (Cone 1991). Dyson, in an appreciative review of Cone, criticizes Cone for prescribing self-respect and self-esteem without "giving a sharp or substantial analysis of the social resources for such qualities and the political and economic reasons that prevent their flourishing in many urban black communities across the country" (Dyson 1993:262). One might add that King's Christianity and Malcolm's Islam constitute a difference that can never be overlooked.

10. "Selfishness" seems to me to be a quite inadequate description of liberal "vice." As I have often argued, the liberal commitment to "disinterestedness," characteristic of utilitarian and deontological moral theory sponsored by liberalism, is quite self-denying. Liberal (capitalist) economic practice and theory may undercut such disinterestedness, but even in economics liberalism can be quite "egalitarian"—everyone has the same worth as determined by the ability to make money.

11. For a wonderful exemplification of memory as moral art, see *Colored People: A Memoir,* by Henry Louis Gates Jr. Gates has the courage to elicit the world of segre-

gation, thus reclaiming those lives as part of the story of "the people." His book begins with a letter to his daughters explaining why he wrote the book: "I am not Everynegro. I am not native to the great black metropolises: New York, Chicago, or Los Angeles, say. Nor can I claim to be a 'citizen of the world.' I am from and of a time and place—Piedmont, West Virginia—and that's a world apart, a world of difference. So this is not a story of a race but a story of a village, a family, and its friends. And of a sort of segregated peace. What hurts me most about the glorious black awakening of the late sixties and early seventies is that we lost our sense of humor. Many of us thought that enlightened politics excluded it.

"In your lifetimes, I suspect, you will go from being African Americans, to 'people of color,' to being, once again, 'colored people.' (The linguistic trend toward condensation is strong.) I don't mind any of the names myself. But I have to confess that I like 'colored' best, maybe because when I hear the word, I hear it in my mother's voice, and in the sepia tones of my childhood. As artlessly and honestly as I can, I have tried to evoke the world of the fifties, a Negro world of the early sixties, and the advent of a black world of the later sixties, from the point of view of the boy I was. When you are old enough to read what follows, I hope that it brings you even a small measure of understanding, at long last, of why we see the world with such different eyes . . . and why that is for me a source both of gladness and of regret. And I hope you'll understand why I continue to speak to colored people I pass in the streets" (Gates 1994:xv-xvi).

I am sure Gates would be the first to acknowledge that his loving remembrance of the world of segregation is possible, as his own account of King suggests, because of the courage of Martin Luther King Jr.

12. "History," as Fish well knows, is a tricky notion. His use of the term in this context begs for further analysis. I do not think he means to reproduce the notion of "history" so prominent in history departments, whose members believe they are telling us "what really happened." Cornel West offers some fascinating reflections on these matters in his *Keeping Faith: Philosophy and Race in America:* "What I find seductive and persuasive about Nietzsche is his deep historical consciousness, a consciousness so deep that he must reject prevailing ideas of history in the name of genealogy. It seems to me that in these postmodern times, the principles of historical specificity and the materiality of structured social practices—the very founding principles of Marx's own discourse—now require us to be genealogical materialists. We must become more radically historical than is envisioned by the Marxist tradition" (West 1993:266). What one would like to see is such views actually displayed by a concrete narrative. I am sure, moreover, that such issues are crucial for how we think about how "ethics" is to be done.

13. "Race," of course, is a fiction, but part of the pain of our history is that it now has an undeniable reality. How to acknowledge that reality without reproducing the destructive practices "race" names is no easy matter.

References

Beem, Christopher. 1995. "American Liberalism and the Christian Church: Stanley Hauerwas vs. Martin Luther King Jr." *Journal of Religious Ethics* 23, 1 (Spring): 119–133.

Cone, James H. 1991. *Martin and Malcolm and America: A Dream or a Nightmare?* Maryknoll, N.Y.: Orbis Books.

Dyson, Michael Eric. 1993. *Reflecting Black: African-American Cultural Criticism.* Minneapolis: University of Minnesota Press.

Fish, Stanley. 1994. *There's No Such Thing as Free Speech and It's a Good Thing, Too.* New York: Oxford University Press.

Gates, Henry Louis, Jr. 1994. *Colored People: A Memoir.* New York: Alfred A. Knopf.

Hauerwas, Stanley. 1981. *A Community of Character: Toward a Constructive Christian Social Ethic.* Notre Dame, Ind.: University of Notre Dame Press.

_____. 1987. "Will the Real Sectarian Stand Up?" *Theology Today* 44:87–94.

_____. 1994. "To Be or Not to Be a Bricoleur." *Koinonia* 4, 1:105–109.

Hough, Joseph C. 1968. *Black Power and White Protestants: A Christian Response to the New Negro Pluralism.* New York: Oxford University Press.

King, Martin Luther, Jr. 1991. "Speech at Holt Street Baptist Church." [1955]. In *The Eyes on the Prize Civil Rights Reader: Documents, Speeches, and Firsthand Accounts from the Black Freedom Struggle, 1954–1990,* ed. Clayborne Carson et al., 48–51. New York: Penguin Books.

Lischer, Richard. 1995. *The Preacher King: Martin Luther King, Jr., and the Word That Moved America.* New York: Oxford University Press.

Miscamble, Wilson D., C.S.C. 1987. "Sectarian Passivism?" *Theology Today* 44:69–77.

Stout, Jeffrey. 1988. *Ethics After Babel: The Languages of Morals and Their Discontents.* Boston: Beacon Press.

Walker, Wyatt Tee. 1994. "Walk Together Children, Dontcha' Get Weary." *Religion and Values in Public Life* 2, 3/4.

West, Cornel. 1982. *Prophesy Deliverance! An Afro-American Revolutionary Christianity.* Philadelphia: Westminster Press.

_____. 1993. *Keeping Faith: Philosophy and Race in America.* New York: Routledge.

Name Index

Subject Index